NOT YET OVER THE HUMP
AFRICAN AMERICANS INTO THE 21ST CENTURY: A PRIMER

ALSO BY ED SMITH

Where to, Black Man? – An American Negro's African Experience

Resources for Affirmative Action, (co-edited with Joan Cannon)

Black Students in Interracial Schools (2nd edition 1994)

After a period pondering medical school, Ed Smith earned a BS degree in elementary education at Northern Illinois University. Over his long career he has taught second grade through undergraduate school. Following a two-year teaching stint as a Peace Corps volunteer in Ghana, West Africa, he did graduate studies at the University of Wisconsin Madison and Milwaukee, earning the Ph.D. in 1975. Ed has taught in public and private schools, his most rewarding experience being as a teacher at a Jesuit residential prep school where he was the only African American adult "working 24 hours a day helping young black males prepare to take on the HUMP!" Smith has spent most of his professional life working in human relations, equal employment opportunity and affirmative action and as an adjunct lecturer of African American history. He has worked in environments as physically and culturally diverse as Vermont and Alaska.

N O T
Y E T
O V E R   T H E
H U M P

AFRICAN AMERICANS INTO THE 21ST CENTURY: A PRIMER

OPINIONS

Ed Smith, Ph.D.

JAED PUBLISHING CO.
FAIRBANKS, ALASKA

JAED Publishing Co.
P.O. Box 81152
Fairbanks, Alaska 99708
Printed in the United States of America

Library of Congress Cataloging in Publication Data

Smith, Ed.
    Not yet over the hump African Americans into the 21st century: a primer / Ed
Smith. – 1st ed.
    Includes bibliographical references.
    ISBN: 0-9641446-0-3 (pbk): $14.95
    1. Civil Rights. I. Title.
Library of Congress Catalog Card Number: 94-96135

Book and cover design by Lisa A. Valore, Art • Design.
Cover illustration by Kate Wallum.

ACKNOWLEDGEMENTS

For staying the course and keeping the pursuit of truth(s) and authenticity as
beacons despite almost overwhelming enticements from far left and right, I am
continually inspired by Ishmael Reed, Toni Morrison and Lerone Bennett, Jr.

For a true and tested friend who refuses to let me quit, I am eternally grateful
to Joan Bertrand.

For believing in this book even when her organizational bosses at a press
where she is Series Editor, rejected it, I am grateful to Dr. Geneva Smitherman
of the Michigan State University Department of English.

DEDICATION

To the women of the world for it is they who will save
humanity—if it is to be saved;

To America's black and white women for only they can save
America from itself;

And to these particular women for having rescued—saved—the
author at critical junctures: Eula Mae Smith, Lula Nixon,
Mrs. Green (my high school counselor), Mary Louise Sequel,
Iris Kapil, Barbara Boseker, Linda Martin Grayson,
Dorothy Larkin, Shirley Stone, Betty Thompson, Peggy Morley,
Carolyn Smith McNellis, Irene Bouzek, Chotty Riness,
Connie Deer, Julie Dagnon, Monica Giganti, Joan Bertrand,
Virginia Louise Nixon, Vera Scott, Erna Wright, Mary Lee Welsh,
Jean Johnson, Roberta Armstrong, Phyllis Bronstein, Leslie Martin,
Penelope "Rose" Pegis, Bonnie Williams, Dorian Ross, Ruth Clark,
Mae Blivens, Annemarie Kuhn, Vivian Burton,
and Mary Kauffman.

❀

And to Jahi and Kwame who, in their time,
will also need to be saved.

Table of Contents

Chapter I ❀ 19 – 76
America in Brief...Through a Pair of Black Eyes

Highlights – Explores the question of what America is and how it became so from an African American perspective. Examines the critical role of success in wars and evolution of Christian denominations as barometers of success. Overviews social pathologies such as high rate of illiteracy, treatment of young and elderly, and the disabled as unfinished agenda. Is critical of immigration, political action committees, handling of crime. Points to strengths inherent in "the" American character.

Chapter II ❀ 77 – 177
African America...The Way We Are

Highlights – Examines the general Black condition in the waning years of the twentieth century. Gives particular attention to the role of law enforcement and the courts; family, youth, education, and health; economic status, political leadership, emergence of Buppies; blacks as professional soldiers and athletes; black women and men; blacks and the media.

Chapter III ❀ 178 – 214
The Hump and Beyond

Highlights – Is the future bright or bleak for African Americans, is the central question. What actions might African American communities and their leaders take to enhance all of our prospects for surviving in the twenty-first century?

Appendix ❀ 215 – 217

Bibliography ❀ 218 – 236

PRAYER

"Once they tell us, Jehovah, that in the great shadows of the past thou hast whispered to a quivering people, saying, "Be not afraid." He watching over Israel slumbers not nor sleeps. Grant us today, O' God, that fearlessness that rests on confidence in the ultimate rightness of things. Let us be afraid neither of mere physical hurt, nor of the unfashionableness of our color, nor the unpopularity of our cause; let us turn toward the battle of life undismayed and above all when we have fought the good fight grant us to face the shadow of death with the same courage that has let us live. Amen."
> Psalms 121
> W.E.B. Du Bois, *Prayers for Dark People*

I am still evolving from being treated as three-fifths of a human, a subpart of the white estate.
> Patricia Williams, *The Alchemy of Race and Rights: Diary of a Law Professor*

Preface

"Racism is the nation's number one mental health problem."
Bertram Brown, M.D.
Former Director National Institutes of Mental Health

Increasing numbers of Black behavioral scientists are beginning to understand that the dominant thrust in what has become known as "Western civilization" is racism.
Black Psychiatrist Frances Cress Welsing

"...and still our society will not—or can not—accept responsibility for the pervasiveness of racism. In recent years, not only have we refused to face our responsibility, we have also tacitly agreed not to discuss racism as a real issue. To the extent that we agree to avoid discussion, we agree to ignore its existence and its consequences. We engage in a conspiracy of silence that promotes the ill effects of racism and reduces the opportunities for change and progress."
Nitza Hidalgo, et al, ed, *Facing Racism in Education*

At a time when high government officials, certain prominent university scholars, even presidents of major colleges and U.S. Supreme Court Justice Sandra Day O'Connor, are making bold assertions about "race no longer being a major factor" in the lives of most black Americans, and when only the muted voices of the National Urban League, the Joint Center for Political Studies, and a few other "race" organizations dare risk exposing the contradictions continuing to drive the American psyche, it is appropriate that a different perspective be added to the chorus of voices.

Middle-age is said to be a time when men and women go through all sorts of wrenching mental and, for women, physical changes, sometimes causing bizarre and perplexing behavioral shifts. The up-side of this period in an individual's life is the ability to use hindsight as a way of looking into the future.

At age fifty-one, I finally came to the full realization that it is ultimately okay *not* to be white. That even though we blacks continue to be in the underbelly of American society and will likely continue to be there beyond the twenty-first century, on an individual level there is absolutely nothing about being white that should so attract our attention that we continue to engage in mental and physical evasions of our own individual selves for the sake of imitating or seeking approval from what turns out to be an illusion when seen at close range, what black Columbia University Professor Patricia Williams calls the "illusion of inclusion." Which simply means that beyond the paleness of their skins, and the obvious advantages accruing to it, whites struggle with the same

9

conditions of living: They live, breathe, love, hate, cry, laugh, hurt, and die. They make war, love, and babies. The black protagonist in the Chester Himes' short story "All God's Chillun Got Pride," came to an intimate if intellectual understanding of our similarities:

> That if he ever made an honest crusade into abstract truth and viewed Negroes and whites in physical, spiritual, mental comparison, detached from false ideologies and vicious, man-made traditions, dwelling only on those attributes which made of what he saw a man, and not of what his forebears might have been nor what he claimed to be by race, he would see, aside from pigmentation of skin and quality of hair, little difference in anatomy, mentality, and less difference in soul. He would see the same flesh, the same bones, the same blood, the same ability to walk upright, differentiating them all from other, and supposedly lower species of animals, the same organs of reproduction; he would see the same false convictions, taught by the same teachers and learned in the same ways, the same capacity for good and evil, for viciousness and generosity, for lust and philanthropy, he would see the passions in both compelling them to rape, steal, maim, murder, he would see the impelling urge for wealth, the destructive desires for power, the seeds of untold lies and the skeletons of deceits, he would see the same knowledge gleaned from the same founts; and when he looked into their souls and saw all the rotted falseness of ideologies imposed upon them all so that the few of any race could live and fatten from the blood, sweat, and tears of the many of all races, all the corruption of religions and philosophies and laws by which they all chained themselves to spiritual and physical slavery, and dedicated their offsprings for untold generations to ever-recurring horrors, for the life of him, God be his solemn judge, he could not have told the black from the white.

A character in Safire's novel of the Civil War *Freedom*, put it well when he mused that whiteness may suggest "purity and honor" but it also makes one think of "cold and death". Our only reasons for envy should be their greater access to opportunities society makes available, which whites claim as a birthright, and the *relative* security of person and property they enjoy.

> Sometimes I feel discriminated against, but it does not make me angry. It merely astonishes me. How *can* any deny themselves the pleasure of my company? It's beyond me.
>
> Zora Neale Hurston, *"How It Feels to be Colored Me"*

The value of this book is that it speaks of African American life in such a way that the reader can bridge the twentieth and twenty-first centuries. While I foresee a static underclass existence for large numbers of blacks, I also see changing attitudes and social structures in black communities. In the twenty-first century we blacks will have come to realize that our only chance for survival is to ignore some of the sham attractions which have taken too much of our attention and resources in the past. We will have finally come to understand that no matter the achievement of an individual, the world still respects the person who is affiliated with a *group* that commands respect. We will understand, for instance, that there is strength in buying a home in a black neighborhood thereby contributing to the stability and viability of black communities. We will come to know likewise that the meaning of physical beauty is not confined to light skin color and straight hair but spans the entire range of our variegated selves. More of us will come to agree with conservative economists like Thomas Sowell who have argued that other minority groups who have "made it" in America did not do so by having social assimilation as an initial priority on their agenda. They did it by engaging in group effort, particularly in the economic sector.

This is a book for young people—the under-thirty group. For it is they whose children will need to—will *have* to!—come to grips with a world not of their making, a world much more complex and confusing than the world of their parents. At the turn of the century, the U.S. Labor Department reports, minorities and women will make up two-thirds of new entrants to the workforce, and immigrants will for the first time since the First World War "represent the largest share of the increase in the population and the workforce." We will have a population mix inconceivable to early generations; and American youth will have to know how to cope with this profoundly New World. Black Americans will occupy a critical niche in the scheme of things.

These youngsters will not be able to rely on much of the writing of the last twenty years of the twentieth century for reliable information or guidance. Three of the most popular white American writers of the 1980s and 1990s, for instance, have virtually nothing to say about black Americans in their autobiographical writing even though each was in a unique position—for a white person—to make such observations.

The three writers are Lee Iaccoca of automobile industry fame; Andrew Greely, the "Parish Priest", and Lewis Grizzard, perhaps the South's greatest humorist since Mark Twain.

Iaccoca could not have avoided exposure to strong sentiments about blacks in his Italian upbringing, for with the Irish, Italian-Americans are considered by blacks to be among the most racially biased. Surely what he became as an adult, and as one of the nation's foremost corporate leaders, had to be influenced by his childhood experiences. Yet he is silent on race. (Except for brief references to Bill Cosby and Jesse Jackson, Mr. Iaccoca extends his omission streak into his second book *Talking Straight*—although the thoughtful reader will credit him for listing jobs as his number two priority "If...(he) Were President.")

Chicago has been appropriately labeled the most segregated large city in America. Andrew Greely, a 'Back of the Yards' Irishman, must have imbibed much racial prejudice from an area of the city known for its violently anti-black sentiments and actions. For decades no black would dare even walk through the area. As a Chicago resident for a time in the 1950s this writer was certainly aware of territorial limitations! It has traditionally been the Howard Beach of the Midwest! Yet Greely, an otherwise bright, well-informed, compelling writer and observer of the American social scene, completely ignores the matter of race in his popular autobiography. That "race" was a manifest feature in Greely's childhood neighborhood is revealed, in an oblique way, when he mildly castigates a neighbor who, on a government questionnaire, freely and "legitimately" admits his Dakota Indian heritage, "while in the neighborhood...he claims only to be Irish." If a dab of "Indian blood" had to be denied there is all the more reason to regard as highly suspect the absence of any mention of race as a factor. On relations between blacks and Irish Americans, James Baldwin made the interesting observation that a black man and an Irishman could be friends anywhere in the world except Boston (and Chicago, he could have added).

Our third prominent writer has even less reason to exclude race as a factor in his early life. Hailing from rural Georgia where "race," ala blacks, was, and is, a central factor in daily life, it is difficult to explain how Lou Grizzard, the popular Atlanta humorist and newspaper columnist, could exorcise such a vital area of Southern life from his autobiography. His only reference to "race" was mention of the Ray Charles – Willie Nelson collaboration on a record album as the ideal form of racial integration!

To deny the black experience of their own lives is a sad testament to the political intrusion of "racial" politics into the American literary arena. That these are best-selling authors—Iaccoca's autobiography alone sold six and one half million copies—who enjoy broad influence among American and international readers only compounds the omission.

But to omit the reality of the black world in print is not to negate its very real existence. To assert that race is no longer a factor in gauging the degree of well being of the black community simply serves as wish-fulfillment and ostrich-like evasions. Pick up any black newspaper on any given day and the headlines scream of race-related actions. For example: A copy of the June 16, 1990 edition of the *Los Angeles Sentinel* had been left by a patron in my barber's shop. It carried these headlines, on *one* page: "Ejected Black Customers: Airport Shops Makes Record Bias Settlement"; "Assessor Sued for Racism—Again"; "Math Teacher Says Blacks are 'Dog-Like'"; "Professor Charges Racism"; "Chicanos' Letter Draws Blacks' Ire"; "Suit Filed Challenging Minority"; and "Judicial Panel Mum on Discipline Case" (involving a black female judge).

Almost three years later to the day, and two years after the Rodney King incident, the same paper (picked up in the corner barber shop) carried a front page story headlined "Carson Family Will Receive $330,000 in Police Brutality Case." The story reports the unjustified beating of members of a black family (including a professional football player) following a routine traffic stop.

One of my purposes in writing this book is to leave the young reader of the twenty-first century a perspective on the black experience in America which is lacking in so much of mainstream writing in the last two decades of the twentieth century. It is my hope that these decision makers of the next century will have more than the tattered and incomplete record of popular writers and unprincipled political leaders for guidance; for they, unlike many of their parents, will not be able to conveniently ignore the black world.

> "But mostly we agreed that gettin' through the Battle of Hue' City without being blown away was like gettin' caught in a storm and tryin' to run between the raindrops without gettin' wet."
> Dale A. Dye, *Run Between the Raindrops: A Novel of Vietnam*, 1985

"Come and I'll tell you" tickles the ear.
African Proverb

Introduction

I do not feel myself to be, nor could I ever succeed in feeling like, a cold recorder of what I see and hear. On every professional experience I leave shreds of my heart and soul; and I participate in what I see or hear as though the matter concerned me personally and were one on which I ought to take a stand...
Oriana Fallaci, *Interview with History*

The general proposition of working for the world's good becomes too soon sickly sentimentality. I, therefore, take the work that the unknown lay in my hands and work for the rise of the Negro people, taking for granted that their best development means the best development of the world.
W.E.B. Du Bois, 1893

The black responsibility for the black condition is more crucial now, and more visible, than it has ever been before. There are some whites—there are many—who understand this very well, and welcome it but they do not form a majority of the white population.
James Baldwin, *The Evidence of Things Not Seen,* 1985

By most measures of national progress in the modern world, America has achieved greatness, unrivaled by nations East or West in its possession of great wealth, military supremacy, and endowment of natural resources.

The increased concentration of much of the nation's real wealth in fewer hands (by 1990 one percent of American families controlled almost 42 percent of its wealth, according to UCLA economist Maurice Zeitlin) has not diminished the aura or fact of American economic ascendancy.

But America's true greatness is not defined by military might or its Gross National Product. Many nations through the course of history have possessed the military muscle to do great harm to their rivals and enemies. For reasons peculiar to their geography, economic or military aggressiveness, or the character and personal vigor of their citizenry, many nations have also been wealthier than their neighbors.

Military and economic power and political stability are measures of might but not necessarily of true greatness. America is great because it has the potential of achieving a society unlike any other in the entire history of the political state. For a variety of reasons this nation is in the process of accommodating a vast diversity of peoples—by color, sex, national origin, economic class, and religion and creed. Whether by design, as some of the framers of the Constitution might have claimed, or the vagaries of its unique political history, no other nation in history has ever attempted to be all things to all people while at the same time demanding the respect—if not always unanimous appreciation—of other nations.

Unlike other nations who proclaim themselves democracies but who close their borders to immigration and settlement of people unlike themselves, the United States, even with periodic immigration control acts which severely limited non-white (and at times even Eastern and Southern European) entry, has nonetheless permitted "hordes" of legal and illegal immigrants to pass through the permeable membranes we call borders. That historical openness is today reflected in the multi-colored fabric of its people.

Within this bubbling caldron of melting but still unmelted pot of diverse cultures and "races" lies the great paradox of the Great Experiment. Black Americans have had the most to gain from the opportunities made available but have been able to share fewer of them than any other group.

The reader will note the exclusion of other than black and white females in the dedication. This is deliberate, for only white women (as a group) will have access to the resources, political influence, and potential for independent thinking and action that can make a difference in boardrooms and public forums. Clout! Black women have always been leaders in the human rights struggle but have never had the kind of political muscle their white sisters are increasingly able to muster. As a group, brown or Latino/Hispanic women, while large in number, appear as still too particularistic and culture bound. Further, they remain too deferential to the whims of their openly chauvinistic mates and the dictates of an authoritarian church. Former Reagan administration official Linda Chavez is not untypical of middle class Hispanic women who have left the barrio. She advocates total assimilation (presumably physical) of people of color into the white mainstream seemingly in disdain for anything of value in "minority" cultures. Her marriage to an Anglo is also not untypical. Native American women are few in number and the leaders among them have shown no inclination to invest in the concerns of blacks or other minority groups on a national scale. Moreover, problems "down on the reservation" are of such magnitude as to be almost overwhelming. Furthermore, anti-black prejudice is not unknown among Native Americans in the modern era. Black writer Ishmael Reed was surprised when an American Indian leader told him of the substantial anti-black prejudice in some Native American communities.

Exceptional leaders have emerged from the ranks of Asian American women (as from the other groups of course). Though few in number they have truly challenged traditional male dominance as well as societal problems. Their numbers have never been proportionate to that of African American and white female leaders, however, and it is unlikely that Asian American women, in all their diversity, will be of significant influence in the political and economic struggles to come. The rate of "out-marrying" among Asian American women; e.g. Japanese American women marrying white men at a rate greater than marriage to Japanese men, and the degree of tradition bound behavior in most Asian American cultures precludes active leadership by women around broad

14

social issues. In thinking of tradition and Asian women one thinks of Gandhi's description of the typical Hindu wife:

> A Hindu wife regards implicit obedience to her husband as the highest religion. A Hindu husband regards himself as lord and master of his wife, who must ever dance attendance upon him.

A gross generalization but instructive.

The principal motivating factor for writing this book lies in two sources. The first is that on two separate occasions two of America's most eminent black writers could not, to my satisfaction, answer a question put directly to them by the author. To wit, "As you are the acknowledged eyes and ears of the black community, our most prominent observers, where do you see black America heading in this country?" Each of these prize winning writers, (one the late James Baldwin), on separate occasions, declared, in almost the same words, "We have survived, and we will survive." That response may have been acceptable coming from a church preacher or hopeful grandmother; that it would come from a man and woman (Maya Angelou) universally hailed as our best, at a time when, in the view of many black observers, the black community is on the verge of sheer collapse, is distressingly disappointing. For if they don't know or don't have any guidance to offer, one wonders, who does? Who speaks for black America?

Equally distressing and inexplicable is the spate of articles and books heralding the decline of racism as a determinant of importance in the general welfare of black Americans. Beginning with black sociologist William Wilson's *The Declining Significance of Race*, certain prominent commentators have dethroned race as the culprit. A personal friend of the author, like Wilson also of the city of Chicago, has asked rhetorically: "If Dr. Wilson thinks race is unimportant, why is (he) referred to this way: "a black sociologist…department head of the Sociology Unit at the University of Chicago." Why isn't he just "Sociology Professor, Department Head, U of C?"

She adds that "I had the impression (after hearing his lecture) that Dr. Wilson had everything except a mirror." One well known white government official from the Reagan administration wrote that "The fact is, racism no longer accounts for the problems faced by most members of minority groups." The impact of race was not even among the seventy-one trends noted by the respected World Future Society's "long-term trends affecting the United States," or among its "hopes and fears" list. As late as 1992 the intellectual Jarid Taylor could boldly assert that "racism has declined dramatically in virtually all areas of life."

While the sociologist later moderated ("clarified") his views, it is probably fair to say that Race and Racism are not popular topics among whites (blacks can never avoid them) in contemporary America. But wishing something away doesn't in fact make it go away. There is simply too much obvious evidence— overt racist acts on our best college campuses, "riots" in Florida and Louisiana, and on and on—to ignore. Unless the American public demands truth from our

15

leaders and objective reporting from those who would inform us, the nation is destined to replay some of the worst mistakes of the past.

> All America lies at the end of the wilderness road, and our past is not a dead past, but still lives in us. Our forefathers had civilization inside themselves, the wild outside. We live in the civilization they created; but within us the wilderness still lingers. What they dreamed, we live, and what they lived we dream.
>
> T.K. Whipple, *Study Our Land*, quoted in Larry McMurtry, *Lonesome Dove*, 1985

What follows is a statement of the American racial scene as I see it. It is opinionated, sarcastic in places, cynical, hopeless mostly, hopeful here and there; it is unapologetic to whomever is the target; caustic; damning in its condemnations; and, finally, a labor of urgency to be added to the few remaining voices who still believe Martin Luther King's question of a generation ago imminently timely: "Where Do We Go From Here! Chaos or Community?" I am in tune with the Hispanic legal scholar formerly of Stanford who, critical of white domination of civil rights scholarship, proclaimed, "Readers of the present volume should be aware that I do not apologize, and indeed proclaim with pride that (my) work is "self-conscious, ethnocentric, ... angry... contentious... (and) controversial." I also share the sentiment of poet Langston Hughes who, in an earlier time, warned the reader:

> We younger (African American) artists who create now intend to express our individual dark-skinned selves without fear or shame. If white people are pleased we are glad. If they are not, it doesn't matter. We know we are beautiful. And ugly too. ...if colored people are pleased we are glad. If they are not, their displeasure doesn't matter either. We build our temples for tomorrow, strong as we know how, and we stand on top of the mountain, free within ourselves.

At an even earlier time, in an 1847 speech, Frederick Douglass demanded the right to openly criticize the land of his birth declaring he "will hold up America to the lightning scorn of moral indignation," making "no pretension of patriotism," thus "discharging the dirty of a true patriot."

Minority advocates are singularly accused of narrow-mindedness by white colleagues and the general (white) public. To the degree that our sharp focus is compelled by dark forces inimical to our very existence that touch us individually and collectively in very personal ways, we simply have no choice in our selection of priorities nor in how they are presented. Many of us, like Law Professor Patricia Williams *want* our readers to *feel* our passion and our personal hurt: "Writing for me is an act of sacrifice, not denial...I deliberately sacrifice myself in my writing. I leave no part of myself out, for that is how much I want readers to connect with me. I want them to wonder about the things I wonder about, and to think about some of the things that trouble me." Insofar as much of the literate public relies on the opinions of "objective" scholars, I offer the view of my friend Iola on experts and their statistics, arrived at after reading the disparate conclusions of two sociologists studying the same phenomenon: "...it seems that an (informed) opinion is as likely to be correct as research statistics."

> Baldwin believed, "that you had to accept, totally without rancor, life as it was and human beings as they were, which meant injustice was commonplace. But at the same time you also had to accept that 'one must never, in one's life accept these injustices as commonplace but fight them with all one's strength'. It meant keeping your heart free of hatred and despair and not succumbing to the fever, the rage in the blood that he had experienced..."
> W.J. Weatherby, *James Baldwin: Artist on Fire,* 1989

> "If you want to dislike me because of the color of my skin, fine. But make no movement or effort whatsoever to infringe upon my rights, because if or when you do that you will have hell to pay. It's that simple."
> CNN anchor Bernard Shaw in interview with *Black Issues in Education,* June 6, 1991

A work such as this book features numerous generalizations. Mature readers will understand the limitations inherent in attributing to every individual characteristics ascribed to the group. Nevertheless, as Patricia Williams has pointed out, "the simple matter of the color of one's skin so profoundly affects the way one is treated, so radically shapes what one is allowed to think and feel about this society, that the decision to generalize from such a division (into black and white) is valid." I take exception to novelist Saul Bellows' proclamation that he "is a Jew, and American," and that he "speaks for all men". I am confident only that the views expressed herein represent the thinking of a large number of African Americans, and, as such, should be of interest to all people who would be informed about an important piece of Americana.

> In battle, your perception is often only as wide as your battle sights. Five participants in the same action, fighting side by side, will often tell entirely different stories of what happened, even within hours of the fight. The story each man tells might be virtually unrecognizable to the others. But that does not make it any less true.
> Col. David Hackworth, U.S. Army (Ret.)

This book is an exploration into some of the forces that have shaped American history and set the stage for relations among the various constituents of the "pot" for generations into the twenty-first century. Among the topics and themes discussed in the present volume, those outlined below are of great import if the reader is to gain an understanding of the place of American blacks in the coming decades.

❀ The single most powerful indicator of black well-being throughout the nation's history has been the quality of leadership within major institutional sectors.

❀ Anti-black prejudice and racism are one of the several principal features giving definition to the American character.

❀ Forces internal to the black community act as powerful obstacles to the achievement of black progress.

❀ The black underclass is real and will include a greater proportion of blacks in the next century.

❀ The black middle class has grown in absolute numbers but is no more acceptable to masses of whites or any more secure in its status.

❀ A measure of the social and economic health of minority groups in America is the degree of well being of its young males.

❀ Blacks must take more responsibility for the course of their own lives, collectively and individually.

❀ Federal equal opportunity laws and affirmative action programs have benefitted whites and non-black minorities more than they have blacks.

"The man who is right is a majority. He who has God and conscience on his side, has a majority against the universe. Though he does not represent what we are, he represents what we ought to be."
Frederick Douglass

CHAPTER I

America in Brief...Through a Pair of Black Eyes

It is easier to count the census, or compute the square extent of a territory, to criticize its politics, books, art, than to come to the persons and dwellings of men, and read their character and hope in their way of life.
Through the Years With Emerson

To be born in a free society and not be born free is to be born a lie.
James Baldwin

As a relatively young nation, America is both easier to understand and more difficult. Manifest Destiny and the idea of progress are understood by people the world over as two forces driving the American character. The difficulty arises from our unparalleled diversity. Unlike almost all other nations, America is home to just about every imaginable color, "race", and ethnic heritage.

This chapter discusses the bright side of the American success story as well as shortcomings which point to continuing problems which must be overcome if the nation is to become a true "beacon for the world". Wars and geography explain much of our success; prejudice and greed have caused most of our failures.

Whatever America has become in its brief two hundred year history is not to be ascribed to a continuum reaching back to Western Europe, with which it is often grouped. Despite industrialization and modernization, Western European democracies remain highly stratified by class and "blood" with few real opportunities for those not born to wealth or status to move into the arenas of real power. The United States, by contrast, while stratified by wealth to some extent, and certainly by race, has a history of much buffeting by internal energies propelling it in ways unpredictable, and unprecedented as to outcomes. Through it all a grand, sometimes grandiose, vision of what America ought to be has served to keep competing diverse interests from tearing the whole into fragments. Success in the American Revolution and a written Constitution unlike any ever thus far adopted insured not only Manifest Destiny—from "sea to shining sea"—but the inevitable coming together around a common "battle cry" of all the disparate populations and interests making up the "pot".

War and National Unity

Without question, America's wars have played a significant role in welding diverse peoples into a nation. The Revolutionary War resulted in individuals, for the first time, thinking of themselves as Americans. Even the monumentally disruptive Civil War did not diminish,—for many U.S. military officers who had fought for American interests in Mexico, and who were to lead the Confederate forces—allegiance to the *nation*. They were almost to a man, as the historian Bruce Catton reported, torn between loyalty to the nation and a personal affinity for their native states. Robert Lee suffered this internal tug of war and remarked that "secession is nothing but revolution," vowing to "carry no arms against the United States," yet seemingly contradictorily allowing that "it may be necessary for me to carry a musket in defense of my native state, Virginia." His fight was not a fight against the United States, but, early in the war, *for* Virginia. Nor was his a fight to preserve chattel slavery which, to him, was an anachronism. Lee wrote that slavery "is a moral, social, and political evil." Confederate president Jefferson Davis "loved the Union" but "had to cast his lot with his state." Celebrated Confederate General "Stonewall" Jackson biographer John Bowers said that Old Jack's wife wrote of him that "'He was strongly for the Union, but at the same time he was a firm States-right man…(who) maintained that it was better for the South to fight for her rights in the Union than out of it.'" Albert Sybley Johnston and others openly wept out of love for the Union even as they resigned their commissions and headed south to lead the forces against that same Union. "Love of the Union" was the rallying cry born at Bunker Hill, Lexington, and Yorktown.

Neither Lee nor Stonewall Jackson, nor most Confederate leaders, believed in the institution of chattel slavery, and went to great pains to explain that their fight was not for the purpose of prolonging that "troublesome" way of life. Catton argues in *Reflections on the Civil War* that few soldiers on either side— Union or Confederate, officer or enlisted—really cared about the institution of slavery. Of the Southerners, he wrote, "the vast majority of soldiers…did not come from slave-owning families, never expected to own slaves themselves and to the very end indignantly repelled suggestions that they were fighting in defense of slavery." Indeed, former Confederate Army guerilla leader John Mosby claims that after the war, confederate generals who fought to preserve slavery even if holding personal disdain for it, had become "Preeminent national heroes…North and South."

Contrary to the thinking of many blacks, northern whites were, at best, indifferent to the plight of blacks, slave or free. John Gauss points out that many whites, among them Abolitionists, who wished blacks freed "thought them inferior nonetheless, and had no desire to live and work with them." Ironically, according to Catton, many Northern whites, like most Southerners, would rather see slavery continue because they "could get along with the black man as a slave much better than they could get along with him as a free person." C. Van Woodward, "Dean of American Historians," has written that even historians who wanted to see slavery abolished believed in "white supremacy...(and held) anti-negro assumptions." Sinkler notes that "much of Northern life and "thought before the Civil War was rather Negrophobic."

William Lloyd Garrison, along with Frederick Douglass, a leader of the anti-slavery movement, could not find a place to speak at the University of Michigan, notes J.H. Kidd, a student at the time. Garrison was forced to the "lower part of town...(where) he was set upon by a lot of roughs, who interrupted him with cat-calls and hisses, and made demonstrations so threatening, that, to avoid bodily injury, he was compelled to make his exit through a window...It was not safe for an 'Abolitionist' to free his mind even in the 'Athens' of (Ann Arbor) Michigan." (Put in this historical context current race related problems on that campus do not come as a surprise.)

U.S. Grant was no partisan for black freedom. Catton said "he despised abolitionists; his wife was an owner of slaves" and even he "owned a field hand." To Grant's credit it should be noted that this slave was manumitted at a time when the Grant family was hard up for cash and could have realized a thousand dollars from the sale of the slave. Also, on Grant's headquarters staff was a colonel who was a full-blooded Cherokee Indian. A photograph of Grant's staff reproduced in the *Civil War Times Illustrated* (Feb. 1990) clearly shows Col. Ely Parker, Grant's secretary. Yet, as President, Grant called for extermination of the Indian, actor Marlon Brando told television correspondent Connie Chung.

That Grant was not as Negrophobic as most of his fellow Northerners was demonstrated following the heroic combat conduct of green black troops at the battle of Milliken's Bend, Mississippi, where, according to Sinkler, he praised black soldiers, asked for more, and in a General Order directed white troops to "aid in removing prejudices against them." He also said that "the Negro are easier to preserve discipline among than our white troops." (When examining black recruits for the newly formed 54th Massachusetts Regiment, Surgeon General Dale reported that "the barracks, cookhouses, and kitchens far surpassed in cleanliness any I have ever witnessed, and were models of neatness and good order.")

Participation in a disciplined military lifestyle makes one out of many. Perhaps the most poignant example of the welding of America's diverse groups by the success of the Revolutionary War was the popular Irish doggerel chanted by Union foot soldiers:

> To the flag we are pledged
> All its foes we abhor.
> And we ain't for the nigger
> But we are for the war.

Historian Burchard comments that some "Billy Yanks" had more "practical sentiments" in a marching ditty:

In battle's wild commotion
I won't at all object
If a nigger should stop a bullet
Coming for me direct.

John Jakes points to the most important fact of the Civil War, one which must be acknowledged if we are to fully comprehend contemporary racial politics and sociology: "Despite Lincoln, despite the radicals, despite amendments to the Constitution, white America remained racist after the war."

The point I make here is that a union, a nation, was an inconceivable outcome of the mix of early settlers who came to call themselves Americans, had not they achieved success in the war against Great Britain. Later victories over Indian nations and other darker peoples followed by the victory over Nazi Germany and Imperial Japan ingrained both a sense of military invincibility and racial superiority. War is more than an instrument of policy and "politics by other means." Success in war brings people together. "There is no success like success." Success in war defines who we are in a way no other political instrumentality can. Catton argues that in fact the ultimate value of the Civil War was that the Union victory solidified the nation and prevented dissolution into warring political entities—

The North American Continent was not Balkanized; the geographic unit that made possible the wealth and the prosperity of later days was preserved. Beyond that, the country made a commitment to a broader freedom, a broader citizenship. We can no longer be content with anything less than complete liberty, complete equality before law for all of our people regardless of their color, their race, their religion, their national origins; regardless of anything. We all have to fare alike.

So, America became a nation through the instrumentality of war. And the European settlers became Americans. And they became "white" by virtue of conquest over "darker races", slave and Indian. Europeans, James Baldwin wrote, have not historically thought of themselves as "white"; they have been French, English, Dane, Italian, and so on. It is only in the context of settler society, particularly in America, that it became necessary to become "white". Jewish novelist Saul Bellow commented that civilized Europeans exhibit little racial prejudice upon arrival and are able to "conveniently lodge their not fully mastered biases in the free-for-all USA." But as racial prejudice is a complement of the general white American ethos, immigrant Europeans were, and are, obliged to take on race prejudice in the same way they had to adopt other "survival" tools.

Religion as Instrument of Bonding and Toleration

Success in war can account for a national identity but it cannot be the sole factor accounting for national success or progress. Perhaps the best illustration of America's astounding success from the perspective of democratic philosophy

22

lies in the arena of religion. From time immemorial nations—whether called tribes, socialist, communist, kingdoms, monarchies—have achieved much of their national unity through a dominant religious motif. Even where other systems of belief were tolerated and splinter groups or sects were unmolested by the State—very few in number!—in no other modern nation did such an array of "religions and denominations" achieve the degree of freedom permitted in the United States.

For some religious groups, toleration had to be won through trial, tribulation and blood, as Hofstadter has observed. That they also called themselves Christian in a self-proclaimed Christian nation did not save them from the wrath of their fellows. Joseph Smith and his successors were chased from the East out into the Utah salt flats where no other whites wanted to live, believing it uninhabitable, dodging bullets, tar and feathers, and opprobrium, all the way. That abominable period notwithstanding, today the Church of Jesus Christ of Latter Day Saints (Mormons) is one of the wealthiest and most influential non-Jewish religious groups in the country, with an estimated eight million members worldwide in 1991 and billions in assets. The material achievements of American Catholics is paralleled by the economic success of Mormons on the organizational level. Mormon power in Utah and several other western states is omnipresent, dominating political as well as economic life. (Mormon treatment of blacks is covered in a later section.)

Equally successful are the Amish. Hostetler observes that the anabaptists (including Amish) came to ruin between the Thirty Years' War and the War of the Palatinate, which ended in 1697. It was a terrible time:

> The devastation of war, plunder, and fire was followed by famine and pestilence. People ate roots, grass and leaves. Some resorted to cannibalism...The bodies of children were not safe from their mothers.

Hounded by "Church and State," they were "burned at the stake...(and) some were placed in sacks and thrown into rivers."

The Amish were very nearly eliminated; and if any had survived in Europe as of this writing they would not recognize the practice or belief of their American brothers and sisters. Far from being viewed as an "obscure sect living by ridiculous customs," after being chased out into the Atlantic and into America, the Amish are now seen as an almost godlike people, and as "islands of sanity in a culture gripped by commercialism and technology run wild." Like Joseph Smith's, Jacob Ammann's "quiet people in the land" have done well.

The success story goes on. Jews are far and beyond the most prominent success story among "minority" religious groups. Quakers, with their "meetings" and pacifism, also had their problems in Europe and later in America; yet no one argues with the fact of their acceptance into the American religious landscape. Early Roman Catholics were accused of blind allegiance and obedience to the Pope—"Romanism"—; they had become by the late twentieth century mainstream Americans who can even join the Ku Klux Klan!

As historians have recognized, geography itself was a principal factor in the success of some of the early "extremist" religious sects. Blessed with vast unpopulated (except for Indian nations which came not to count) stretches of "free" land, the nation could tolerate if not integrate the "infidels". Had the Mormons been unable to migrate west, it is highly unlikely they could have survived the onslaught of physical abuse they suffered in the East. And had not the Amish held to a personal and group discipline which characterizes their lifestyle, their demise would have been equally predictable.

The latest chapter in the religious equation is the emergence of Jerry Falwell's Moral Majority which, in the wake of the Jim Bakker and Jimmy Swaggart scandals, appears to be in decline. In the zenith of its popularity millions of Americans flocked to the banner of "returning to the basics," legitimizing a literal interpretation of the Bible, and pouring tens of millions of dollars into the coffers of the righteous. In the 1990s it was overshadowed by the more secretive Christian Coalition.

The important thing to understand in this discussion is that while religious tolerance never reached the level many Americans would like to believe, diversity of religious groups could have but did not on a national level divide the nation into warring camps to the extent that the political entity itself was threatened. Like success in war, religious tolerance became a bonding substance rather than the nation-wrecker it might have become. That an American president in a "Christian" nation could almost poke fun at organized religion at a time when few questioned the Christian label is itself a testament to the degree of religious tolerance. When asked what his religion was, Abe Lincoln is said to have replied: "When I do good, I feel good; when I do bad, I feel bad; and that's my religion."

Much has been written about the place of religion in the history of African Americans in America. What is assuredly known is that no matter the motives of those who controlled the lives of black Americans—in slavery or after—and denied, promoted, or encouraged religious worship among them, the Christian Church has been their most influential social institution. And it may yet be that the tolerance of religious belief and worship may become for blacks what culture and secular institutions became for others.

Leaders: The Presidents

Religious diversity and tolerance is one of the grand foundation columns of the United States. Another, with equally turbulent historical twists, is the quality of national leadership. Often overlooked by all but "revisionist" historians is the conspicuously contradictory political behavior of men who came to occupy places of great honor on the scrolls of America's leaders—men who were great statesmen, orators, military heroes, "captains of industry", and religious and educational pioneers. Put another way, they were leaders who have taken us down two wholly contradictory paths, beginning with the Founding Fathers (there were no *mothers* among them). On the one hand, guided presumably by democratic principles and revolutionary zeal, a group of "true intellectuals" led by the likes of Jefferson and Madison, produced two of mankind's most revolutionary documents—the Declaration of Independence and Bill of Rights. Yet, as Michener has a character explain in *Chesapeake*, these same men of great erudition and passion were Southerners and slaveowners. Of the first twelve U.S. presidents, nine owned slaves. Thus, those documents which eventually came to be hailed as beacons of liberty and freedom for hundreds of millions of the world's oppressed were framed not with the goal of "liberty and justice for all" but to serve the purposes of those already "in", namely white male Protestant property owners.

That the revolutionary leadership had no intention of extending coverage of its "sacred principles" to blacks became obvious as certain enterprising blacks attempted to force their way into the "pie". Businessman Paul Cuffee, a war hero, having met all the official qualifications for exercising the franchise, in an impassioned plea to the Constitutional Convention, said:

> If you are fighting this war because taxation without representation is tyranny, since we (blacks) are taxed and we are not permitted to vote, we don't think we should pay our taxes...

Without explanation, but perhaps for "disturbing the peace," "they were thrown in jail". So would any of the other five thousand black revolutionaries fighting for independence making the same request. Vexed that her husband John and other Revolutionary partisans could so glibly and hypocritically tolerate and protect slavery, Abigail Adams remonstrated that "it always appeared a most iniquitous scheme to me to fight ourselves for what we are daily robbing and plundering from those who have as good a right to freedom as we have." Eminent historian John Hope Franklin has written that the Founding Fathers welcomed black combat soldiers yet "were not willing to extend to blacks the rights for which they fought in the war." A situation which, as we shall see, followed each of America's wars.

The matter of national leadership is critical to understanding the evolving "place" of African Americans in contemporary American society. Black leaders of the 1980s accused Ronald Reagan of following the lead of past presidents who publicly proclaimed their personal abhorrence to racial discrimination—certainly in its most virulent forms—but whose actions appeared to give lie to those pronouncements. Because Jefferson, Washington, Madison and other Founding Fathers—"none of them," in Franklin's words—could imagine blacks as equal *human beings*, the nation witnesses a Howard Beach, Cummings, Georgia, and Amherst and South Central L.A.

Strong anti-black sentiments have characterized virtually all the nation's leaders as well as the general populace. Our most learned and philosophically democratic leaders are no exception. The esteemed and universally loved Benjamin Franklin had great disdain for darker peoples, asking, in *Observations Concerning the Increase of Mankind*, circa 1751, why should we (whites) "darken" the people of America: "Why increase the sons of Africa, by Planting them in America, where we have so fair an opportunity, by excluding all Blacks and Tawneys, of increasing the lovely white?" Thomas Jefferson, perhaps our most intellectual president, set the tone for presidential sentiment regarding race, noting in the massive *Notes on Virginia* that while he could not definitively confirm scientifically that blacks were on a lower level on the scale of evolution, he had a "suspicion" that they "are inferior to the whites in the endowments of both mind and body." (While there is not unanimous agreement among historians that Jefferson in fact took the mulatto Sally Hemings, his wife's half-sister, as a mistress, there is sufficient agreement that Hemings mothered several white-fathered children; and her descendants are convinced.) In denying that Jefferson could or would have engaged in such philandering his descendants join with those of other famous white men, eg., North Pole explorer Admiral William Peary, who wanted no connection to that darker part of their heritage, ignoring that wherever white men (and men of other hues as well) have journeyed they have invariably left behind reminders of their passage. Jefferson was perplexed with his own contradictions. To affirm black humanity and solve his own evident guilt he needed, he wrote, "to see proof that nature has given to our black brethren talents equal to those of the other colors of men ...," unrelated to their "degraded condition." Like others who believe in racial supremacy (but far less charitably than Jefferson), he must have suffered acute anxiety when introduced to Benjamin Banaker, mathematician, astronomer, and assistant surveyor who laid out the design for the District of Columbia. Banaker, of course, was black.

Honest Abe, the Great Emancipator, believed that whites were and would always be superior to blacks, and he could not see how the two groups could ever live in the same space in a state of harmony and equality. (Even so, Lincoln had a black bodyguard, Ferdinand Schavers, from 1861 to 1863.) It has been reported that Abe's son Robert was so disdainful of blacks that "he refused to let them wait on him or touch his luggage, car, or any of his possessions. Blacks who did got their knuckles whacked with his cane." (Those who emphasize that the major platform of the Republican Party at its founding in 1847 was abolition of slavery, often fail to mention that, as James Bilotta reports, the Party's leaders were to a man, believers in Negro inferiority. Bilotta adds that "racism was at the core of their political beliefs and goals.")

> Lincoln and Garrison, John Brown and the Alcotts they were the same—aflame with one true mockery of freedom, truth, and faith but not for brotherhood.
> Margaret Walker, "Five Black Men...and Ten Will Save the City"
> a poem

Our more recent presidents have harbored similar sentiments toward blacks. Theodore "Teddy" Roosevelt, perhaps our most ardent presidential proponent of individual courage and personal responsibility, followed black troops up San Juan Hill and allowed they were excellent fighting men. He also denigrated blacks with the claim that to "mingle the races" by permitting "social equality" would mean "suicide for the white race". In his acquiescence in the "legal" lynching of black soldiers in Brownsville, Texas, Roosevelt demonstrated an unwillingness to do more than "speak softly and carry a big stick." After more than fifty years these men, the lynched and the illegally discharged survivors, were exonerated. After black and white federal employees in the District of Columbia had been working together for fifty years in "peace, harmony, and friendliness," the Ph.D. intellectual Woodrow Wilson, through a "stroke of the pen" (an executive order), resegregated the federal civil service costing blacks thousands of jobs (which were at the time the only non-professional route into the black middle class). Wilson did not regret to send black soldiers off to World War I to help make the world "safe for democracy". He further showed his race bias by openly weeping in sympathy for the white "victims" after viewing the racist film *Birth of a Nation* at a private White House showing. In his important essay "Propaganda as History", historian John Hope Franklin deemed "*Birth of a Nation* the midwife in the rebirth of the most vicious terrorist organization in the history of the United States." The Klan. Former Virginia Governor Douglas Wilder has noted the passionate criticism Herbert Hoover came under for "the mere inviting of (black) Illinois Congressman Oscar DePriest's wife to a social gathering," some state legislatures even "threatened sanctions."

In the memory of Americans living in the 1990s the nation's chief executive officers have by and large tended to be more subtle but no less prejudiced than their predecessors. The aristocrat Franklin D. Roosevelt exhibited the degree of his concern for racial justice by approving the continued segregation of the Armed Forces and advising complaining blacks that justice for them would have to wait until Germany and Japan surrendered. Even with wife Eleanor's prodding he refused to support an anti-lynching law. His greatest concession to racial equality was to establish the Fair Employment Practices Commission, a concession forced by a threatened "March on Washington" by Sleeping Car Porter's Union President A. Philip Randolph. This time around Eleanor had her way (with covert encouragement by Mary McLeod Bethune and other black leaders). Establishment of the Fair Employment Practices Commission (FEPC) drew many blacks into the Democratic Party; yet, according to economist Thomas Sowell, Roosevelt's New Deal policies did not materially help large numbers of blacks, that, because, in Sowell's words, the "ratio of black income to white income *fell* during this period." The war industries of World War II were in fact the cause of black economic gains, not Roosevelt's policies, a fact lost on many blacks and whites.

John F. Kennedy, whose likeness the author has seen hanging alongside that of Martin Luther King, Jr. in many black American *and* African homes, also had to be persuaded by fast-moving domestic political events to act in the name of racial justice and fairness. Nothing in the record of "might have been" had JFK survived his first term is convincing of a dramatic turn on behalf of civil rights. To John Kennedy's credit, however it must be conceded that he and his brother Robert were responsible for creating a political atmosphere conducive to accepting the changes that were to come later. (Kennedy's charisma was worldwide. Hackworth noted during a military tour in West Germany that adulation for JFK was so great among Germans that an observer would have thought he'd been elected *their* president.) Most important for African Americans, they were able to confront as no previous administration had dared the racist recalcitrance of the FBI's J. Edgar Hoover. It was left to Kennedy's unlikely successor, Lyndon Johnson, to become the twentieth century's great emancipator. Hailing from a staunchly segregationist social background, himself early in political life a "dyed-in-the-wool" segregationist (historian John Hope Franklin notes that Johnson voted against every civil rights bill to come before him through the 1957 congressional session), LBJ saw history in the making, jumped aboard the "Freedom Train" and rode to glory on the courage of his equal opportunity laws and executive orders. He, more than the boyishly charismatic but hesitant Kennedy, should be remembered for his signal contributions to the furtherance of human rights and the fulfillment of the pristine promises of the Declaration of Independence and the Bill of Rights.

LBJ was followed by a president from whom blacks had little reason to expect much. Despite his politics Richard M. Nixon made several curious contributions to the forward thrust for equal employment and educational opportunity for minorities and women. He strengthened affirmative action regulations and signed the Education Amendments of 1972 extending the benefits of previously enacted civil rights legislation to women, and was a strong supporter of minority business enterprise. But "Tricky Dick" was no paragon of virtue regarding minority rights. In his view blacks were "jungle bunnies" who were inherently inferior intellectually to whites. (He was also reported to have strong anti-Semitic feelings, yet was forced by Jewish economic and political clout to follow the practice of appointing Jews to high government and diplomatic positions...The reader should understand that presidential appointment of Jews is not a modern phenomenon. George Washington initiated the "practice" when he accepted financial assistance from wealthy Jews, perhaps in exchange for his vigorous denunciation of religious bigotry). On Nixon's "hit list", as revealed by the White House Tapes, was black Michigan Congressman John Conyers, whose transgression was revealed in a one-liner: "He likes white women"! In a post-president interview Nixon said:

> A lot of people are just as racist now (as back in the 1950s) but it's not fashionable anymore...You can't talk about blacks like you once did...The racism has receded, I think. But it's there and it always will be there.

Following Nixon, Ford appeared to be a non-leader, following more than leading. Nothing of note occurred during his brief administration to give any hope to blacks or women. His successor, Jimmy Carter, who, like Johnson, had roots deep in southern culture, and, also like Johnson, achieved visible gains in the civil rights arena, most notable in appointments of federal judges. One suspects that Carter's thinking on civil rights had more to do with religious conversion to Born Again Christianity than philosophical or political considerations. Former President Reagan, the man whom Camille Cosby told Spelman

College's 1989 graduating class was "this century's worst educated president," probably did more to resist the evolutionary movement toward openness, fairness, and racial justice, than any chief executive since Woodrow Wilson. It will be well into the twenty-first century—barring miracles (which do happen!) before the retrogressive shift in attitudes and white social behaviors instigated by Reagan are again challenged and reexamined. Marilyn Yarborough says of the Reagan administration that it was fixated on an illusion that discrimination no longer exists, "that somehow, somewhere, the slate was wiped clean." The worst kind of wishful thinking. All of that notwithstanding, Reagan's first administration provided some $15 billion to minority businesses.

Many black Americans viewed George Bush's administration with mixed emotions. Unlike his predecessor, Bush is seen by many as being personally free of race prejudice or ill-will toward blacks. While both his appointment of Colin Powell as Chairman of the Joint Chiefs of Staff and Clarence Thomas to the U.S. Supreme Court are acknowledged as politically motivated, many also hold the view that such gestures spring from deep personal commitments. On the other hand, many view Bush's tinkering with the civil rights bill (which the President signed with great reluctance in 1991 after an earlier veto) or massaging the agenda of conservatives all along the political right continuum and signalling, as did Reagan, that bigotry, not equal opportunity, was the new order. In failing to take into account the vast reservoir of anti-black prejudice remaining in white America, Bush, again like Reagan, set a tone apparently amiable to the haters and manicured David Dukes.

Actor Kirk Douglas has raised the interesting point that most American presidents, while elected to represent all the people—"all faiths, all colors"—will join private, segregated and Jewish-restrictive clubs once they are out of office. Carter is probably the only ex-president whose sense of morality and ethics would prohibit such hypocritical conduct.

> Why do holders of high office so often act contrary to the way reason points and enlightened self-interest suggests. Why does intelligent mental processes seem so often not to function?
> Barbara Tuckman, *The March of Folly: From Troy to Vietnam*

But why should blacks hope or presume that American presidents are, or should be, any less racially prejudiced than the population over whom they preside? After all, warns Blauner, "Race and racism...are central to the economics, politics and culture of this nation." While some historians such as Lerone Bennett, Jr. have argued that the virulent racism accompanying and growing out of chattel slavery was absent in the early years of the black presence in the colonies, (as evidenced by the presence of black "men of means": ship builders, merchants, and other entrepreneurs, many of whom employed *black and white* workers), by the mid nineteenth century both white racial superiority and white Christianity were believed by most whites to be the higher good for the entire world. White, in Horsman's words, "was a superior race, and inferior races were doomed to subordinate status or extinction." No president, even of the intellect of a Jefferson could free himself of the binding ligature of white racial superiority.

The liberal theory of political leadership in democracies is ludicrous in light of the indebtedness a president carries with him into the Oval Office: he owes a debt to the wealth which financed his victory, in the view of Will and Ariel Durant; to the political and social attitudes of white voters whose votes he required; and to an unspoken but understood code of conduct which will keep him there and perhaps assure his re-election. (The male gender is used deliberately here.) Lincoln and Kennedy paid the price of severe non-conformity, becoming genuine heroes only after violent deaths. The monastic Thomas Merton explained this phenomenon:

> Every society honors its live conformists and its dead troublemakers.

Leaders: Industrial and Economic

Political king makers were not alone in harboring ill will toward black Americans. Rulers of economic empires have been equally (some would say more guilty since they control millions of jobs) responsible for denying opportunity. Wealthy and powerful white supporters of Booker T. Washington, men such as Andrew Carnegie and Roger Baldwin and John Rockefeller, believed implicitly in Negro inferiority and denied critical financial support to schools trying to provide true higher education to early descendants of slaves.

These early "robber barons" spawned ideological descendants. When famed black photojournalist Gordon Parks was beginning to receive professional recognition he was given an introduction to the art director of *Harper's Bazaar*. Looking forward to meeting Parks but not realizing he was black the director, who was Jewish and sympathetic to the black cause, had to say, "I must be frank with you. This is a Hearst organization. We can't hire Negroes," even though he was personally "embarrassed and terribly sorry." A tycoon of a later era, Coors Beer Chairman, William Coors, once exclaimed that though blacks had the drive, they "lack the intellectual capacity to succeed, and its taking them down the tubes." He also felt that Africa never offered the world anything of value (except for its mineral wealth) and thought black Americans ought to be grateful for having been "rescued" into slavery and brought out of the Dark Continent. Coors family watcher Russ Bellant believes that the Coors family's apparent capitulation to a more enlightened perspective on race matters is really a smoke screen to cover a move to a higher not different level of ultra right conservatism. To Bellant, selling beer to "new markets"—racial minorities, gays and lesbians—generates revenue that goes to "promote theories that would roll back the political and social gains made in the past thirty years: and "funds right-wing groups (such as) Heritage Foundation, Hoover Institute" and Anti-democratic forces in Africa. There is no possibility, from Bellant's point of view, that Angola's rebel army led by Savumbi's UNITA, could have been the anti-democratic instrument of subversion and terror that it is without massive covert support from Western sources, for example.

In 1986 a newspaper in a so-called progressive Southern city—the "Black Mecca of America"—disclosed that several powerful banks in the city had conspired to deny access to home mortgage and improvement loans to blacks. *Any* blacks. Ability to pay the loan was not a factor, for all blacks were screened out. (For this story the newspaper won a Pulitzer; but an important editor was forced to resign not long after.) In 1991 the Federal Reserve revealed that the practice is widespread concluding that "dramatic disparities in loan-rejection rates" along racial lines, no matter the income of black applicants, were apparent.

Americans have not really appreciated how one individual (usually a male) can deny entire segments of the population access to society's goods and services. Another example: One white man, simply on the basis of his personal prejudices against Alaska Natives, persuaded a major public body to close a fishing area that was the economic lifeblood of Natives in this area. That it was race prejudice not the desire to conserve resources was revealed in diaries he kept.

Another example is Charles Lindbergh, America's aviation hero (and Adolph Hitler worshipper.) Shortly after completing his epic solo flight in the *Spirit of St. Louis*, Lindbergh remarked that aviation was the preserve of whites. It was, he said, "one of the priceless possessions which permit the white race to live at all in a pressing sea of yellow, black and brown." A legacy of Lindbergh's sentiments is that in 1991 of 50,000 commercial pilots in the U.S. less than 300 were black, representing only 0.6% of all major airline pilots. One black pilot who sued and collected damages from a major carrier said "White men think it's a white man's job."

This extreme racism isn't entirely dead, however, and it appears in some of the most unlikely places. For example, a wealthy white industrialist and donor to an upper Midwest college makes a substantial gift which had to be returned when the college trustees learned that the donor had personally mailed hate literature to racially mixed families, some of the flyers reading "…a dog breeder would not think of producing mongrel dogs, so why should the human race be mongrel?" (An important black professional of that state told the author that he had received one of these flyers, adding, "and I was married to a *black* woman!") A white student in my Black History class related how his wealthy industrialist uncle remarked that his Alma Mater (Notre Dame) was having an off-year because too many blacks were on the football team. The wedding of racism, power, and wealth is one of the principal obstacles to progress for blacks.

Leaders: Education and Science

Racist attitudes have not been confined to military, political, and industrial leaders, of course. Racism in education, within the foremost ranks of university scholars, went hand in hand with racism among the nation's less erudite leaders. Some of America's most respected scholars and academic leaders were far less polite than Jefferson on matters of race. I.Q. test pioneer Lewis Terman said of non-whites that "The 70 to 80 I.Q. is very common among Spanish-Indian and Mexican families…and also among Negroes." And like Jefferson he believed "Their dullness seems to be racial…and cannot be wiped away by any scheme of mental culture."

Stephen Jay Gould's classic work *The Mismeasure of Man* documents a convincing history of racism in science in the American academy. From the conscious racial bias of a Cyril Burt who, Gould states, "faked data" to arrive at predetermined conclusions, to other equally prominent scientists who had biases that were "unknowingly influential" in their work, American science (which in fact was birthed by pre-American European biological determinism) has not been a friend to a genuine quest for truth or to nonwhites, particularly blacks, who were usually assigned to the very lowest rung of the genetic pecking order.

Most striking in Gould's work is the sheer physical revulsion many leading scientists felt for blacks. Gould provides a striking illustration in the career of the "great Swiss naturalist" Louis Agassiz (a name familiar to American college students from introductory science courses). Agassiz, who never even saw a black person before emigrating to the United States, thereby having no first-hand experience from which to draw negative attitudes, nonetheless "experienced a pronounced visceral revulsion" when he first encountered blacks. In a letter to his mother, which Gould claims is usually omitted or paraphrased by historians in accounts of Agassiz's life and work, the great scientist expressed his true feelings; here quoted in length from Gould because of the clarity it brings to the matter of "scientific objectivity":

> But truth before all. Nevertheless, I experienced pity at the sight of this degraded and degenerate race, and their lot inspired compassion in me in thinking that they are really men. Nonetheless, it is impossible for me to repress the feeling that they are not of the same blood as us. In seeing their black faces with their thick lips and grimacing teeth, the wool on their head, their bent knees, their elongated hands, their large curved nails, and especially the livid color of the palm of their hands, I could not take my eyes off their face in order to tell them to stay far away. And when they advanced that hideous hand towards my plate in order to serve me, I wished I were able to depart in order to eat a piece of bread elsewhere, rather than dine with such service. What unhappiness for the white race—to have tied their existence so closely with that of negroes in certain countries! God preserve us from such a contact!

For the remainder of his life Agassiz crusaded against any sort of black-white social interaction and remained wedded to the fiction of black inherited inferiority. Calling intermarriage a "sin against nature" and "shuddering against the consequences," Agassiz used his high visibility as a respected even acclaimed Harvard scientist to promote a mythical science. And even as he neared death when many reputable scientists began to "regard his as a rigid and aging dogmatist,"…"he remained a hero to the public" and "his social preferences for racial segregation prevailed."

Agassiz and Terman's legacy is carried forward by academic intellectuals such as Arthur Jensens, Michael Levin, Richard Herrnstein and, in Canada, J. Phillippe Ruston, prominent Professor of Psychology at the University of Western Ontario.

It is indeed difficult to discern a qualitative difference between conclusions reached by these eminent academic scientists and those of Adolph Hitler, who, in the infamous manifesto *Mein Kampf*, allowed for the Negroes' kindest disposition" but warned the their native intelligence was of such a low level that "all assimilation, all education is bound to fail on account of the racial inborn features of the blood."

The principal point of Gould's book is that science and scientists do not exist in a vacuum uninfluenced by culture and the events of the time. Psychologist Arthur Jensen's resurrection of the theory of inherited black intellectual inferiority, and its wide acceptance among the white public and within some academic circles, is as much influenced by the political and social context in which it was generated as was those of the earlier biological determinists. "Science," Gould warns, "is a socially embedded activity."

> But I was inspired to write this book because biological determinism is rising in popularity again, as it always does in times of political retrenchment. The cocktail party circuit has been buzzing with its usual profundity about innate aggression, sex roles, and the naked ape. Millions of people are now suspecting that their social prejudices are scientific facts after all.

While biological determinism has worked to the disadvantage of some European groups—particularly southern and eastern groups who were deemed less intelligent by test scores—it is blacks who have been the brunt of scientific racism and to whose great detriment it has been because of its "evident utility for groups in power."

The list of "scientific racists" is long and includes prominent names like Carlton Putnam, Carlton Coon, William Shockley, and the latter day statistics manipulators Arthur Jensen and Michael Levin. When the lay public looks to respected scientists for truth they all too often ignore University of California at Berkeley's Ronald Takaki who cautions:

> Like everyone else, scholars have ideas and beliefs about human nature and society. Their conceptions of what the moral universe is or should be, how people behave and should behave, what America is and what is should be, influence the ways they frame their questions, select and examine their evidence, and draw their conclusions.

A recent "craze" in higher education is the Palestinian immigrant Edward Said's *Culture and Imperialism* wherein the case is strongly made for a wholistic assessment of how conquered peoples are portrayed by their new rulers. Arguing (as has numerous African Americans from late 19th century onward) that "all aspects of society participated (in the subjection) including artists and writers," Said posits that only when we admit that even as we enjoyed the best of Western art and literature, we have to openly confess that much of it complemented the more racist programs of political, military, religious, and education leaders. Said notes that some of the white West's most sacred literary icons, such as Rudyard Kipling and Joseph Conrad, "provided the moral grounds for colonial expansion." Kipling's still widely popular *Kim*, then, is both "a work of great aesthetic merit" and a "novel that takes as a given 'the inferiority of non-white races, the necessity that they be ruled by a superior race. Though raised by a black woman, Jack London was an ardent bigot.

Reaching back into historical antiquity, most tribal peoples have proclaimed themselves "the people", the best of the human race. Indeed, many groups such as the Eskimos and Plains Indians gave themselves names which, literally translated, meant "the people." So, it may be understandable that American whites adopted the racial arrogance which had characterized the thinking of early groups, though "race" was not the criterion of superiority. In any case, white attitudes of racial superiority have a long history. The Founding Fathers, military leaders like Civil War hero General "Li'l Phil" Sheridan, who said the "only good Indian is a dead Indian," savages without civilization. Down to Vietnam, where, according to Charles Anderson, who was there, the general American attitude toward the Vietnamese was "we Americans left the highest standard of living in the world, we came ten thousand miles to one of the most fucked-up countries there ever was to save these people from communist brutality and to show them how to raise themselves to our level of civilization." Further, these white soldiers believed "in the superiority of white skinned peoples over yellow-, brown-, and black-skinned peoples."

"It's their (Indian) buffalo ground." "No it ain't, Irishman. That's ground open to any man what's got the balls to make his claim on it."
Terry Johnston, *Dying Thunder*, 1992

Interestingly, a group of skinheads gave the same answer responding to a question on the July 22, 1993 Jane Whitney Show. They want the northwest United States as a "White Homeland." When asked how they would deal with the Indians whose ancestral home this land is, they, in unison, replied, "We deserve this country because we will fight to take it."

Along with Manifest Destiny, success in war, and religious tolerance, anti-black racial prejudice has been a cornerstone of America's historical march. It defines as much as any other feature of national life what America is as a nation, and it has spawned so much of the social misery we know as African American life. Some of that misery, and the promise and faith interwoven with it as in a helix molecule, is the subject of the following section.

Question: Do I think all white people are racist, evil, bad and corrupt? No, but those who are, are clearly in the majority and are the ones who hold power and determine the future of my children and my neighbor's children.
Haki Madhubuti, *Black Men: Obsolete, Single, Dangerous?*

Many otherwise bright, even brilliant, and, in their minds, morally upright, men and women all too often become distinctly rabid on matters of race. Probably the greatest harm this group (and the millions who would imitate them) has done to African Americans, above all the nation's other social groups, is to deny us our individuality. While "these people prized the notions of individuality and excellence above all things," Donald Smith wrote in *The Freeman*, it is clear that on matters of race and black humanity their eyes were not watching God!

Dubois put it well:

In propaganda against the Negro since emancipation (and before) in this land we face one of the most stupendous efforts to discredit human beings, an effort involving universities, history, science, social life, and religion.

Race Related Violence

Violence is as American as cherry pie
H. Rap Brown

Violence as an instrumentation of greed and prejudice is a well documented force in American life and history. H. Rap Brown is joined by respected scholars in pointing to the function of physical force as a means of securing objectives. "By any means necessary," as a slogan was uttered by Malcolm X but was in fact one of those unspoken codes known to all Americans and practiced by most in time of need. Catton has written that:

There is a rowdy strain in American life, living close to the surface but running very deep. Like an ape behind a mask, it can display itself suddenly with terrifying effect. It is slack-jawed, with leering eyes and loose wet lips, with heavy feet and ponderous cunning hands; and then, when something tickles it, it guffaws, and when it is made angry it snarls; and it can be aroused much more easily than it can be quieted.

America is a land where violence is an acceptable alternative in getting things done, even as it meets with unanimous public opprobrium. Hofstadter's claim that "racial mixture" is the "fundamental determinant of American violence" is far too narrow in scope to explain the vast arena of violent behavior which is not even remotely related to "racial mixture" or any other aspect of race relations. While touched upon later in this chapter, non-race related violence is not central to the thrust of this work.

Race and Mob Violence

Catton's descriptive personification of the "rowdy strain" in American society perfectly characterizes a form of white violence well known to African Americans. This spontaneous-appearing collective violence is seen in the now infrequent (though not disappeared) Southern style Saturday night lynch party, mob massacres of blacks in Detroit, St. Louis, New York City, and other Northern cities during the early decades of the twentieth century (not forgetting the "draft" riots of the Civil War Era that took thousands of black lives, children included. In *A Treasury of Civil War Tales* Webb Garrison called it "one of America's worst riots," participants numbering in the "hundreds, then thousands then tens of thousands", adding that "some who were convicted of killing a black received sentences lighter than those usually handed out for stealing a side of bacon." That mob violence against blacks is not a thing of the past can be seen in the racial incidents occurring since the inauguration of the Reagan administration—Howard Beach; Amherst, Massachusetts; Cummings, Georgia; Los Angeles; and so on. For the first time, racism has flared on the nation's most prestigious college campuses, accompanied in some instances by the formation of *white* student unions (as if these institutions were not already "white".)

Some areas of the country where blacks had traditionally fared better have now joined the rest of the country in displaying the deeply rooted racism. This writer recalls an incident in a "liberal" midwestern city, home to one of the nation's most respected public universities. Three black men joined an otherwise all-white picnic party at a public park. Somehow an altercation developed between one of the visitors and a white male. Ten minutes into the argument a mob scene developed, the ensuing chase with shouts of "kill the niggers" reminiscent of a classic Southern lynch party. The three blacks barely escaped with their lives, saved by the actions of one who in fleeing grabbed a butcher knife from a table and held the mob at bay until they could all reach the safety of their car (itself almost overturned in the escape). One later told the author: "It seemed that all of a sudden they were screaming and running towards us with blood in their eyes." White women and children as well as men joined in the chase.

Somehow Thomas Merton captures the quintessence of a mob:

> No one is so dangerous as a respectable person with a sense of outrage. Once aroused, a square can easily turn into a skinhead.

Yet as irrational as mob violence appears to be it has a material basis which black Americans, in particular, would do well to understand. In the American context, racially motivated mob violence is related to *power*, to who has it and the extent to which they will go to keep it. The presidential National Commission on Causes on Prevention of Violence described how power relates to violence:

> Men seeking to seize, hold, or realign the levers of power have continually engaged in collective violence as part of their struggle. The oppressed have struck in the name of justice, the privileged in the name of order, those in between in the name of power.

In the history of blacks in America, expressions of violent opposition to their demands for the rights of citizenship has appeared in various guises depending on the time and place. Nixon was correct in suggesting that in the 1970s and 1980s it was not "fashionable" to openly espouse racist causes or utter racist comments—at least not in certain company. La Franchi found that even in Texas whites "don't find it acceptable to acknowledge racism." On the overt level, blacks no longer have to worry about a Governor Vardaman who in 1907 exclaimed with exuberance: "if it is necessary, every Negro in the state will be lynched; it will be done to maintain white supremacy." Or a Bilbo from Mississippi who once said that he "would rather see civilization 'blotted out with the atomic bomb than see it slowly but surely destroyed in the maelstrom of miscegenation, interbreeding, intermarriage, and mongrelization'." Or a U.S. Senator Ben "Pitchfork Ben" Tillman of South Carolina who openly told how he and his partisans controlled blacks: "We took the government away (from black Reconstruction officials). We stuffed ballot boxes. We shot them."

Neither do we, in most places it is to be hoped, any longer have to worry about being lynched for wishing to open a grocery store in a *black* neighborhood as happened to a black businessman in Memphis in 1892. In 1927, in the wake of a trumped-up rape charge, the black neighborhood in Tulsa, Oklahoma was bombed from the air (Philadelphia was not the first!), leaving nearly one hundred men, women, and children dead and 4,000 carted off to internment camps with most of their material possessions, including many prosperous businesses, confiscated (West Coast Japanese were not the first, either). Billed as the "Negroe's Wall Street" for its success, the black business district was destroyed by whites because "envy bred hatred of the blacks."

Vardaman, Bilbo, and Tillman knew that racial oppression of blacks was about maintaining white supremacy; about power. Longtime observer of the American racial landscape, Lewis Killian commented that many whites throughout the nation will use extreme means to protect their turf and privileges and are "unwilling to share their schools, neighborhoods, their unions, and their tax dollars..." with blacks. Ex-Harvard Professor Derek Bell comments that many whites will suffer self-deprivation if it means confining black progress.

Race and Violence by Individuals

There is another level of violence in American society, of course. It is violence on the individual level. It can be racially motivated or simply stem from any number of other causes. The person committing the violent act can belong to an organized hate group or act alone out of a racial motive. A case in an upper midwestern city illustrates the point: A white man in his early twenties drinks beer with friends in an ethnic neighborhood bar, becomes inebriated and decides he wants to kill a nigger, drives his car to a predominately black area of town, sticks the .45 automatic out the car window and shoots—and kills—the first black person he sees, who happens to be an elderly woman. After doing only four years for murder, he becomes a Born Again Christian and a poet. (This author was introduced to the reconstructed white supremacist when he guest lectured during the 1970s.)

Joseph Paul Franklin, with membership in a racist organization, traveled the country killing black men (and at least one white woman) who appeared to have social ties with white women. He traveled to one midwestern city to assassinate a Jewish judge whom he felt had been too lenient in sentencing three black teens convicted of raping a white school mate. Not conveniently locating the judge's house, he shot and killed a black man and a white woman who were leaving a car at a shopping mall (and who, it was later revealed, were merely friends). Army private Joseph Christopher left a similar trail of murdered black men in New York. His crimes were made more heinous because his victims' hearts were "cut out after they died." None of his victims were involved with white women; they were simply black men who symbolized "evil" to a deranged mind. As were the seven black women murdered in Kansas City. In the same manner of the murder of blacks by a white South African policeman whose father had taught that blacks were not human.

In 1981, in Mobile, Alabama, two young white men did it the "old fashioned way." They lynched an eighteen year old black male by hanging him from a tree branch (and for the first time a court awarded the victim's mother substantial Klan property, in addition to long sentences for the murderers. The Invisible Empire, Knights of the Ku Klux Klan, perpetuators of a violent attack on marchers in Forsyth Count, Georgia, in 1987, suffered a similar fate. A federal court in 1993 ordered the group to essentially turn over all its assets to the marchers or their representatives, including names of 11,000 subscribers to the *Klansman*. Collecting monetary damages from convicted racist perpetrators of violent crimes is becoming a common and effective legal tool of Southern Poverty Law Center attorneys, as reported in its *Law Report*.)

Law Center attorneys filed lawsuits against White Aryan Resistance leaders Tom Metzger and his son John as accomplices in the murder by Skinheads of an Ethiopian student in Portland. Tom Metzger was later held liable by the Court and ordered to pay damages that the Center averred "would break W.A.R.") The NAACP alleges that the 1988 "suicide" of a fourteen year old black youth in Columbia, Missouri, was also a lynching.

A white supremacist being tried in Ft. Lauderdale, Florida, for murdering a prostitute demanded he be allowed to wear a Klan robe in court and be addressed as "Hi Hitler" (he didn't realize the salutation was actually "Heil") in all court documents. (*Birmingham News*, Feb. 13, 1994).

American neo-Nazis Gary Lauck, known as the "farm-belt Fuehrer" has a program to deal with blacks and Jews. For Jews he would apparently favor extermination if they refused to give up their alleged power. For blacks according to George Rodrigue in a piece appearing in the *Birmingham News* (2/11/94), he would give blacks money to voluntarily expatriate.

"We could say, 'Here's $5,000 more than you could make with selling drugs or crime or whatever you do. And you can take this money and a plane ticket or, after a certain time, a concentration camp and a bullet in the head.' Then, you know what they'll decide."

"He killed a White woman, who was seven months pregnant with a child from a Black man, and he drowned her two-year-old daughter who's father was also Black." This is how the Columbia, South Carolina, *Black News* reported one of the more heinous race crimes. After a string of thirteen murders, most of which gave vent to his anti "race-mixing" delirium, Donald "Pee Wee" Gaskins was convicted of rigging a bomb to a toilet seat and murdering a black man in his own cell. *Black News* headlined "Gaskins first White to be executed in South Carolina for killing a Black". That such a crime could be committed in 1991 is testament to how close America and the South are to what novelist David Ross called in *White River* our animalistic origins.

The reader will note that I have not included Bernard Goetz in the above discussion. The omission is deliberate. While I agree with New York City Police Commissioner Benjamin Ward that white racism explains much of the pro-Goetz furor, I am also painfully aware that such incidents happen not only to the Goetzs of America's cities but more frequently to other blacks, not uncommonly to defenseless elderly black men and women. I will have more to say about black-on-black crime in a later section; but put in Goetz's place, I and many other blacks would have reacted as Goetz did. On this particular subject, our thinking is more in line with former Philadelphia Mayor and Police Chief Frank Rizzo who said that a conservative "is a liberal who got mugged the night before." Many blacks feel the same way about the gang-rape (a "wilding") of a white woman in New York's Central Park by black and Puerto Rican youths.

Black Americans have to be on guard against a wide array of possible physical attacks. From other blacks; from race neutral individually motivated assaults by whites; from unjustified mishandling by police authorities; and from organizations committed to maintaining, like Pitchfork Ben Tillman and Governor Vardaman, white supremacy at any cost. It is this latter group to which we now turn.

The stick in your neighbor's house is no use against the leopard at your door.
African Proverb

Organized Racism

8 Held in L.A., Charged In Plot to Start Race War
Fairbanks Daily News Miner, July 16, 1993

As preface to my comments about white racist organizations, it should be noted that these are terrorist organizations (though the media rarely labels them as such) that have been historically committed to violence as the major weapon for achieving their goal of continued white domination. As such, no legitimate claim can be made on their behalf that they are simply exercising the First Amendment right to free speech, or that they must be permitted to run terrorist training camps under the protection of the Fourth Amendment. (I am a life member of the National Rifle Association, and I would not have Americans disarmed, by the way, for I believe strongly in this Constitutional guarantee. The problem we blacks have in this connection is that a significant number of whites wish to retain that right exclusively for themselves, some even claiming the Second Amendment does not apply to blacks. The actor Eddie Murphy made this point graphically in the movie 48 Hours when he allowed, to a country-western crowd in a bar, "I'm your worst nightmare, a nigger with a badge" and a gun. Many whites are obviously afraid that, contrary to most of our history in America, we will one day turn those muzzles away from ourselves and toward them, a more rational but highly unlikely, occurrence.)

If Communists can be outlawed because revolutionary overthrow of the legitimately constituted government is integral to their doctrine, then white terrorist groups, the only race based violent groups in the nation, should be banned on the strength of their known history and ideology. While the media rarely if ever labels neo-nazi and Klan type organizations terrorists, black historian John Hope Franklin has appropriately dubbed them the most vicious terrorist groups in the history of the nation. The ban should be extended to include people like David Duke who exchanged his Nazi swastika for a Klan robe and who now claims three-piece-suit respectability as a member of the Louisiana State House. That many Americans can label Libya's Khaddafy a terrorist and not at the same time discern terrorism in white supremacist organizations defies logic.

Klanwatch warns that Duke is even more dangerous with his recent political success for supremacist groups are busily scheming how they might duplicate it in other areas of the country. Duke's 45 percent of the Louisiana vote in the 1990 U.S. Senate race served to give other racists added hope. Duke's unsuccessful 1991 bid for Governor of Louisiana was "not really an occasion for relief," wrote columnist Anthony Lewis. With almost half of his more than $1 million campaign fund coming from outside Louisiana and the wide exposure of his effective use of anti-black code words—affirmative action, welfare, big government-national politics will be profoundly changed. One of the "dozen Alaskans who gave a total of $800 to Duke's... campaign ... "calls the Ku Klux Klan the greatest organization ever formed and blames all the ills of the world on a conspiracy of racial minorities and international cartels." This supporter is also anti-Semitic and says "I'll gladly tolerate the other races as long as they stay in their (place)." Another supporter, a retired engineer in Massachusetts, voted for Duke because he's an advocate for white rights, explaining:

> The Republicans take care of the rich, the Democrats take care of the blacks and David Duke takes care of the whites—no one else is for the whites. I think civil rights have ruined this country. Black people don't want to work. They are taking over all the housing projects. This country is ruined...

David Duke is a racial demagogue serving what former campaign aide Bob Hawks called his three gods: "David Duke, money, and power." In a Reader's Digest article sub-headed "Will voters support him in large numbers when they learn what his business really is?, Ralph Bennett paints Duke as an accomplished hustler who would use any vise and go to any lengths to become somebody. White racism is simply the vehicle; so is electoral politics, for as Duke told Hawks of his plans for the 1992 presidential bid (even while then campaigning for governor), "I don't care whether I win or not...I'm not doing it to get elected; I'm doing it to get those funds out of Washington. Man, that'll be clear money."

In his perceptive book *David Duke: Evolution of a Klansman*, Michael Zatarain reveals a curious combination of constituencies accounting for Duke's success. That his suburban New Orleans legislative district is more than 99 percent white is no surprise; nor is its 65 percent Roman Catholic religious affiliation. The surprise is that the district boasts "the highest educational level in the state," has Democrats and Republicans, and "include some of the wealthiest people in Louisiana." Zatarain says such a constituency is "tailor-made for David Duke" and his National Association for the Advancement of White People. Duke won his legislative seat despite open opposition "from two United States Presidents and the Republican National Committee."

Perhaps an even greater surprise is that Duke's district is in a parish whose sheriff is of "Oriental descent." This same law enforcer was the object of national headlines in 1986 when it was disclosed that he ordered his deputies to "stop and question" *any* "blacks found roaming white neighborhoods."

White supremacist groups have proliferated during the current generation, particularly during the years of the Reagan administration. From an active roster of about five million in 1925, Klan membership has declined to probably fewer than 10,000 nationwide. Obviously, numbers alone don't tell the whole truth. Far from the Southern backwoods communities in which the hooded villainous "protectors of the race" used to ride to their cross burnings and lynchings, the contemporary Klansperson can be found in three-piece business suits, working in banks and other occupations of status, and are almost as likely to be female as male. In contemporary America Klaverns are as likely to be found in states such as Massachusetts, Wyoming, Alaska, and Nevada as in Alabama, Mississippi, and other states of the Old Confederacy. The modern Klansman most certainly is present in correctional institutions and the military—with concentrations on Navy warships, Marine units, and Army elite commands. Glen Miller, who has headed various white racist groups including the white Patriot Party, is a decorated Vietnam combat veteran with service in the Special Forces (Green Berets). A black ranger, when asked, since he was such a good trooper, why he did not join the Special Forces, replied, "Naw, I thought about it but decided not to because the Berets are full of redneck Southerners."

Before 1985 no Northerner had ever been Imperial Wizard of the Klan. By 1986, one of the more important Wizards not only hailed from above the

Mason Dixon Line, he was also a Roman Catholic, also a first. This new leader, Farrands, has been quoted as saying:

> Oh heck, I love the colored people. I love the ones in the South more than the North. Why? Because they're farther away. Ha-ha!

It has not been many years ago that Roman Catholics in the South had almost as much to fear from the Klan as blacks.

Even more improbable, Klan membership now includes individuals with Hispanic surnames. And *most* unlikely, an admitted Jew has been accepted into membership. (Of course, he "dropped" his Jewish affiliation, he said, on joining.) In early 1989 another Jew, masquerading as a Gentile had his "cover blown"—he was an Imperial Wizard and was promptly dismissed. He vowed to continue with the Klan by forming his own national organization. A few years ago another Jew joined the Klan and committed suicide when his ethnic affiliation was discovered. A 1991 edition of *Klanwatch* reported two separate incidents where Jewish skinheads had been assaulted, one clearly an attempted murder, by their gentile comrades when their religious identification was revealed. The point here is that who is "white" has been redefined so that formerly excluded ("dubious") whites are now in the mainstream. In a segment of the popular television series *Tour of Duty*, the leader of a budding white racist clique asks the Hispanic machine gunner whose side he was on during an incipient racial confrontation with black grunts, thereby implicitly granting him the right to choose to be white.

> In this context, definition of "white" becomes an issue. Andrew Hacker makes an interesting observation: …it should be clear that the question is not "Who is white?" It might be more appropriate to ask "Who may be considered white?" since this suggests that something…permission is needed. In a sense, those who have already received the "white" designation can be seen as belonging to a club, from whose sanction they ponder whether they want or need new members, as well as the proper induction of new admissions.

Being in the racial mainstream, Kochman points out, means being able to "represent the cultural patterns and perspectives of the dominant racial group." It is evident that in late twentieth century America former "out" groups such as Hispanics and Jews are now "white" enough to qualify for membership in this exclusive club. Italian American Klan leaders like Bill Riccio revel in their acceptance and are among those making the wildest of assertions. Riccio's memorable statement about the Atlanta child murders must have endeared him with his followers. He was happy because:

> Little niggers grow up to be big niggers, and that's 20 of 'em we won't have to kill later.

Jews don't escape his wrath; there must be a "Final Solution", and he is "not going to hang up my robe until the last Jew is deported to Palestine or executed." The reader is reminded that these sentiments came not from the 1950s or earlier hate peddlers but from the latter quarter of the twentieth century. What columnist Mike Royko said about the earlier race terrorists still applies to some parts of the country:

> The beady-eyed look had seized control of a big part of the country. They were America's version of the beer-hall thugs who followed Hitler in Germany...violence, terror, bigotry and ignorance...

The Klan and its fellow traveling "brother" groups such as W.A.R. (White Aryan Resistance), the Order, Aryan Nations, Identity Churches, and Church of the Creator have an explicit agenda: all non-whites must be deported or corralled into places of the supremacists' choosing. Wyoming's Klansman congressional candidate Daniels opts for broad scale deportation, including, presumably Native Americans. Aryan Nations leader Richard Butler takes the issue a step further in declaring "the United States was founded for the white race", and he is prepared to encourage a race war to retrieve or achieve it. As Cheryl Sullivan has reported, the leaders of contemporary white terrorist organizations aren't interested in the "old labels of respectability which used to cover their criminality"—terms such as "law abiding and patriotic"; indeed many hope to overthrow the government by violent means.

Americans of all colors and backgrounds should read Thomas Martinez's *Brotherhood of Murder*, for with frightening clarity and simplicity he describes how close The Order came to realizing its goal of an America so totally terrorized that *The Turner Diaries* recipe for a race war was only a hair's breadth away from being achieved. One is forced to ask how is it that our law enforcement agencies were so unaware of what was going on until it was almost too late. By 1992 others were continuing the Order's penchant for using criminal means to secure funds. Two white men who "robbed banks to fund a white supremacist group's war" received long prison sentences in Oklahoma, as did Phineas Priesthood leader Elijah Thody who "robbed banks to fund...white supremacist group's war on the federal government."

In 1991 *Klanwatch* reported major Klan organizations in thirty-three states. States such as Oregon and Washington which are not known to have active Klan groups do have considerable racist violence originated by other white supremacists like the Skinheads. Acts of racial violence have risen sharply over the past decade. The U.S. Justice Department's Community Relations Service, which monitors racially motivated violence, reported that between 1985 and 1986 racist attacks increased by forty-two percent. New York alone witnessed 796 racial assaults between 1984 and 1986. On college campuses reported incidents of racial violence increased from 14 in 1985 to 56 in 1987. The Northwest Coalition Against Malicious Harassment reported to the U.S. Justice Department a 70% increase in hate crimes between 1989 and 1991. (The Northwest Coalition includes the states of Idaho, Montana, Oregon, Washington and Wyoming.)

Racially motivated violence is no longer restricted to the Southern states or to areas of low socioeconomic status. Boston has a long history of white racist assaults on blacks, despite its reputation as a major center of intellectual endeavor. It has the reputation among blacks which warns that in certain areas "no black man dares to go." The extent of racism in Boston was revealed once again in the 1989 Stuart case when a white man (Stuart), in attempting to cover *his* murder of his wife and a self-inflicted gunshot wound, blamed a black man, knowing that such an allegation would unleash an instantaneous police dragnet indiscriminately directed at all black men. The inevitable in fact happened, and the ploy would have worked had not his own brother revealed the truth: Stuart planned the perfect murder (for Boston) hoping to collect on a $1 million insurance policy on his wife. When interviewed some time after the truth of Stuart's ruse was made public and the police condemned for terrorizing the black community, a public official stated "We *wanted* to believe" Stuart. (Massachusetts, and Boston in particular, have a peculiar history for blacks. In calling for black military recruits for the 54th Colored Massachusetts Regiment, the great African American Abolitionist Frederick Douglass exclaimed that "we can get at the throat of treason and slavery through the State of Massachusetts. She was first in the War of Independence; first to make the black man equal before the law; first to admit colored children to her common schools. She was first to answer with her blood the alarm cry of the nation when its capital was menaced by the Rebels...")

Despite its liberal veneer attributable to its position as home to great academic and cultural institutions—and the Kennedy Clan (can anyone recall any Kennedy denouncing racism *in Boston*?)—Boston is an anti-black city. That *Money* magazine would classify it as one of the ten best places in the nation to live (1988 survey of 300 best areas) suggest a racist exclusion not uncommon in surveys which purport to claim creditability, and is reminiscent of the photographer who was fined by his publisher whenever he submitted a photo of a street scene that included blacks, as reported by *Heritage* magazine.

In the Midwest small farmers are wooed by Posse Comitatus; in the West Aryan Nations, The Order, Arizona Patriots, and the White Aryan Resistance dominate. Killian notes that conservative white Southerners have to their delight found "many allies in the lilly-white suburbs of the North and West." In late 1991 the 58,000 whites of Dubuque, Iowa, made national headlines by using burning crosses, intimidation and harassment to tell the world it wanted no more blacks to join the 331 already living there. In the summer of 1993 whites in a public housing project in Vidor, Texas, ordered desegregated by a federal court, chased out the few blacks who had dared to move there, and, according to one, endured "derisive yells, threats and oppressive fears" which "had become too much to bear."

Where Can Blacks Live in Peace?

In this connection, blacks still debate about the "best" and "worst" places to live in the country. Periodically *Ebony* magazine does a special story on the country's *best* areas for blacks, (always omitting Alaska, the nation's best-kept secret for blacks!) in keeping with its tradition of accentuating the positive. This writer's list of *inhospitable* places for blacks include the City of Boston; Metropolitan New York and Buffalo; Chicago's suburbs and all of southern Illinois; Milwaukee and much of rural Wisconsin (home of Posse Comitatus); Wyoming; Utah and other places where Mormons have political and financial hegemony (*Megatrends* author John Naisbitt relates how he, a Mormon, led a movement to desegregate lunch counters in Salt Lake City "ten years before others did it in North Carolina"); parts of Los Angeles and most of Southern California (The May 15, 1993 arrest of eight white supremists who planned to assassinate Rodney King, "spray" the oldest black church in Los Angeles with machine gun fire and sent a letter bomb to a rabbi-which motivated the arrest-came as no surprise. What was more noteworthy was that the group came from four California counties and represented at least four different supremacist groups.)

In fact and in lore, Texas is a violent place to live—for whites and blacks. Because it is such a mixed bag for blacks economically—with some blacks in places like Dallas and Houston enjoying high status—it is considered as a special category. The negative on Texas for blacks is the uneven dispensation of bad law enforcement, which appears to administer "justice" to blacks in ways no white would tolerate. Which embellishes the state's violent image. Journalist Willie Morris told David Frost that "violence is an almost gleeful thing (in Texas)…there's a passionate kind of joy in…Texas violence."

Texas is the state where the Klan is bold enough to stage a march on an important holiday for African Americans—Juneteenth Day; and the state where a black man spent 5 years in prison for stealing a package of cigarettes and a white man convicted of being party to the murder of a black man, got 10 years probation; and where, were not national media attention focused on the matter, a white teacher who used an article from *Ebony* magazine in class likely would have had her contract non-renewed.

Texas is the state of the gun. With an average of four guns per person Texans possess more than 16 million lethal weapons. Mark Potok reported that "Texas is the only state where more people were shot to death in 1991 than killed in car crashes." In 1993 a group of Texas lawmakers sponsored a bill to legalize carrying a concealed weapon.

In terms of its livability for blacks, Texas is probably the biggest enigma among the states. Civil War General Sherman's reported quip that if he "owned Texas and Hell…(he'd) rent out Texas and live in Hell" (so great was his disdain for the Lone Star State), provides a backdrop on the conflicting images and experiences blacks have of that vast state. So, even as a recent governor is the subject of the ire of black Texans for refusing to fire his top legal aide for allegedly saying "I do not want anymore minorities serving on juries in Dallas and Houston", it is in those very cities where minorities have made the greatest gains.

Former Texas Congresswoman Barbara Jordan, who ought to know better, told photojournalist Brian Shanker that Texans respect only the individual: "A Texan believes that the individual is powerful…I believe that I get from the soil of and the spirit of Texas the feeling that I, as an individual, can accomplish whatever I want to and that there are no limits...," and it is true that the novel *Lonesome Dove* revealed a black Texas ranger in the nineteenth century, decades before integration.

There are simply too many black *individual* Texans whose skin color, not their individual talents or shortcomings, have given lie to Ms. Jordan's notion for it to be other than wishful thinking of the worst kind. On a flight between Dallas and San Antonio the author of this book had a "Texas experience" when a white male passenger riding coach class verbally (and loudly), objected to a black man (me) riding first class. The flight attendants were shocked into stunned embarrassment. What a L'Amour character said about Tucson in *The Lonely Man*, could well apply to Texas, from a black perspective:

"All this town needs...is more water and a better class of people."

A buddy answers:

"That's all hell needs."

(With the 1990 election of a liberal female governor black Texans were hoping for a more progressive attack on racism.)

During the Civil War, Congress debated moving all freed slaves to Texas. The bill (Senate Bill 45), sponsored by Kansas Republican Senator James Henry Lane (an "anti-slavery zealot and favorite of...Lincoln"), would have set aside all of Texas West-southwest of Austin as the black homeland—"Territory of the Rio Grande." One hundred years later, Nation of Islam founder the Honorable Elijah Muhammad, also wanted Texas, and other southern states, as an African American homeland.

The litany of bad news continues. Mississippi excluding Jackson; rural North Carolina; parts of Pennsylvania; southern Indiana (which once had an avowed Klansman as Lt. Governor) and Ohio; all of Missouri and Kansas; Miami, Dade County, and Southern Florida in general (Charles Cobb chronicles the turn of fortunes for Miami's African American community. From having comprised one-third of the signers of Miami's original charter, making up prosperous segment of the community, to, by 1992, the city's poorest people, poorer, according to Cobb, "than blacks in 23 other urban centers."), and all of Louisiana outside New Orleans. Any state which gives almost half its vote to a white supremacist is by definition hostile to blacks. Much of the rural south remains unchanged from pre-Civil Rights Era. In traveling around the country to research *Blue Highways*, William Least Heat Moon discovered that blacks in Selma, Alabama were as a group in about the same economic condition in the 1980s as they were in the mid-1960s when that southern city was the center of Civil Rights activity. A friend, recently voluntarily transplanted back to her native Mississippi makes the same observation.

By the early 1990s Portland, Oregon, had become the Boston of the West Coast, leading the northwest in hate crimes by 1991. In point of fact, racism in Oregon reaches back before statehood, according to Stephanie Coontz. She documents the plight of African American George Washington Bush who helped found Puget Sound which was later incorporated into Oregon territory, which prohibited black settlement. Since Bush and his family had saved so many white lives in 1852—he gave them "wheat for food and planting"—a special law was passed in 1854 exempting Bush and his family "from the black exclusion law."

It is this writer's opinion that blacks may simply wish to abandon some American cities, not simply try to become separate entities within them as blacks attempted in Boston and talked of doing in Milwaukee. (The novel *Negotiations* explores the separatist idea in some detail.) Joining Boston on the list of the unredeemable are New York City, Miami, Milwaukee, probably Portland, the entire states of Missouri, Kansas and Utah, and Southern California.

Regarding New York City, NFL football star Lawrence Taylor has said:

Ever since I've gotten to New York, I've had to hold everything back. I'm playing in a white man's world. I know that. So I've held it back-until now. I've seen things in New York that are 100 times worse than anything I ever saw in the South, in Virginia, where I grew up. New York is a time bomb. I wouldn't want my kids growing up there. If something doesn't happen son, it's going to be a hellhole.

Atlanta ("the City too Busy to Hate") is even more of an enigma than the state of Texas. Long acclaimed as the most progressive Southern city for blacks, a recent black mayor, responding to a question about the city's homeless, declared that 80 percent of the city's residents were doing well. Questions remain: How can the city be doing so well when it can be the scene of a genocidal string of murders of black children, mostly males. How can a progressive city also be discovered to have a racist conspiracy to deny blacks home loans? How is that a personal acquaintance from the "movement" of the 60s tell this writer recently that the only reason his daughter, graduate of a prestigious Eastern college, has not been able to secure employment other than supermarket cashier, is because of her dark complexion? (New Orleans, Charleston and the District of Columbia join Atlanta here in practising a color caste code historically just short of that found in South Africa.) And, finally, if Atlanta blacks are so well off, why did former President Carter call a press conference in late 1991 to announce Atlanta as "the second poorest city in the nation" and inform listeners of his intention to turn from his worldwide mission of encouraging building low income resident owned homes to focus his efforts on Atlanta? Sherman left more than ashes in Atlanta on his "march to the sea". There is a legacy of denial and pretense that defies reality. Black political leadership, a black middle class anchored in the professions and business enterprise, and enviable black educational institutions do not necessarily equate with general prosperity.

The Atlanta child murders raise serious questions: Where was law enforcement and why did it take so long? No black person with whom I have discussed this subject, including the late James Baldwin who did an investigative report, believes that Wayne Williams' arrest and conviction solved the mystery of the massacre. (In 1991 William Kuntsler and several other prominent defense attorneys petitioned for a new trial for Williams.) My personal theory is that the murders were committed by persons desiring membership in white racist organizations, which, being so heavily infiltrated and "snitched" on by informers under pressure of law enforcement agencies, imposed a permanently binding membership "fee". And who is more defenseless than a poor, almost nameless, black male child? In the *Turner Diaries*, white males who want to join the Organization are required to bring in the head—"not the body—of a black person..." The seventeen "mystery" murders of black women in Missouri also come to mind.

Contrasting the almost comic coverage of the Atlanta child murders with the "media.... obsession with sensational slaying" of "the smiling face of the attractive, blonde victim" (a "suburban homemaker") of homicide in 1992, leaves little doubt about which act of horror has garnered more public attention.

White Youth and White Supremacy

Most disappointing and frightening is the involvement of increasing numbers of white youth in white supremacy organizations and activities. To the surprise of many observers, the Skinhead phenomenon burst upon the racial landscape with a force not witnessed since the 1920s. What's original with the 'heads is their youth and willingness to use violence as their only weapon. (Hollywood recruited a stellar cast, including Chuck Conner and Barbara Bain, to produce the 1988 film *Skinheads*, a revealing but not entirely accurate depiction of personalities who join such racist groups.) One commentator called the Skinheads "the most active, influential and dangerous supremacist organization operating in America today." In one writer's terms, "Some of the most violent members of the white supremacist movement today are teenagers—kids who shave their heads, wear Nazi tattoos, dress in black stormtrooper boots and operate in small gangs."

Recognizing their value in injecting "life" into organizations almost out of business with lethargy, old-line white supremacists like Richard Butler and Edward Fields are ecstatic with the appearance of these "shock troopers". White supremacist youth are the backbone of contemporary racist violence. Fields says they were the "biggest surprise...and were a majority in the Cummings, Georgia" confrontations. White youth perpetrated violence on college campuses (so much so in one midwestern state that the state legislature considered passing a law "requiring automatic expulsion for students who commit racist acts"). Ninety percent of those arrested in 1988 were under 21. Like the Skinheads, many of these youth believe "We are the last remnants of white purity."

Racist organizations are hard at work recruiting the next generation of "soldiers", not only in the South but on the West Coast and in New England, where "Connecticut is the most volatile state." Skinheads are recruited by the

Klan to distribute its "Final Solution" booklet. In Texas nine teenagers from affluent families, all honor roll athletes, calling themselves "the future Aryan Lords," promised that "Democrats, communists and niggers shall perish under our wrath." Turncoat Aryan Nations member Floyd Cochran expressed surprise at seeing "middle-class kids, fresh from the suburbs," instead of "white working-class young people from the big cities" flock to Richard Butler's compound.

That young whites are so prominently involved with terrorist groups should come as no surprise, however. As comedian/actor Eddie Murphy sees it, "some of these people (racists of the 1960s) are still around. They have children who have children, and some of them have the same values as those who sprayed the (water) hoses." They are the children of the stone throwers on Chicago's West Side, Boston's South Side, New Orleans, Little Rock, and other cities that experienced desegregation and bussing strife. They are the Howard Beach (this widely publicized incident became the storyline for the 1990 television movie *Equal Justice*) young men, one of whom when convicted showed "absolutely no remorse", said the presiding judge. The leader of the group even had a black girl friend!

Class bias is unknown among them for some of their members are the sons, and sometimes daughters, of some of America's wealthiest families, some of whose older members equate civil rights and equal opportunity with Communism. And they are the offspring of the sheet metal workers in New York City who succeeded through legal trickery in keeping their union lilly-white; and the Alabama State Troopers who, equally adroit in outmaneuvering federal court orders, managed to deny equal employment opportunity to blacks for decades. It is clear that while competition for dramatically dwindling resources, such as jobs, is a factor in some of the "new racism," as the Durants suggest in an essay on the "law of biology," it is equally clear that blacks cannot put as much faith in the younger generation of whites as some of us had hoped; for many, our greatest disappointment. Moral love is no more likely to be found among the young as among their elders.

> To love a thing means wanting it to live,
> To hate a thing means wanting it to perish.
> > Confucius

Any black person in any section of the United States can be subjected to white racist violence. The only realistic defense is suggested by the writer Maya Angelou:

> Since you're black, you have to hope for the best. Be prepared for the worst and always know that anything can happen.
> > *The Heart of a Woman*

During the course of writing this chapter, I finished reading Laura Palmer's *Shrapnel of the Heart*, a collection of letters and other "remembrances" left at the Vietnam War Memorial. As I finished this remarkable book, I couldn't help but ask: How is it that people with so very much love can hold within the same breast so very much hate?

We professional educators have long been interested in attitude development in the young. It is known of course that parents and peers are influential attitude peddlers and that social institutions such as the church and school play pivotal roles, one traditionally reinforcing the other. We are also reluctantly coming to the realization that formal teaching of righteous moral values, around which healthy attitudes should develop, are, in the modern world, more often than not simply overwhelmed by the impact of "informal" teaching that goes on all around the young. This informal inculcation or imbibing of attitudes comes from the media, particularly television, peer associations, and even from some of our prestigious preparatory schools where one researcher found that students are taught two sets of codes of conduct. On the one hand they are taught to follow the Golden Rule, and on the other, "He who has the gold makes the rule," is the implicit but forceful message.

Racism as Attitude

I grew up believing that racism was a consequence of ignorance. But 80 percent of the students at Brown had finished in the top 10 percent of their high schools. If they were racist, the nation was doomed.
Peter Hamil, "Black and White at Brown," *Esquire*, April 1990

Attitudes towards race have been generously studied by many able psychologists and other social scientists, and their work is readily available. To retain the comprehensive scope of the present work, the reader needs to understand some prominent features of racist attitudes which have affected the behavior of whites in this country.

Racism is *the* compelling priority for blacks, because, as Frank Aukofer has written, it "exists as the meanest of streaks in American society, stubbornly entwined in attitudes and institutions from the 'nigger' jokes told by white children to the agencies established to protect the people". Racism is still so much a part of white America's thinking that as recent as 1978 fully one-fourth of American whites admitted feeling that "blacks have less native intelligence than whites." (A gross underestimation, most blacks and honest whites would argue, when whites who don't make an open admission are counted and researchers are becoming aware of the "games" people play with attitude and opinion pollsters.) Andrew Hacker writes that "most white people believe that, compared with other races, persons with African ancestors are more likely to carry primitive traits in their genes." Perhaps this attitude explains why some whites can believe that "many of the nation's black leaders have been of predominately white ancestry," their "white" genes making the difference, according to F. James Davis.

That random sampled whites should hold such feelings should come as no surprise since even white intellectuals sometimes admit to their prejudice. In a famous 1963 essay, the managing editor of the prestigious liberal magazine *Commentary* lamented in "Your Problem and Mine," eloquently describing his visceral objection to white female-black male intimacy. Trying to come to grips with the obvious brilliance of his house guest James Baldwin, novelist William Styron "still possessed a residual skepticism: Could a Negro *really* own a mind as subtle, as richly informed, as broadly inquiring and embracing as that of a white man?" (Styron later recanted and offered an apology—but not an admission of racist thinking. In a collection of essays honoring Baldwin, he wrote of his earlier remarks: "My God, what appalling arrogance and vanity!") Editors of the liberal *New Republic* join former President Richard Nixon in believing that racist attitudes continue to dog white thinking despite the civil rights gains of the 1960s. There is an unbroken line from Jefferson to Styron.

The white American attack against the black claim of divinely—bestowed membership in the human family has been broad-based, affecting all social institutions, consistent, and unremitting. Millions of white Americans will carry the legacy into the twenty-first century.

(Where else but in America could a white man be awarded disability compensation—$231.47 to be exact—"to compensate for his fear of working with blacks"? Whenever he had to work alongside blacks he suffered a nervous breakdown! Where else could a white woman, mugged by a *lone* black man on a Miami street, develop an "irrational fear of (all) black people, collect $50,000 disability compensation over five years not for her injury but her fear because "she cannot function in an integrated workplace," and requests from the state an additional $200,000 in workmen's compensation for permanent disability? The woman testified that "she is especially afraid of 'big, black males'." The state of Florida agreed she had a legitimate claim, but the opposing attorney demurred saying, 'if we are to award…money, then every Ku Klux Klansman should be awarded money because they, too, have an irrational fear of black people'. Where else but in America would white apprentice and journeymen electricians say "No" and simply leave the worksite when they discovered their job boss was a black master electrician, as they've done in the nation's capital, as told to the author by the black tradesman?)

Squeaking Christianity

While observing Muhammad, I have often thought that if everyone just had ten percent of his faith in God this world would be a much better place for all people of all colors and religions.

Howard Bingham, Muhammad Ali photographer and friend, 1993.

Attitudes are related to values. Are there moral values we as Americans collectively share in such a way that, say, a "man from Mars" could, upon landing in New York, then sauntering off to Birmingham, Atlanta, Jackson, and continuing on to southern California after whistle stops in Idaho and Fairbanks, Alaska—exclaim "Ah, this is how Americans feel about...?"

Just who is an American? Is there an American *character*? A Gallop survey conducted in the early 1980s provided a clue. According to that study, compared to Japanese, Italians, West Germans, and French, we Americans take pride in our work, would go to war in defense of our country, are proud of our nationality, and believe in God. Black political scientist Charles Henry assumes at least verbal acceptance of the American creed by most Americans. Documents embodying this set of beliefs are the Declaration of Independence, the Bill of Rights and the preamble to the Constitution. Specific rights held dear by most Americans include "life, liberty, and the pursuit of happiness; property rights; the right of free speech and assembly; equality under law; and the principle of power deriving from the consent of the governed." (Christians would add a belief in the Ten Commandments.) Essentially what the Gallop survey found was that despite our obvious diversity and differences, we have, as noted previously, achieved a unity unique in the world. "Out of many, one." That unity has consistently contained anti-black prejudice.

The contradictions remain, and will loom larger in importance as our social and economic problems multiply. The values we say we have cherished may well be stretched beyond the point where their retention will be functional—even given the contradictions between much of what we say and what we actually *do*. So long as Americans could "keep the faith" and believe that the world would be assuredly better for their children, especially if "we" worked hard and were frugal, expanding economic opportunity would take care of the rest. Catton saw the pitfalls of this wishful thinking years ago:

Something is indeed gaining on us, and it is nothing more or less than the unhappy fact that what people have been encouraged to want is somehow a good deal less than what they actually have.

Not even most *white* parents can assume that their children's lives will be *as well off* materially as their own, let alone *better off*. The Wall Street Journal has noted that Americans are "losing faith" in the capability of the nation to sustain the rise in living standards most Americans have enjoyed since World War II. The Golden Years are gone. Perhaps forever for most of us.

Some contradictions within the American moral fabric predate by centuries, and eclipse by centuries, the contemporary economic quagmire across the races, of course. The major moral dilemma which has always faced and plagued America lies in the religious realm. It revolves around the estrangement of words and deeds; or, put another way, the interpretation of the "Word". (It would appear that only the Quakers—Friends—was able to overcome this duality, certainly on matters of race, over time.) Christianity, to which most Americans claim some degree or affiliation or allegiance, preaches and teaches brotherhood, yet it has historically blatantly denied the full benefit of its salvation to black and other dark-skinned believers in its God. The American Indian writer Vine Deloria, Jr., perhaps the most incisive critic of Christian treatment of minorities, suggest that "Christians either do not believe in resurrection, or they exclude non-whites from their heaven," (in the same way most exclude minority, certainly black Christians, even decorated war heroes, from their cemeteries).

While the white Christian treatment of non-whites has, on the whole, been despicable, Deloria's most damning criticism is directed at Christianity's direct participation in "politics by other means"—War—to bring about peace on earth (another contradiction):

> If one were to take the last two thousand years and the events of that period as representative of the validity of the Christian religion in bringing peace on earth, then there would be little question that the religion is incapable of working any significant peaceful change in men or their societies. That period has been filled with continual warfare, conquest, bloodshed, and exploitation...Much of it was Christian pitted against Christians...not just against minorities.

Other commentators have linked Christianity with barbarous conduct toward racial minorities. Historian Jack Forbes notes that "the sixteenth century perpetrated the greatest genocide in history," resulting in mid-century of fewer than 10,000,000 of the estimated 80,000,000 native inhabitants of the Americas. Alaska news columnist Fred Pratt notes that Alaska Natives—Indians, Eskimos, Aleuts—numbered about 80,000 before contact with whites. "A century and a half of slavery, murder and disease dropped this to less than 20,000 by the turn of this century..." It has taken Alaska Natives almost a century—to the 1990 census—to recover such that its population is about 80,000 again, very few of whom are without some white genetic heritage. A bitter legacy remains: According to the Alaska Native Blue Ribbon Commission, Natives suffer birth defects caused by fetal alcohol syndrome (FAS) at twice the national average, a suicide rate four times the national average (with males between 20 to 24 having a rate 14 times as high), a homicide rate matching suicides, and lead the nation in accidental death. Virtually all this social pathology is alcohol related. "If the word genocide has ever been applied to a situation with some accuracy, this is here the case,"he adds. The 1937 book, *The Tree*, was even more explicit noting that when Christian whites "could not prevail by honest war or justice, then broken treaties, economic sanctions, exile (Native Americans were exiled to Africa as well as Europe, according to Forbes), whiskey, entire destruction of the buffalo herds and ruthless suppression of tribal life, customs, religion, language and arts, eventually accomplished the desired results."

In Alfred Silver's fictional account (*Lord of the Plains*) of Canod's Great

Northwest Rebellion of the late nineteenth century, the struggle of native Metis (white-Indian people and their descendants) to keep possession of their lands against encroaching whites, an Indian ally told the Metis leader: "I have quit the missionaries. I am no longer a 'Good Indian.' He said that when he was young the Manitou used to give the people of the plains all they needed to live a good life. But then the missionaries came and told them there was a new god now and the Manitou had grown too weak to provide for his children. So Poundmaker and his people went over to the new god, and since that time the buffalo have disappeared, the antelopes and deer and even the rabbits have been just about hunted out, and the children are dying of hunger and cold—so Poundmaker decided he was going back to his old god because even if the Manitou's grown weak as the whites say, he can't do any worse than the Christian god has." Christianity as organized religion has been a paradox for America's racial minorities. How it has been viewed is revealed in these two commentaries.

As a group, blacks have always enthusiastically and uncritically rallied to the Christian banner, and have been some of its best soldiers, theologically and militarily, and will continue to be. Indeed, Marcus Garvey, the first African American nationalist to enjoy broad appeal, claimed blacks had the original claim to Christianity, arguing: "…whilst the white and yellow worlds … persecuted and crucified Jesus, the Son of God, it was the black race through Simon … who befriended the Son of God and took up the Cross and bore it alongside of Him up to the heights of Calvary … the Cross is the property of the Negro in his religion …" A 1982 Gallup Opinion survey concluded that "blacks as a group appear to be the most religious people in the U.S." However logical and rational the criticism of persons like Deloria, (and this writer) and however great the need for blacks to reassess our allegiances and address the pronounced hypocrisy of the Christian Church (and other religions including Judaism), the die is cast. There is no creditable evidence to suggest that blacks will abandon the spiritual beliefs of their heritage. "I will not be moved," in the words of the old Negro Spiritual, says it all. Furthermore, the southern Civil Rights Movement demonstrated how Christianity can be employed in the cause of righteous social change, although that period also taught the limits of its usefulness.

The reader may wish to contrast Poundmaker's latter sentiments on Christianity to the resiliency expressed in a March 11, 1990 letter to the author from Iola. After explaining how the "Me" generation of blacks had forgotten the Church and much of its teaching:

> Now Ed, what is sinking sand as opposed to solid ground? "On Christ, the Solid Rock I stand, all other ground is sinking sand." Christ gave a way of life. We are not able to keep straight in Christ's way…but there is a need to try! It gives a solid base for society.

Despite the misuse and deliberate misapplication of Christian principles to African Americans throughout our history, Iola's belief in the ultimate victory of

Christianity is shared—and has always been—by a great majority of America's black population.

> I think, that as a people who have had to deal with the absurdity of being Black in America, for many of us it is a question of God and sanity, or God and suicide.
> Cornel West to bell hooks

Liberal commentators still point to 11:00 a.m. Sunday morning as being the most segregated hour in the nation. Gustav Niebuhr entitled his important *Atlanta Constitution* article "Sunday Morning at 11 Remains Most Segregated Hour of Week" The liberals, black as well as white, castigate American religious bodies, especially Christian, for perpetrating the very ills they are by doctrine supposed to be helping cure. Black and white don't mingle in many Christian congregations (nor in Jewish synagogues) in this country, and there is little integration of religious associations at the national level.

Well, in the view of some of us, separation in worship across racial lines can be good or bad. To the extent that segregated worship is a mirror of society where blacks are deliberately excluded from interaction across racial lines (no black church has ever denied membership to whites), there is legitimate cause for concern. But to the extent that black church services, particularly Protestant though increasingly Catholic, also, differ in ritual and ceremony from that of their white counterparts, many blacks prefer their own church, even if it means not being able to "network" with white individuals who may provide or have access to certain goods and services in the non-religious arena. For those whites or blacks who wish to worship in integrated settings, impediments imposed by race should be removed.

Much of the ritualistic behavior of black churchgoers so brilliantly chronicled by Zora Hurston in *the Sanctified Church* and other works still occur as integral components of ceremony in most fundamentalist African American churches. Recognition of "style" differences in religious music across race lines is reflected in the Gospel Music Association's 21-year rule of separating two broad types of gospel music corresponding to black and white performers. Poet *(For My People)* and novelist *(Jubilee)* Margaret Walker has claimed that black and white worship is fundamentally different in terms of outcomes". ...the white preacher is talking about personal salvation...(not about) the brotherhood of man...(whereas) the black church preaches a social gospel."

Whatever the eventual outcome of religious worship across racial lines, Christianity as an institution of influence in world affairs is going to have to come to grips with its own racism. In the past, Deloria reminds us, Christian missionaries have all too often been the vanguard for murderous exploitation of non-white peoples. African leaders of the early post-colonial period used to quip that when the missionaries first came "we had the land and they had the Bible; now they have the land and we have the Bible." These early "messengers" often claimed land as well as souls in the name of God. Like other non-white intellectuals of the late twentieth century, Deloria does not ask that the Christian Church atone or offer expressions of "guilt for remote sins," however infrequent they might have been made. Rather, he wants the white church to become the vanguard for a new relationship between races, which can only happen when "contemporary attitude(s) toward aboriginal peoples" and other minorities are changed. The church can exercise a tremendous influence here— if it would.

That organized religion is not likely to be in the vanguard of any movement toward increased acceptance and appreciation of minorities, blacks in particular (this distinction is critical), is evidenced in continued segregation by race more than by ritual; lack of interracial cooperation within religious denominational associations; the fact that Mormons, despite their recent "abdication" of exclusive white right to the priesthood, continue to view blacks as racial pariahs; (*The Book of Mormon* is replete with derogatory references to black skin color, e.g., "dark and loathsome," "vapor of dark" skin); that it has taken the Roman Catholic Church centuries to appoint a black American bishop; and that few white church leaders on the local level dare to associate themselves with progressive racial causes. It is a sad commentary on the state of the American church when a pastor gives a "prayer for racial peace and harmony in the United States," but cannot reveal to his parishioners that the prayer is in honor of Martin Luther King, Jr., out of fear that "it might offend some of his parishioners" and perhaps result in his loss of a livelihood, as happened to several white pastors during the 1960s. In a *Playboy* interview, Martin Luther King, Jr., told Alex Haley that one of his earliest, most surprising and disappointing discoveries as a civil rights leader was failure of Southern Christian ministers to join his cause. What King's years of theological training had not prepared him for was that most white & black Southerns read from different Biblical texts. It was a fatal flaw in King's education. One problem with Stephen Carter's *The Culture of Disbelief* is how to cope with that class of individuals who also want to return to behavioral expression of *religious* belief but whose interpretation of doctrine lead them to a hiearchical, superior-inferior, ordering of the human universe. If a white supremacist (or black supremacist, for that matter) group claims divine instruction as basic for its views on race relations, why is its view not as legitimate as Carter's which attributes secular *political* connotations to such expressions. Whose interpretation of the Holy Scriptures is valid?

Along with the Church of Latter Day Saints, the Catholic Church is seen by many blacks as being most bigoted. One prominent black minister told a midwestern news reporter that "the Roman Catholic Church in America looks white, thinks white and feels white. It prays white, worships white and in relation to black people, believes preeminently white." The Church's own "renegade" black priest, Rev. Stallings of Washington, D.C., who has formed his own black congregation, expresses identical sentiments. (Rev. Stallings left the Catholic Church in 1989, founded the African American Catholic Congregation, and in 1991 "ordained" Rose Vernell, a black former nun, the Church's first female priest. By early 1992 Rev. Stallings had established other "alternate temples" in several cities with large black Catholic populations.)

How white religious groups view blacks affects more than who sits next to whom in a church or synagogue. Mormons, Jews and Catholics control billions of dollars of assets and jobs in the hundreds of thousands. (With an estimated 8 million members worldwide in 1991, and some 4.5 billion in annual collections from its members, the Mormon Church is arguably an economic giant.) In the long-term, it is lack of black access to these resources that blacks can legitimately criticize rather than bemoaning being segregated in places of worship. When a Mormon employer refuses to hire non-Mormons, as many of them have reputedly done, or "corner" markets in Mormon dominated areas of the country, then blacks as well as other non-Mormons suffer. (The Mormon dominated University of Utah hired its first non-Mormon president in 1991.) The twenty-first century will probably see surfacing some antagonizing problems between Mormon, Jewish and other power blocs in the United States.

> Being a melting pot for diverse cultures and heritages has always been one of America's greatest strengths. We don't have time to waste fighting one another on the race issue. We should love one another. If we can't do that we should learn to get along with one another now. The few diehards remaining should recognize that we are stuck with one another. Let's link arms and form a winning team.
> H. Ross Perot

But for all of that, African Americans wish to see an end to the dilemma of word and deed. University of Colorado Professor Wallis King put it well in a public television broadcast: "All we are asking of America is to be what it puts on paper." Inasmuch as white Christianity has a history of hypocritical behavior towards blacks, the simplistic cautions expressed by a character in L'Amour's *Calloway* suggest the vigilance blacks should bring to overtures from white Christians.

> A man who starts imagining that others think good because he does is simply out of his mind.

> When feeding time comes around there's nothing a hawk likes better than a nice fat, peaceful dove.

> I believe in forgiving one's enemies, but keep your hand on your gun while you do it, mentally at least...

America: From Bad to Worse — And (Perhaps) Getting Better

Racism in religion, racist violence, and leaders harboring racist sentiments toward non-white Americans, are symptoms of a deep sickness in American society. As if racist manifestations of prejudicial attitudes were not enough, we are as well plagued by problems *not* directly associated with race but which compound the already fragile existence which many non-whites face.

An Illiterate Population

Topping the list of national problems is illiteracy. In political theory democracies are said to need for their stability and economic health a literate, educated citizenry. Only an informed populace can make informed decisions in the voting booth, the "sacred" instrumentality for insuring proper conduct and policy by representatives who rule in the halls of legislatures, the courts, state houses, and the White House.

But are we an informed citizenry? Twenty-seven million adult Americans are functionally illiterate, and can't, according to the Coalition for Literacy, "read a bedtime story to a child." In absolute numbers whites outnumber all other groups combined in illiteracy rate. Illiteracy is taking a toll on American industry. At a Motorola plant in South Florida, almost two-thirds of applicants for entry-level jobs couldn't pass a fifth-grade math or a seventh-grade reading test. Owens and Lopez estimate that one of three major corporations have to teach basic skills—the "3 R's"—to their workers.

Of the vast majority of Americans who do read, they spend only an average of sixteen minutes a day reading; nine of those minutes are "spent on the sports and comic pages". A poll released by the National Association of Broadcasters revealed that more than fifty percent of Americans say television is "their only source of news and information." Among the most popular non-news reading Americans do are pulp romance novels, Louis L'Amour westerns and mysteries by Agatha Christie. Stephen King and a few other popular modern authors can be added. Hardly a well rounded reading list for a nation whose citizenry must be able to make informed judgments and decisions.

My personal opinion is that "emotion comes before reason" in the decision making process, particularly where matters of race are the issue. As we have seen with presidents and industrial leaders, all to often the literate, well-read person, with a college degree, is no more likely to make a rational, objective, judgment or decision as the unlettered. Thus explaining how throughout the nation's history so many political, military, educational, and business leaders were quite rational on all matters save race. The connection between literacy and prejudice—rather, the outward expression of it, is valid to the extent that one *hopes* that education in the sense that Alfred Lord Whitehead described it would predispose an individual to rely *more*, instead of less, on certain objective criteria, informed by a broad consensus of valuing, in arriving at judgments. (The ideal is exemplified in the case of retired Army Colonel Hackworth, who, orphaned at an early age, had only a very racially bigoted grandmother to teach him about "race". Yet it is clear from Hackworth's words *and* actions that study and interaction with African Americans and other non-whites virtually eliminated any racial prejudice he might have imbibed from his otherwise "grand" grandmother. Racial prejudice *can* be unlearned or overcome. Another, even more vivid, example is the family of ex-Klan members who appeared on the Oprah Winfrey Show during the week of January 20-24, 1992. Having spent many years as high officials (the wife was chaplain) of the Southern Knights—the father once considered murdering one of his own sons who refused to join—the self-imposed hatred became so taxing that they had to find another non-racist way to live. For them Born Again Christianity was the answer.)

As matters now stand only "eggheads" and members of the privileged classes devote "real" time to serious reading and study. Fortunately for the future of the nation, organized groups of concerned citizens are beginning to address the problem. Seymour Hirsh's book *Cultural Literacy*, while shortsighted, is a step in the right direction. So are Lee Iacocca's recommendations about everyone reading national as well as local newspapers and news magazines; and local literacy councils are making a difference.

But even good readers, who are informed and culturally literate, are not likely to be spared racial bias and other irrational sentiments when other areas of their lives are not adequately cared for. Slavery and race discrimination, to the contrary notwithstanding, America has in most of its history been the land of abundance. In Catton's time that progress would happen exponentially was a given; and by and large it happened. Even in Grizzard's, the generation following Catton's, the nation came through hard times and "emerged with a glorious victory," and a "deep belief in (the) system."

> (Parents) wanted to protect us. They wanted to educate us. They wanted us to be doctors and lawyers and stockbrokers, not farmers and mill hands...(They wanted) to make certain that, at whatever cost, their children would be spared the adversity they had seen.

Since child labor laws were enacted, and before average life span stretched to the 70 year range, no one could have predicted that our children and our elderly, the beginning and end of the life cycle, would be at risk in the way they are today. No discussion of America in the waning years of the twentieth century would be complete without consideration of our young and old.

Youth: Prosper or Stagnate

Our young people are at risk. And not just the pre-adults or minorities. The faith their fathers and mothers had in "the system" is faltering on uncertain futures. In generations past, young people, upon reaching age eighteen—the "age of majority"—were expected to "hit the road," go to college, get a job, join the armed services, get married, start their own families, and live happily ever after. One symptom of changing times is the "boomerang kids" phenomenon. An estimated 220,000 eighteen year olds now live with their parents, up nearly 50 percent since 1970, according to research done by Kathy Johnson. Many in this group will keep "boomeranging" back home well into their forties.

The displaced boomerang kids are joined by increased numbers of traditionally aberrational children. More than thirteen million of our children are growing up in one-parent families; more than one half of all black children do. Big Brothers/Big Sisters of America predict that sixty percent of all children born in the early 1980s will live at least one year in a single parent home. Chris Spolar reports that on any given night as many as 735,000 homeless people wander the streets; and five hundred thousand of the nation's estimated two million homeless are children. Spolar says of these people that they are "people who have slipped over the edge." For the first time in our history since the Great Depression, whole families are "over the edge" and homeless. If the homeless, those living two households to a dwelling, and those who spend more than half of their income on rent are combined with the boomerang kids, some 15 million Americans are without adequate shelter. In New York City alone 200,000 await public housing, and, at the rate it is currently becoming available, many will be waiting for the next 18 years!

> How ironic this is when we consider that mankind has never been more prosperous and so able to care for its children. Never before has the world gone for so long a period of time without suffering major famines.
> Elasah Drogin, *Margaret Sanger: Father of Modern Society*

One way many otherwise concerned observers evade dealing with systemic issues which may explain some of the problems of our youth is to point to the lives of great people who started in humble circumstances. Out of the worst of adversarial conditions, they say, the world will always produce giants. A Winston Churchill whose father "considered him dull" and unlikely to ever achieve in school. Or a Pablo Picasso who could barely read at age ten. Or an Albert Einstein whose teachers said he was "dumb" and who had poor math skills as a child. America, they say, will continue to bring forth a Thomas Edison who had decidedly poor math skills along with a serious hearing impairment. Before becoming president, "Honest" Abe Lincoln failed in business twice, (was) defeated in various legislative races seven times...; had a sweetheart die, (and) suffered a nervous breakdown". Army General U.S. Grant failed at everything except for marriage and war. The black woman Madam Walker did the unthinkable by becoming the first American female millionaire early in the twentieth century.

A discussion of black children follows in the next chapter; suffice to say here that as a nation, America cannot afford to wait on "luck," fate, or "a throw of the dice" to thrust our children onto paths where their potential might be allowed to blossom and their contributions to the "general welfare" assured. Our changing family patterns must not preordain our children to a stagnated and unconstructive adulthood, many locked in what Spencer Rich called a "self-perpetuating underclass". Somehow, no matter the absence of a parent, we must encourage a return to certain values even where former structures supporting them are absent. Vermont neurologist Kenneth Crongoli warns that the nation's "primary institution should be the family, not the individual; and that in a rational society, children must be held more precious than careers." If we viewed our children in that manner the one-third identified by Crewdson as abused would not themselves grow up to be abusers and a drain on national resources. The Commission on Work, Family and Citizenship estimates that twenty million of our youth aged sixteen to twenty-four will not only not enroll in college but will come to make up a large segment of the permanent underclass. Twenty-two percent of our children and adolescents suffer from some form of mental or emotional disorder. And in absolute numbers more white youths are at risk than blacks.

In our brief discussion of America's youth, it should not be presumed that poverty alone is disruptive of healthy physical and mental development. Wealth poorly used can be as stifling as lack of money. "Corporate raider" T. Boone Pickens regards inherited wealth an albatross both because too many with wealth "are often terrified they are going to lose it" and they tend to shower *things* on their children instead of giving "them the opportunity to earn a paycheck", thereby *earning* self-respect and enhancing self esteem. We can teach our children what Parish Priest Andrew Greely says his lower middle class parents taught their children: respect for excellence.

> You respected excellence, perhaps not always the man who was excellent, but the excellence he possessed..whoever was good at what he did, we were taught, deserved our admiration.

> Respect for excellence and its pursuit did not mean that you had to be excellent. You did your reasonable best. You didn't quit. If you failed, that was all right too, so long as you didn't quit. (Parental) approval was not conditioned on performance, it was conditioned rather...on trying.

Neither wealth nor poverty guarantees excellent performance. In that regard, notwithstanding the obvious benefits accruing to children of wealthy parents, all children start the race in the same place. In *Bendigo Shafter*, L'Amour says, "Nobody is anybody until they make themselves somebody."

The Elderly: Productive or Profaned

We are a nation of the young and increasingly very "old". There was a time not too many years past when to live to the age of fifty years was to be old by current definition. To have reached the age of fifty was also considered a blessing borne of luck or "breeding". In the late twentieth century, to be elderly is not old "when life is still flowing along like a song," the wall plaque over my grandmother's ice box used to read.

But life does not flow like a song for too many of our "new" elderly. Among the two-and-one-half million chronically mentally ill Americans a large percentage are senior citizens. Fully one third of the poverty-ridden are elderly, according to the findings of a long-term study of poverty conducted at the University of Michigan. Mental stress due to fixed incomes and cutbacks in entitlements at the federal level are spawning an epidemic in suicides of older

Americans, particularly white males. Medical care costs have become prohibitively high, and preventive health programs reach only a minority of the elderly population. American political bodies and the medical establishment have not kept pace with the need. Former Colorado Governor Richard Lamm has observed that, compared to some European nations, "We spend money on doctors and over-built hospitals and they spend money on health..." Almost $700 billion was spent on health care in 1990. Almost half the citizens of the country receive some form of benefit from the federal government—Social Security, Medicare, food stamps, representing 39.1 million of the nation's 83.6 million households. The majority of these recipients are white and increasingly elderly.

Elder abuse is becoming epidemic in America. A report released by medical researchers in May, 1990 disclosed that an estimated one and one-half million elderly persons are abused each year, often by members of their own families!

Gerontologists and researchers who study the elderly predict that not far into the twenty-first century senior citizens will constitute close to fifty percent of the nation's population. To the extent that the country's policy makers and the medical establishment begin to promote independent living, as far as practicable, for the elderly, will be the degree to which our general welfare improves. Seventy year old Art Krug, a retired truck driver who has ridden his bicycle around the world, is not the only elder who is independent, healthy, and capable of adding spice to the life of the nation. Ninety-two year old Antonio Lopez-Olano was not alone in being able to live quite well independently, even in an abandoned building—until a social agency forced him into what amounts to a nursing home. Of this move the old gentlemen said:

> What you did when you brought me out of my house and brought me in here...I was a man. Now I am a boy. You try to do good things, but no good...all my things, I don't want them anymore. I used to love my books—now I don't want them anymore...I'm going to the hospital to die.

A friend has written how when her 80 year old mother first began visiting her each day, the mother would spend all her time sitting in the kitchen staring out the window. Now that she knows she's a useful member of the family, she helps care for great grandchildren, accompanies her daughter to club meetings and theatrical productions and, in general, enjoys life.

Discrimination in employment of older Americans is now prohibited by federal law. It's a good law. Yet discrimination in employment is only one means of keeping senior citizens out of living gainful, productive "sunshine" years. Denied in many places the opportunity to work with the young in school settings, they leave us not having had the opportunity to fully share their wisdom, skills, and wit—an ages old function of the "old-timer". A New York physician isn't alone in praising his grandfather, who "was more helpful than my parents, teachers or school counselor" in both helping the grandson become a medical doctor and in "passing on" ethnic lore and traditions. Our elderly can enrich all of us if they are brought in from the obscurity of retirement communities and urban cold water flats.

The over 50 age group will number an estimated 80 million by the year 2000; (President Bush joined 31 million other Americans by turning 65 in 1989) and will control about half of the nation's disposable income. While policy makers may procrastinate about addressing the needs of the down-and-out among them, where most black elderly fall, the larger number with resources, represented by membership in the American Association of Retired Persons, will not be forever denied or ignored.

The Disabled: Help at Last

The other traditionally "outcast" group, numbering many elderly, that is beginning to receive deserved attention is the disabled. Numbering about 40 million, two-thirds of the "able-bodied" members of this group are unemployed, making them the most disadvantaged and discriminated against minority group in the nation! A terrible waste of another valuable national resource. With passage of the Americans with Disabilities Act of 1990, Congress is finally giving a degree of recognition to the problem. Where would the field of physics be if England's Stephen Hawkins, by peer consensus "the world's greatest theoretical physicist," if his severe disability (as of this writing he has lost use of speech and all mobility except for one thumb which allows him to continue to work!) had automatically excluded him from participation? Of course, there are thousands of individuals with disabilities who, despite the odds, have made significant contributions to their communities and to the world. So many more would if some of the remaining barriers to their full participation were removed.

This brief overview of the American social landscape concludes with a short discussion of several other areas of American life that impact the welfare of African Americans. Immigration, political action committees, the environment, crime and drug abuse, have been matters of much public discussion and debate over the past decade; and much confusion still attends any attempt to design policies and solutions to their more deleterious effects. My aim is not so much to explore these matters but to state a perspective on them and to give the reader the benefit of my opinion on how American citizens might go about doing something out of their own self interest to resolve them.

Immigration: A Time For Reconsideration

Immigrants only hours off the boat, while subjected to scorn, were allowed to assert their superiority over black Americans.
Andrew Hacker

They came through Ellis Island, "where *Giorgio* becomes *Joe*, *Papparailu* becomes *Palmer*, *Evangelos* becomes *Evans*, *Goldsmith* becomes *Smith* or *Gold*, and

Avakian becomes *King.*" So, with a painless change in name, and in the twinkling of an eye, one becomes a white American.

> ...But the Irish became white when they got here and began rising in the world, whereas I became black and began sinking. The Irish, therefore and thereafter—again, but one example—had absolutely no choice but to make certain that I could not menace their safety or status or identity; and if I come too close, they could, with the consent of the governed, kill me. Which means that we can be friendly with each other anywhere in the world, except Boston.
>
> James Baldwin

America is a land peopled by representatives from every nation on the planet. Fueled by the despoliation of war, famine, religious intolerance, and just plain adventurism, they have comeby "nook or crook", legally and under cover of darkness, defying sharks (including the human variety!), barbed wire, anti-personnel mines and ditches, machine guns, treacherous seas, law, and other obstacles thrown in their path. More than 16 million came from Europe between 1892 and 1924, alone, so great was the attraction of the New World. Christopher Columbus and Hernando de Soto, each in his own way, had opened vast new vistas to the imagination where before only blank spaces and visions of "dropping off the edge" of the earth had sufficed as explanations to the question "What's out there?" At a much later time former President Lyndon Johnson gave a succinct version of the great lust:

> My plane has landed on many continents. The wheels have never stopped and the door has never opened that I have not looked upon faces which would not liked to have traded citizenship with me.

No other nation in the history of the modern world has held such broad appeal.

To be sure, the United States government has encouraged some to come more than it has others. In fact, America, and Canada, Australia, and New Zealand, literally saved Europe by becoming outlets for a land hungry and, in many places, a starving and warring Europe. There is simply no way the Irish or English populations would have grown in the numbers they have without an Americas or South Sea Islands to migrate to. Ireland's 1848 Potato Famine would have decimated the Irish population had not America opened its doors. Ireland, Germany (from which America actively sought immigrants to settle Texas), and other European countries simply could not support larger populations even without natural or man-made calamities. Without the opening of the western hemisphere to European exploration and settlement, what is called the white population of the world would have remained even fewer in number, even though it might well have still become the ruling "race". (James Baldwin convincingly argues that before coming to America, "no one was white...They were Poles," French, English, Irish, Dutch, etc. He adds that we blacks were *not* black either!) Germans and Irish, long dominated the rolls of American immigrants (and of these, according to Greely, Catholics became the "most successful gentile ethnic group".)

Put simply, Europeans, Western Europeans in particular, have always received a warm welcome here. (And many whites still believe, of course, that "America is a white man's country.") Following the abortive 1956 Hungarian Uprising, the United States accepted 30,000 of the losers. When the ragtag followers of the Cuban dictator rode into Havana in 1959, all but about 750 of Cuba's 15,000 (white) Jews fled to our shores with no more than mere formalities waiting at the border. Yet, as Trans-Africa's Randall Robinson points out repeatedly, no prominent American has ever even hinted at bringing to America some of the starving millions of Africa, or the earlier victims of the fratricidal war in Biafra (eastern Nigeria). Between 1975 and 1991, for instance, America accepted for asylum over one and one-half million *legal* immigrants, only 11 of those black, these from Haiti.

To stymie immigration of Haitians, despite charges of racism by Congressman Charles Rangel and others, another boatload of Haitians was returned in November 1991 and Charles reported in the January 1992 edition of the *National Geographic* that of the almost 24,000 Haitians seeking entry since 1981, "only 20 have been brought ashore to seek asylum," a figure that does not include the more than 100 AIDS infected Haitian detainees a federal court ordered admitted in June 1993, and other darker peoples of color, the U.S. Immigration and Naturalization Service has even concocted a new label for classifying immigrants. If they are "economic" refugees, they are denied entrance; being a "political" refugee is preferred. One can't help but wonder whether the immigrant parents of Lee Iaccoca, Michael Dukakis, Ed Koch or ex-Vermont Governor Madeline Kunin would have been, under these guidelines, permitted entrance. And no one seems to have questioned the status of the five hundred thousand Poles who fled to the West between 1983 and 1987.

Yet even with the favoritism shown white immigrants, before the twenty-first century is well underway "racial and ethnic groups in the U.S. will outnumber whites for the first time," reported *Time* in "Beyond the Melting Pot" (April 9, 1990). The U.S. 1993 immigration quota for sub-Sahara Africa is zero. And no matter the official and unadmitted intentions of some to "keep America white," America will not remain white, at least not in the traditional meaning of that term. By the year 2000, a few short years away, the nation will be one-third non-white.

At the same time that Haitians and Africans are excluded, (CBS News Correspondent Richard Thredkeld reported on "Eye On America" (June 24, 1993) that in addition to legal immigrants and the illegals caught, "Tens of thousands...sneak into this country every year," most of them nonwhite. The Chinese boat people are only the latest and most visible), other dark complexioned peoples are welcomed—if not with open arms at least not intercepted by Coast Guard cutters and turned back homeward or allowed to land only to be incarcerated indefinitely in prison-like holding pens. During the decade of the 1980s more than 8 million new immigrants arrived, 6 million legally and a rough-counted 2 million illegally. Asians and Latin Americans made up more than 80 percent of this wave. In Bush sponsored legislation in 1991 a 40 percent increase was authorized. Somehow American whites are redefining "acceptability" while still believing they are maintaining a "white" nation. Moreover, the world is getting "darker". Rosenblum reports that "during 1987, as many children will be born in Turkey and Egypt as in all 12 countries of the European Common Market...(and) Third World countries grow at rates up to 4 percent a year." As in America European whites are living longer but not reproducing themselves at a level "necessary to replace present numbers." Thus the combination of massive increases in Third World populations and declining "white" populations will mean ultimately, that whites as we know them will disappear.

America may indeed become the harbinger of things to come for the "white race". Much of Europe is in bad shape economically, and if past practices prevail, America will open the doors wide for them. Public Television reports that Northern England, for example, is an economic wasteland with an over-supply of skilled people with few jobs available. White South Africans are increasingly trying to emigrate, going to Australia in large numbers and knocking on the immigration doors of America. Even with widespread sterilization of black South African women, reported by *Essence* magazine in March 1987, these white South Africans realize that the days of white hegemony are numbered and will go the way of the dodo bird! (Of course, many white South Africans are leaving because they too are disenchanted with apartheid.) The rising European racism against formerly welcome Third World immigrants, most of whom come from former colonies, will not save Europe from the "de-white-nization" process. And America can not issue visas fast enough to hold onto a white majority into infinity.

Ethnic and racial strife are not limited to America and Europe, of course. In Africa and elsewhere ethnic, if not racial, hatred and conflict have been, and, in some places, are, characteristic features of the society. In Sri Lanka, Japan, Nigeria, and Australia (which was settled by exiled British convicts and other outcasts, people Kenneth Turan called the "human trash heap" of England, who slaughtered the Aboriginals by the scores, and whose descendants "hunt them...to this day." The Longshoreman-Philosopher Eric Hoffer told a television commentator that America was also "settled by the (European) scum of the earth.") Indeed, the author once met by chance an immigrant Australian, a scientist employed by an American university, who confided that as a young-ster, before he "knew better," he joined others in taking potshots at the natives on trips to the Outback. Australia only recently "scrapped the Immorality Act which outlawed intermarriage," although as in America and other white domi-nated lands the intent of such laws was to prevent interracial liaisons between white women and native (or black) men, leaving white men free to practice interracial lovemaking at their whim. The Yvonne Gooloogongs and so-called half-breeds ("breeds", in the vernacular) are the result. Australia at one time forbade immigration of non-whites, notwithstanding their own origins in im-migration. In New Zealand the "pakeha...white majority...are riffraff, the flot-sam and jetsam of British culture." Yet they control the country and have dominated the native Maorians. In Africa there is strife across ethnic lines most glaringly in Liberia's ethnic (not *civil*) war. Israelis and Palestinians war over territory; and Indians in much of South America are under siege and on the verge of becoming extinct. Like the DooDoo Bird!

Not alone because of the potential for international conflict, (such as the bombing of New York's World Trade Center and the June 24, 1993 arrests of several immigrants on charges of conspiring to commit other terrorist acts), America must adopt a policy of *no more immigrants*—of any coloration. The only exceptions should be selected diplomatic refugees such as defectors from communist regimes and other unfriendly governments; a few experts we absolutely cannot do without; and the rare exceptional humanitarian case. Under these guidelines a Peter Jennings, for instance, would be denied legal entry for immigration purposes. No compelling justification can be offered for his admittance; I could never be convinced that out of what must be thousands of trained journalists in this country not one of equal (or greater!) competence could be found to read the evening news. In hiring a Polish immigrant as a police officer *prior* to his becoming a naturalized citizen, the action of an Alaska municipality is equally puzzling, especially since the department had only two black officers in 1990, one of whom, a veteran on the force, was fired in 1991. So is hiring a Russian Jewish immigrant to head the theatre department at one of the state's public universities.

Other jobs are going to foreigners and immigrants which should be targeted for Americans. In 1985 some 8,000 Israeli engineers were working and living in the United States. Philippine doctors and nurses dominate health care work in many public health facilities; an immigrant Filipino female supervises multi-million dollar construction projects for the State of Alaska. Many government departments in Alaska's capitol, Juneau, are dominated by Filipinos. American college students are much more likely to encounter East Indian, Australian, Israeli, and Pakistani teachers than they are black, Hispanic or Native Americans. Hundreds of other foreign nationals have moved into administrative leadership positions in our educational institutions. (In an earlier era W.E.B. DuBois painstakingly chronicled (*The Philadelphia Negro*) how immigrant Germans, Italians and Irish displaced blacks in catering, domestic service and other traditionally "black" jobs, devastating what had been a stable middle class in the City of Brotherly Love.)

With respect to college teachers and administrators (these need never be "imports"), the only exceptions under the guidelines I propose would be scholars recruited in the national interest, one-of-a-kind historians like England's Paul Kennedy and theoretical physicist Stephen Hawkins. Where Americans cannot be recruited in sufficient numbers to staff our "hard science" faculties, such as computer science and some engineering specialties, foreign nationals (holders of "green cards") should be recruited on an interim basis with conditional visas. Colleges, and the U.S. government itself, if necessary, would, in such circumstances, offer the necessary incentives to attract Americans into disciplines with personnel shortages.

With the multicultural mix available within the United States, no scientist or engineer from another nation can bring anything substantially distinctive to justify a recruitment from abroad.

There are other compelling reasons to severely restrict immigration beyond what the new Act provides. Not many Americans seem to realize it, but the most recent wave of aliens from Asia and South America are having a serious impact on the employability of blacks and other minority Americans. While it may be true that many immigrants take low-paying jobs not really wanted by anyone else (at least, that is the speculation), the fact of the matter is many young Americans between 16 and 24 years of age who would ordinarily be introduced to the world of work through these entry level positions no longer have that opportunity. And lacking a work history, they later find securing higher level employment that much more difficult. Also important is that through the employment of aliens employers are able to keep wages artificially low, depriving (not so much the aliens, many of whom view *any* job in America as a Godsend) blacks and other traditionally disadvantaged Americans an avenue of escape out of dead end lives. This writer is aware of several universities which in the last decade have employed Asian immigrants for most of their low-paying; e.g. custodians, jobs. At one such institution custodians are paid $10-$12 per hour. Immigrants who are allowed to stay and pursue citizenship should be restricted, after attaining status as naturalized Americans, to "bringing in" only close relatives—immediate family. In a cafe owned by a former boat person, the author overheard the owner, in response to a question from her white American brother-in-law about "how many have you brought in now?" say that she had brought over 20 and was working on "number 21." It is not difficult to calculate the numerical if not economic and social effect if every immigrant can sponsor however many "family" members she or he wants to.

One has to ask: If aliens were not hired to do these jobs, who would be? A Tampa, Florida black leader complains that in the past African American Floridians had competition from Jews and Italians, "Now it's the Arabs, Koreans," and seemingly countless other groups grabbing opportunity away from blacks. African Americans are impacted in ways most other social groups are not. After reviewing a study by the Government Accounting Office, John Sullivan reported that in cities like Los Angeles, Miami and New York, immigrants have in fact replaced blacks in certain occupations: janitors in L.A. and in jobs now requiring Spanish language proficiency in Miami, Houston and San Diego. Sullivan cited another study that concluded: "There are tens of thousands of jobs in New York City for which the native born are not candidates."

The *Houston Post* reports millions of dollars going to help Asians adapt— "Chinese immigrants get help with jobs, adopting the culture." This is a city where the Oriental economic presence is almost as prominent as that of the traditional white males. Favoritism towards foreigners is shown in other ways, as, for example, in the 76 percent of financial support that went to non-American students studying for the doctorate in science and engineering in 1986. By 1994 scholarships and other forms of aid to students from the former

Soviet Union will equal or surpass that provided to American minority students.

Community leaders in the black enclaves of Miami's Overton and Liberty City are unanimous in condemning the actions of immigrant Hispanic police officers against African American citizens.

Immigration policies permitting millions to come into this country have other undesirable consequences. Our land is extraordinarily large, to be sure, but increased population pressure on natural resources, and especially on our flora and fauna, can only lead ultimately to a diminution of the quality and amount of resources available for use and enjoyment. In 1960 the U.S. population stood at 200 million. By March of 1990 it had reached 250 million. One estimate projects 392 million by the year 2100.And who wants America as congested as an India, Japan or China?

A *positive* contribution of Third World immigrants is staffing faculties of historically black colleges. *All* of these institutions depend on foreign nationals, principally Asian, to bring their teaching corps up to accreditation standards, since the supply of black Ph.D.'s never could meet the demand. Since the 1960's predominately white universities, which can offer greater financial incentives and research facilities, have depleted the pool of candidates. Thus, permitting entry to these aliens is in the national interest.

Beyond the issue of resource diminution, it is important to ask: Just who are these people who are pointing their way to the "Land of Honey"? What impact will they have on what we have come to think of as American? We know that the pattern of immigration has shifted, in recent years, away from white domination. By 1988 almost eighty percent of new immigrants came from Asia (about 43 percent), Mexico, and the Caribbean. It is noteworthy that Africans comprised only about three percent of this group. (*Ebony* magazine has reported only 170,000 African immigrants in the U.S.).

Perhaps the question to ask is not who the immigrants are but *who is an American*? Saul Bellow and others have suggested that being an American means having some important things in common. "There are things that (Americans) *should* know," Bellow asserts. John Gardner has written that "A great civilization is a drama lived in the minds of a people. It is a shared vision; it is shared norms, expectations and purposes." While there is insufficient research on this subject at this point in time to permit definitive statements to be made, there is ample anecdotal evidence to suggest that Americans ought to in fact be very concerned about the matter. Some examples: neighborhoods in a large southwestern city where homes for sale are advertised in Japanese (a new brand of segregation?); in many large cities Koreans, Lebanese, Pakistanis, and East Indians, displacing small black business people and causing social strife; foreign nationals teaching in American universities who have little facility in the English language, many with good theoretical training but lacking experience in application.

The most damning criticism about the new immigrants is that most come from countries where class and caste are ingrained and immovable barriers.

They don't hail from democracies. India, for example, from which a large contingent of foreign national college faculty comes, is perhaps the most caste bound society in the modern world. It is a land where individuals are born into permanent niches in the pecking order. An *Untouchable* will always be just that; even though in post-Independence India he may be able to drink from the same water well as a higher caste person. Not even India's first Prime Minister, the very popular Nehru, could significantly change the system of caste. His appointment of a highly educated *Untouchable* as President, and the expansion of educational opportunity to provide greater access for *Untouchable* children, while laudatory, were gestures intended to reorder basic attitudes toward caste and the *Untouchables*, in particular. His well intended programs notwithstanding, these darker skinned Indians (it should be noted that Indians in general consider themselves descendants of Caucasians) will always be at the bottom of the heap. They are India's niggers. Black writer Kesho Scott discovered pronounced anti-black prejudice among East Indian immigrants in this country.

In India caste is joined by extreme male chauvinism as evidence of anti-democratic transfers to the United States. More than a few American universities have experienced difficulties arising from attitudes toward race and sex exhibited by their imported faculty. Moslems from Iran and other Middle Eastern nations have similar attitudes about race and sex. For those African Americans who favor Arabs over Israelis in the Mideast conflict, they should know that blacks have been enslaved by Arabs for centuries and that black Africans currently residing in Arab countries are virtual slaves. Mauritania, for instance, has a majority black population yet denies anything resembling equal opportunity to blacks. The Arabs have their own brand of apartheid, one the world press ignores but which is as slave-like as South Africa's. The Arab disdain of blacks is transported to the United States through Arab immigrants.

Many immigrants who achieved citizenship through the naturalization process proudly boast that they are now "American". Yet, on the rare occasion when one dares ask the question: If I became a citizen of Japan, for instance, would I then be *Japanese*? The impression conveyed through stunned silence is its own answer. A recent television program featured an American woman, married to a Japanese farmer, who, after some fifteen years residence in rural Japan, knew most of the rituals—"how far to bow on a given occasion", but who was quick to admit that she was American and could never be Japanese, despite her apparent acceptance.

> But citizenship is more than paper—it's a connection to a community—not just a formal state. (It's) an inter-generational sense of responsibility, a sense of sharing in the community's past and future fulfillment of obligations.
> Martin Heisler, U. of Maryland

With the rapid growth of poor and seriously disadvantaged whites in America, there is a growing consensus among blacks *and* whites that the time has come to put brakes on the flood. The country simply cannot accommodate them. Former college professor and U.S. Senator S.I. Hayakawa formed U.S.

English to fight attempts to make Spanish co-equal with English in the United States. Actions by the National Lawyers Guild and others to have federal courts force local governments to treat Spanish as though it shares equal status with English will only further the cause of the "stop immigration" lobby.

On the matter of the meaning of immigration to African Americans, there is not much to be hoped for. In a guest column for the *Washington Post* naturalized East Indian Natwar Gandhi wrote of the "vitality" immigrants bring to this "promised land", saying "the fresh new stream keeps the old water from stagnating." In his glowing tribute to the vitality of the newcomers (and his thinly disguised glee for being able to flee an unattractive homeland) nowhere does he acknowledge the burdens immigrants such as himself bring with them. Certainly, from an African American perspective, there is nothing in the record to suggest that *we* are gaining allies or that democracy as a political ideal will be strengthened.

An ad for the movie *Alien Nations* matches my sentiments on immigrants: "They have come to...live among us. They've learned the language. Taken jobs. And tried to fit in. But there's something about them we don't know."

Controlling immigration will be a major federal government priority in the opening decades of the twenty-first century. Public disclosure during 1993 of a wave of illegal Mainland Chinese, each of whom pay a much as $30,000 for the ride, landing on our shores aroused the American people and the Clinton administration to action on the immigration issue.

But we cannot build a safe and secure world unless we can first make Americans strong at home. It's our ability to take care of our own at home that gives us the strength to stand up for what we believe around the world.
Before the presidency in Robert Levin, *Bill Clinton: The Inside Story*, 1992

The Japanese Connection

Japanese influence is arguably most detrimental. Along with their incredible economic offensive, which An Wang calls the Japanese extension of World War II by other means, (Hackworth goes further saying "Japan is celebrating a belated wartime victory.") the Japanese are among the worlds most tribal and racist people; and their leaders make no real apologies for the racist sentiments they publicly express. Former Japanese Prime Minister Nakasone said of blacks and Hispanics that "they are lowering U.S. intelligence rates". Japanese liberal democratic party leader Michio Watanabe called American blacks "irresponsible" and said that blacks "would rather declare bankruptcy than pay their bills". An international protest had to be mounted to stop the Japanese from making and selling the famous "Sambo" dolls and "Darky Toothpaste". The Japanese cannot be considered potential allies to African Americans.

A new group, Organization for a New Equality, has been established for the explicit purpose of combating Japanese racism.

71

Foreign Investment and Political Action Committees

Foreign investors are making vast inroads into the American economy. A decade ago few could have imagined that foreign investment in the American economy would surpass $1.5 trillion. Japanese investors are among the leaders of the pack; represented by the recent completion of a $1.1 billion automobile assembly plant in Kentucky, and the acquisition of large tracts in farm and ranch land in the American west. This is money, which if withdrawn, "could wreck havoc on our economy", according to " respected economists Martin and Susan Tolchin. In 1988 foreigners owned 4,000 American factories and in that year added four million acres of American farm and ranch land. More ominous is the level of foreign, particularly Japanese, influence in our political affairs. Foreign sponsored Political Action Committees spent $2.3 million in the 1986 congressional races out of a total $132.2 million spent by PAC's. Between 1972 and 1982 PAC's grew enormously in number and influence, from less than 100 to more than 3,000. In the 1990 Senate and House campaigns, PAC's gave more than $120 million to incumbents, according to Common Cause. By the presidential election of 1992 political action committee influence in American political life had become enormous. Albert Hunt explains how the influence works:

> If a member (of Congress) gets $10,000 from the AMA and votes to exempt doctors from FTC (Federal Trade Commission) jurisdiction, we're not saying it's a bribe...But it's just as incredible for a member to say $10,000 makes no difference. In this case, it gives the doctors a decided edge.

Foreign and domestic Political Action Committees are changing the way the American political game is played. While wealth has always been a factor in politics, as the Durants observe, never before have so many narrow self interest economic groups been so influential in American political life. It should come as no surprise that Americans feel estranged from their own government. "Americans have expressed sad and bitter alienation toward those running the society and feel powerless to do anything about." An all-time high of 79 percent of us feel that way, no matter our race, sex, income or age. And if whites feel alienated (61 percent), it's forgone that blacks feel even more so (77 percent). The great danger of PACs is that they influence policy makers in ways almost always detrimental to the poor, and certainly to blacks.

Crime and Drugs

Crime is out of control in large areas of America—where one in four households suffered a violent crime in 1988; a murder is committed every 25 minutes, and most murderers are never caught; where "missing persons" is almost as common as murder; and where serial murder is appearing in areas of the country that in the past had only occasional single homicides. Crime against individuals is matched in magnitude by white collar criminality, exemplified by the Alan Boesky, Michael Milken (In his April 24, 1991, newscast, Dan Rather reported Milken's fine, after a guilty plea, was $600 million, leaving his personal assets in excess of $1 billion!), Charles Keating cases and other high stakes thieves; and organized crime, which the President's Commission on Organized Crime claimed is entrenched in the American market place and is "increasingly using labor unions as a tool to obtain monopoly power in key sectors" of the economy. Only in recent years has a vigorous pursuit of organized crime leaders here and in Italy and Columbia been launched, and it will be some years before the American people will know whether this "festering sore," so much more influential in American life than most Americans realize, has been properly "treated" and exorcised.

Interestingly, the *Atlanta Journal and Constitution*, in an exhaustive investigation of national crime patterns, discovered that it is not the largely black inner cities which lead the nation in violence and social pathology. Rather it's the American west that is the "most...dangerous region...*(where the) rate of violent death among youths in the most isolated parts...are higher than those in big city ghettos, (and people)...have worse health conditions and live shorter lives.*" (Emphasis added.) A June 1991 *Newsweek* report confirmed that serious crimes such as homicide have "skyrocketed" in the nations midsize cities.

President Bush announced a crime fighting program, to cost in excess of $1 billion, put too much emphasis on punishment—new prison cells, law enforcement officers, prosecutors, and judges. America already jails a higher percentage of its citizens than all but two nations—the former Soviet Union and South Africa, surpassing them by 1994. To get at the root of criminal behavior, the nation will have to, in the words of columnist Louis Overstreet, remove the "incentive to commit crime...(and reinforce) the values that preserve and advance a productive and just society..." President Clinton's pledge to fund thousands of additional police officers in the nation's cities prompted a caution from his Housing & Urban Affairs Secretary that this cosmetic approach would only deal, cosmetically, with symptoms not causes.

Drug abuse has reached epidemic proportions in poor and black communities. And the white middle class has felt the pain of the "Coke" craze as well. In 1987 six million of us spent $110 billion on cocaine (the "Big C"). In New York City, in a two month period, over three-quarters of the people arrested tested positive for cocaine use. When mothers will neglect or sell or even abandon their own babies in blind compulsion and when the "White Lady" has the potency of literally making slaves of its users, it is past time for society itself to rebel and declare "war on drugs". An active combination of governmental and educational programs are required to root out not only the users and potential users but the pushers and their high-level, often quite "respectable", suppliers and bankrollers, and the money launderers.

In a nation where by the year 2000, according to Dennis Cauchon, 1 of every

90 adults will be in prison or jail, most drug related; and where, Stephanie Coontz reports, the highest homicide rate in the industrial world has been maintained for 150 years, and where poverty is increasingly "locked in", prospects for national prosperity are very limited. Drug abuse may be symptomatic of something amiss much deeper.

Following former President Bush's lead and pandering to a perceived public consensus, President Clinton announced in his January 25, 1994, State of the Union address a broad attack on crime. As commentators like James Austin and Marc Mauer have pointed out ("Crime 'Explosion' is a Myth", *USA Today*, January 27, 1994), the new President's program will be no more successful than his predecesor's. Both were based on fallacies.

Americans should know these **facts** about criminal activity:

❀ Blacks do not commit most crimes in this country.

❀ Drug abuse is more widespread among whites than blacks.

❀ Ever higher imprisonment rates have not reduced criminal activity.

❀ Mandatory minimum sentences have not reduced the number of "serious" criminals on our streets.

❀ Recidivism (repeat offenders) is not related to length of prison sentences.

❀ Number of police officers per capita is not related to the crime rate.

❀ No serious study has ever demonstrated a causal connection between the death penalty and the homicide rate. What it does **guarantee** is that the executed will never commit another crime of any type!

Former Nixon aide Chuck Colson ex-con, born again Christian and chairman of Prison Fellowship, roundly denounced the Bush-Clinton initiatives as political pandering to am impish and uninformed/misinformed public weary of crime. Broad implementation of legislation like the Clinton bill will not reduce crime, it will only create greater anxiety, leaving those who might have been helped. The public as victim as well as crime perpetrators – worse off than before. Colson, who was a Nixonian "Lock 'em up and throw away the keys" firebrand before serving time himself and learning firsthand the essentially political underpinning of criminal justice, makes more sensible recommendations. Instead of prison, require first-time, non-violent offenders (more that two-thirds of all those sent to jail every year) to work and make restitution. Because mandatory sentencing almost always works to the benefit of the "big time" criminals who can negotiate lesser sentences leaving their underlings to catch the "hard time" low-level offenders should get "alternative sentencing" allowing them to "develop marketable skills, keep their families off welfare and pay restitution to their victims."

The Environment

Care of the natural environment is finally getting the broad public attention it deserves. The Russian nuclear disaster, the unprecedented oil spill in Alaska, and smaller scale man-made despoliation of the environment have galvanized public attention in a way not witnessed since the world realized the awesome potential of nuclear power with the dropping of atomic bombs on Japan.

Western peoples in general, and Americans in particular, have not historically held the same regard for natural phenomenon that Africans, American Indians, and other peoples have shown. For Americans, land has not held a spiritual dimension; it was rather a commodity, very often an obstacle, to be bought, bartered, and despoiled in the pursuit of wealth. It was not "Mother Earth" to be cherished, honored, and lived in harmony with. Long time Alaskan Ray Tremblay, who had to be speaking of *white* men, wrote that "Left to his own devices, man will reduce wildlife to the last mammal, bird, or fish to satisfy his own needs..." African social historian Ali Mazuri has observed that "Europeans are the greatest creators of ugliness in human history...the Goddess of Ugliness...," and novelist Alice Walker adds that white men "have never met any new creature without exploiting, or destroying it."

The most frightening possibility of all in the wanton use and destruction of natural phenomenon is nuclear disaster. Chernobyl will look like a 2.5 Richter earthquake compared to what could and will likely happen if greater care is not exercised in the use of nuclear energy. The draconian possibility arises not from its use but from the half-life of radioactive materials like Strontium-90. All Americans should read Australian physician Helen Caldicott's *Nuclear Madness*. Because we cannot rely on politicians or other leaders to teach us or protect us from nuclear madness, an aroused citizenry must demand responsible behavior from policy makers. We also can not rely on "experts", in the words of Saul Bellow, who have failed " *because they were experts*...They were devoid of humanistic knowledge..." Or as Colonel Hackworth quotes Lord Salisbury, "No lesson seems to be so deeply inculcated by the experience of life, as that you should never trust in experts." (Alice Walker is probably correct in believing that blacks show little interest in nuclear energy matters because many, in fact, secretly, consciously or unconsciously, hope for a holocaust that will destroy all whites—who can't be changed through other means—even when knowing they will also perish in the fiery cataclysm.)

Of more down-to-earth concern for black Americans are the various reports made public in 1992 that revealed an undeniable relationship between being black and the siting of hazardous and toxic waste dumps. It's not just poor communities but *black* communities that tend to attract these death dealing facilities. After studying Environmental Protection Agency (EPA) documents for 1991, *Birmingham Post-Herald* reporter Thomas Hargrove declared "Pollution Hits Black Neighborhoods Hardest, Records Show." Newswriter Bill Kole headlined a study of toxic waste dumping "Nation's Poor and Minorities Get the Worst of Toxic Waste."

"Environmental racism" has been a steady if silent killer of blacks in this country.

Resolution on March 1994 of the issue surrounding siting a toxic waste dump in a black Birmingham neighborhood should become a model for relations between elected officials and citizenry. The Birmingham plant, already built at a cost of $17 million, with approval of a black mayor and predominately black city council, came under fire from community residents as a classic case of environmental racism. Joined in street demonstrations by activists from several black colleges, local groups such as Malcolm X Grassroots Movement and Ujima, though violently dispersed by police (headed by a black chief), persisted until Mayor Arrington agreed to look for another site for the dump. The mayor agreed to a $6.7 million settlement to the private corporation that built the facility. Doing the right thing can be expensive!

CHAPTER II

African America...The Way We Are

For, while the tale of how we suffer, and how we are delighted, and how we may triumph is never new, it always must be heard. There isn't any other tale to tell, it's the only light we've got in all this darkness...
James Baldwin

One thing is certain, whatever was put in the mix before I came along, I have been black since I was born. For those of you who have not had that experience, I can tell you truly that it doesn't make life easier.
K.C. Jones, with Jack Warner, *Rebound*

In 1857, the Supreme Court ruled that the Constitution had been written for whites only. Chief Justice Roger B. Taney affirmed, in the Dred Scott case, that blacks were not citizens and "had no rights which the white man was bound to respect."
Mort Gerberg, *The U.S. Constitution for Everyone*

We grant full citizenship in the World Commonwealth to the "Anglo-Saxon" (whatever that may mean), the Teuton and the Latin; then with just a shade of reluctance we extend it to the Celt and Slav. We half deny it to the yellow races of Asia, admit the brown Indians to an ante-room only on the strength of an undeniable past; but with the Negroes of Africa we come to a full stop, and in its heart the civilized world with one accord denies that these come within the pale of...Humanity. This feeling, widespread and deep-seated, is, in America, the vastest of the Negro problem!
W.E.B. Du Bois, "Still 'A Final Word', The Meaning of All This.

Throw away your crutches and quit complaining because you are black. Don't belch, choke, smoke, and wish for something to go away. Because when you are finished belching, choking, smoking, and wishing, society will still be here.
Barbara Jordan, and Shelby Hearon, *Barbara Jordan: A Self-Portrait*

We will win, because we are on God's side.
Joe Louis in Chris Mead, *Champion: Joe Louis, Black Hero in White America*

Progress: A Mixed Bag

So much has been said and written about we people of African descent that the reader may wonder whether there is some magical genie let loose to spread propaganda about a problematic people who just can't seem to get it together. Indeed, in a *USA Today* special report a prominent black scholar commented that "If there is one growth industry continuing to expand, it's Afro-American history" including "the urban experience, gender, (and) civil rights." With the renewed interest in the status of the nation's African American population, one would think that all is well or surely becoming so. That many Americans believe this to be the case is noted by black University of Tennessee-Knoxville Law School Dean Marilyn Yarborough, who argues that black status is not a "pretty picture," and that the slate has not been wiped clean of invidious racial discrimination.

All appears to be well for some blacks; nothing is well for many, many more of us. America has never been a "well" society for most blacks. Most Americans would agree that the United States continues to be the "home of the brave," and the more informed would not argue with the truth that, except perhaps for the first generation of blacks to touch these shores, America has never been the "land of the free." Any black person who makes a contrary claim, of whatever social or economic status, should be encouraged to spend a night at Howard Beach, Glen Falls (in Philadelphia), Oxford, Wisconsin, Cicero, Illinois, Cummings, Georgia, Dubuque, Iowa, Buffalo, New York, or the thousands of other communities across the nation where blacks are quickly, if sometimes subtly, reminded of their "place."

Older blacks know that reality well, many having experienced personal encounters with America's Howard Beaches. Borrowing the title of a Philip Caputo novel, most white neighborhoods in this nation are "Indian Country" ("any terrain considered hostile and dangerous") to blacks. So many younger "bloods" seem not to have learned the lessons of the past, flaunting what they consider their freedom and usually paying a high cost for their ignorance and arrogance. They have not yet learned what novelist Zora Neale Hurston tried to teach decades ago: "By some measures all black people are the proletariat no matter how many millions of dollars they may possess. Any black person is subject to discrimination no matter how cultured his accent..." It's a lesson that publishing magnate John Johnson knows well, declaring in his autobiography *Succeeding Against the Odds,* that neither merit nor money—both of which he has in great quantity—signifies acceptance of blacks by whites.

For a group whose American heritage "predates that of very large numbers, if not most, American whites," remarked Theodore Cross, "the historical pervasiveness and tenaciousness of racial prejudice suggests the monumental tribute owed Black Americans. "Despite the heavy toll race discrimination continues to exact, our striving proceeds. Writer Peter Bailey says we must be "strong, resourceful, individuals...(simply because we have) survived the constant physical and psychological brutality that has been inflicted on us in this country."

Yet progress seen from the perspective of the abject debasement of our previous condition of "involuntary servitude" has been achieved. Without question. And it is the hope of this chapter to applaud those achievements even as we point to the continuing problems of this American Dilemma. While there is little that is upbeat in the lives of many black Americans, my hope is that a reading of these pages will leave the discerning individual with a feeling that no matter the toughness of the task or the distance yet to be traveled, the African American example will continue to be seen by the world's racially oppressed as a beacon of hope and faith. It's what former Supreme Court Justice Thurgood Marshall had in mind when he said that the U.S. "government was defective from the start, requiring several amendments, a civil war and momentous social transformation to attain a constitutional government and it's respect for individual freedoms and human rights we hold as fundamental today." *And Still We Rise*, Maya Angelou wrote.

This chapter is concerned with some of the major dimensions of the black condition. Though not as comprehensive as some histories and social science texts, it does discuss areas that most blacks have some first-hand experience with, and it does raise questions about the extent of externally imposed as well as intragroup self constraints placed on black individuals. Beginning with a brief discussion of police community relations it revisits black self esteem and self hate as indicators of the degree of self-acceptance blacks have achieved, followed by overviews of family, youth, education, and health; the black economic condition; leadership; Buppies and the black middle class; religion; blacks as professional soldiers and athletes; black women and men; and blacks and the media. The discussion of each of these topics is abbreviated and attempts only to arrive at some understanding of the role played by each and the extent of impact of each on the current status of black Americans. Understanding these somewhat separate and disparate but obviously interconnected dimensions should provide valuable clues to what the group's status may be in the next century.

While I have no desire to burden the reader with a list of statistical indices of our condition, it is important that some of the more salient features be acknowledged. Blacks are about thirty million, or 12 percent, of the nation's almost 250 million—inhabitants or citizens. (The reader should understand that the U.S. census has *never* made an accurate count of the black population. In 1980 almost 1.5 million blacks were not counted, representing about 5% of the total black population. Black males made up a disproportionate share of the under-counted. Census Bureau officials admit an undercount in the 1990 Census though they claim a less serious one.) The black birth rate in 1984 was about twice that of whites (although as Coontz points, birth rates among single black women was lower in 1992 than in 1970, lower than the current white single female rate). Blacks, overwhelmingly young males, comprise nearly 50

79

percent of arrests for violent crimes and make up a correspondingly high percentage of incarcerations. In 1991, 40 percent of death row inmates were black. In almost all violent crimes perpetrated by blacks, the victim is also black. (Contrary to a myth widely held by whites, *they* have little to fear from blacks!) An estimated one half of young black men over age 16 are not working and are functionally illiterate. In some areas of the country black unemployment of the 16 to 24 age group approaches 70 percent. More than half of our children grow up in single parent homes, more times than not led by mothers. In 1982 we lived about six years less than whites, about the same difference as in the early 1950s (although by 1989 the gap had widened considerably, according to a report by the national Center for Health Statistics.) Black income has consistently lagged behind that of other groups including the later arrivals. In 1987 blacks trailed whites by about $14,000 in median income and Hispanics by more than $2,000. Asian income far exceeds that of blacks.

In its stunning but not surprising annual report for 1992 the United Nations Development program outlined a state of affairs of blacks (and other minorities in the United States) that totally contradicts the sentiments of those who deny race is a factor. Among the reports findings:

> "Minorities in the U.S. have a lower standard of living than 30 other nations, while whites in America enjoy a better life than any country on earth.

> "The living standard of African Americans is ranked 31st in the world—on a par with Trinidad and Tobago."

The Enforcers: Blacks Experience of the "Law"

> You cannot really communicate what it feels like (as a black man) to look into your rearview mirror and see a cop behind you.
> Ishmael Reed, *Life*

> The task of a policeman (sic)...is to protect persons and property in a manner that embodies the predominant moral values of the community he (sic) is serving.
> *Supplemental Studies for the National Advisory Commission on Civil Disorders*, 1968

Away from their place of work, by far the most intimate contact many, if not most, African Americans have with whites is through the legal system. If the reader can imagine being confined to a cage where a major source of life-sustaining sustenance—whether material or psychological—is controlled, as in a scientific experiment (or a jail), by forces external to their own environment and where real or perceived threats can induce predictable behavioral responses, much of the African American world would begin to make sense.

Contact with the legal system is not limited to law enforcement or the courts; nor is it exclusively an actual physical encounter or interaction with police officers or judges. In the sense used here legal system encompasses the entire body of laws, policies, regulations, and implicit codes of conduct which governs—and frightens and often bewilders—most blacks in their points of contact with whites. To enroll a child in school for the first time, for instance, can be an ordeal for a parent whose everyday mode of existence has not called for learning the "rules of that game" or interacting as a matter of course with people, especially *white* people, who are in fact strangers who speak a "different" language, have apparently confusing or unknown expectations and who obviously have power over both student and parent by virtue of their status (which includes their skin color). Walking into a bank, military recruiting station, public assistance office, or almost any other unfamiliar place of business is for many blacks like stepping into a different world. And indeed it is; for there is little social continuity between the environments (worlds).

But there is another, more subtle, and more menacing and debilitating, form of contact between black and white. It is a fear born of the knowledge that "white" can and has injured black solely for reasons of race. Believing oneself at the almost complete mercy of another human being who in almost all circumstances has power to do harm is probably the most crippling psychological baggage African Americans have had to contend with. The unremitting, though sometimes unconscious (or at least not admitted), fear, rooted in historical experience, explains much of black behavior which would otherwise seem unjustified, unredeemably paranoid, and pointless. Few whites—a minuscule few—ever manage to make the leap of understanding necessary to comprehend that this form of encounter with the white world undergirds our relations with them *and* with each other. Fear is a powerful motivator! Only blacks who have perfected what retired theologian and poet Johannes Gaertner called *perspicacity*, "a happy medium between suspicion and...naive trust," an ability to see through to the motivations of another, can successfully maneuver this life-long obstacle course.

Where blacks are concerned America is a society largely segregated by race. In fact, asserts black law professor Donald Hill, the nation is integrated "only to the extent that (black and white) *have* to come into contact with one another." (Emphasis added). But race more than the fact of segregation accounts for much of the social pathology in African American communities; and it explains and defines the attitudes of black individuals who live "beyond the pale" of black neighborhoods.

The vast dichotomy between word and deed in the American ethic is evident throughout the nation's social fabric, but nowhere is the contradiction more manifest than in the justice system. As New York State's first black supreme court justice concluded after years on the bench, the American court system, while supposedly the most objective and color-blind institution in the land, has "been little different from other segments of the nation's life." Judge Wright adds that a "campaign of terror has been a constant theme in black life, whether at the hands of justice or the Ku Klux Klan." Through biased arrests, jury selection, sentencing (both length and type of incarceration), and other mechanisms racism has been a critical factor. Indeed, claims eminent historian

C. Vann Woodward, "the absence of Negro judges, jurors, witnesses and lawyers helps to explain the heavily disproportionate number of Negroes in northern prisons."

Support Your Local Police?

"From the 1960's to the 1990's more than half of all the major riots by Black Americans in our cities have been precipitated by police malpractice incidents, including police brutality."
      Jet, May 3, 1993

Long a subject of controversy and debate, police-community relations in black America continues to set the tone for black-white relations in general. If fear is a fact of behavior for many blacks in their relations with what we have called the legal system it's manifestation is even more poignant in relations between African Americans and law enforcement agencies and the judicial system. Because these agencies of government touch the lives of so many blacks, and touches them very often in ways that leave imprints for life, no discussion of blacks in America would be complete without a discussion of the "law" and its impact.

The police and courts have played confusing roles in the lives of African Americans. On the one hand, black communities need quality law enforcement more than any other segment of the nation. Yet these same "protectors of life and property" have been the leading edge for much suffering, fear and hate. Blacks knew long before the revelations of the National Advisory Commission on Civil Disorders that police and the courts were often as much to be feared as any night rider with a robe.

Historically African Americans have been shortchanged by the American criminal justice system. In territories colonized by Europeans, the "mother country" often dispatched her own nationals to "police the natives," sometimes with the assistance of "native" hirelings, as in South Africa. This model of colonial administration has been used by some observers of the domestic scene to describe what happens to African American communities policed by white officers. Despite the amount of "law" and "order" they presume to bring, it is clear that many wearers of the blue (or gray or tan) are not fit to police middle class communities let alone poor black neighborhoods already plagued by a multiplicity of social and economic woes. In San Francisco, for instance, a city considered by many (though by no means, all) Americans to be on the cutting edge of progressive public administration, one psychologist determined that only 10 percent of the police force were "psychologically fit to serve in that capacity." Seventy-five percent of the force divorce their spouses, alcoholism is wide spread, and the "suicide rate (is) 6 1/2 times the national average."

This admission by a former cop is confirmed by another former police officer who adds that "there is racism within the brotherhood." Surveys of black police officers reveal almost unanimous agreement on the high levels of white police racial prejudice. The Southern Poverty Law Center's *Klanswatch* has noted that "white supremacists have traditionally been attracted to jobs in law enforcement." Former Los Angeles police officer turned author Mike Rothmiller reported that during training superiors apprised him of the way it *really* was. "If you want to last here, if you want to survive, if you want to make probation, all niggers are fucked. Don't ever forget that." This same officer added that L.A. blacks were forced to live in a different America, "a police state—a Los Angeles Police Department State."

Police departments have in recent years been obligated by law to abandon gender and race based hiring practices; yet women and minorities hired in the wake of lawsuits and civil rights laws have not fared well in many cases. The "racism in the brotherhood" has caused homicide, refusals by white male officers to share patrols, and various forms of harassment. Case in point: a black female cop gets $90,000 settlement for a claim of harassment by white male colleagues working at a "liberal" university in a "liberal" midwestern city. A black male co-worker and two former white colleagues (who had been harassed off the force for supporting claims of the plaintiff) are also awarded damages. No punitive action is taken against offending officers. This is one of dozens of such instances of continuing discrimination *within* the nation's law enforcement agencies.

Nor have many big-city departments made much progress in hiring. Blacks and Latinos made up about one-half of New York City's population in 1982, yet constituted only about 12 percent of the city's police officers. By 1993 little had changed, prompting *Emerge* magazine to report that the city "has the worst record nationwide on the hiring of African American police officers." In Georgia, years after federal courts ordered quota hiring in Alabama, then promotion of black state troopers, the state's Public Safety Board had to rescind promotion of 22 officers because the outgoing commissioner had violated a court order by the U.S. Justice Department on minority hiring.

Routine arrests, brutality and casual incarceration of black males, in particular, are not uncommon occurrences in America even in the 1990s. (Two prominent instances in 1991 were the arrests of prominent civil rights figure Julian Bond by Maryland police who were out, he said, simply to arrest *any* black man, and the arrest and beating of ex-Atlanta Mayor Andrew Young's college student son by D.C. police.) And not infrequently, when the innocent are saved their salvation is affected by unusual saviors, viz, the falsely arrested, charged, and convicted black engineer in Texas who was saved by CBS's *60 Minutes*; the black Marine, falsely accused and convicted of rape of a white woman, saved by *60 Minutes*. And what of those who don't enjoy almost divine intervention: a black man beaten to death by white cops in Miami's Overton community, the cops later tried and acquitted; an inquest held for a black man arrested on a drunk driving charge and later found dead in his cell concluded he had been killed *in* jail; as in the engineer's case a black man convicted despite eyewitness testimony placing him at work at the time of the crime, but he spends eight years in prison for a crime he never committed. An innocent black woman spends nine years in a Texas cell. In Mississippi from 1990-1993, 23 deaths of young African American men in their cells were officially classed as "self-inflicted suicides."

The Los Angeles Police Chief was criticized "because so many blacks were dying from a vicious 'chokehold' his police officers used to cut off the supply of blood to the brain." Harassment of Black males by L.A. police prompted the late Miles Davis to personally notify police when he purchased a new car. An *Essence* magazine Special Report concluded that the "best predictor for police shootings is race," meaning if you're black, and especially male, your chance of encountering the wrong end of a police service revolver is greatly enhanced (about equal, some would say, to a black man's chances of being the victim of *black* perpetrated homicide). Indeed, as Pinkney argues, black males who live in large cities and have not attended college will almost certainly have a negative experience with the police and criminal justice system "by the age of 25," and are six times more likely than white males to spend some time in a prison during their lifetime.

The March 3, 1991 videotaped police beating of Rodney King in Los Angeles and the alleged lack of proper police behavior in the Jeffrey Dahmer case in Milwaukee came as no surprise to mature blacks. Both places were identified in this book (written prior to both incidents) as among the most inhospitable in the nation for African Americans.

Exposure of widespread police abuse of authority brought to light—again— by the Rodney King incident, does not appear to have significantly curbed harassment of black citizens. There is now even apparent cooperation across state lines by white police to harass their black colleagues as well as those with whom they directly work. A *Jet* report documents such behavior in the northeast—New York, New Jersey, Connecticut, Rhode Island and Massachusetts— and notes that black and Hispanic officers have formed a regional support group to combat it. Black cops have to routinely keep an eye on their white partners even while chasing real criminals.

> When white people hear the cry "the police are coming!" for them it almost always means "help is on the way." Black citizens cannot make the same assumption.
> Andrew Hacker

That few offending officers are ever punished is perhaps the ultimate tragedy. Rothmiller said the L.A. police department "closed ranks around its torturers and psychopaths and protected them." Hubert Williams, president of the Police Foundation concurs that "excessive use of force is at the heart of most of the civil disorders," and adds even when a municipality pays big settlements in brutality cases, the offending cop "often goes unpunished." A University of Florida study concluded that in almost all brutality situations (97 percent) blacks and Latinos were the victims and white cops (93 percent) the perpetrators. The study's authors called this systematic abuse of police power, our "dirty little secret of racism," and noted that neither education nor wealth, urban or rural locality, made any difference in police treatment.

The Federal Bureau of Investigation: Secret Mission

Racial discrimination by and within municipal and other local law enforcement agencies is perhaps understandable when one considers that these are local hires who carry attitudes and values attuned to their immediate locales. They are homegrown. They fulfill the expectations of their constituencies, regardless of the *law*. As for the nation's national police force, most Americans (at least the most naive or uninformed) must have been surprised to learn that the Federal Bureau of Investigation (FBI), an agency with a world class reputation as a police department, sworn to uphold the laws of the United States and the Constitution, was founded and led for it's first quarter century of existence by a man, J. Edgar Hoover, who has been labeled a rabid racist. Garrow, a scholar of the FBI, said "Hoover's racism is...widely documented." In perhaps the most important work exploring relations between the Bureau and black America, Kenneth O'Reilly's " *Racial Matters* " paints a picture of a man obsessed with keeping blacks "in their place." Hoover's politics, in O'Reilly's words, "cannot be held legitimate in either a legal or moral sense." For decades Hoover's FBI had only two black "agents," neither of whom "was trained for anything other than...domestic duties." One was Hoover's chauffeur, the other his "reception-ist for more than thirty years." When Bobby Kennedy demanded the addition of black agents, one, a janitor in the Chicago Bureau, was hired and immediately became the Chicago Bureau Chief's personal chauffeur.

Given the tone set by its illustrious leader, it should have not come as a surprise that the FBI, post Hoover, has been the target of discrimination complaints. A black agent charged racial harassment by white colleagues and was supported by the federal Equal Employment Opportunities Commission. A federal court later found in favor of a group of Hispanic agents who also claimed race discrimination. (It is ironic that on the same day the black agent was accusing white agents of "racial harassment...threats of death, mutilation...and sexual assault (threatened) against his white wife," African American Army Lt. General Colin Powell was being sworn in as the first black presidential National Security Advisor.) In 1990 this black agent was put on permanent disability by the FBI and is assured of more than $1 million over his lifetime. His ex-wife also was awarded a generous settlement.

The FBI's campaign of harassment and vilification against civil rights organi-zations and their leaders during the 1960s has been well documented. The agency's "counter-terrorist" (COINTELPRO) program employed thousands of black informants in its often illegal effort to discredit and thwart legitimate civil rights activities. What is not widely known is that the extent of Hoover's campaign of subversion against Martin Luther King, Jr. and other activists went far beyond what might ordinarily be expected in even a clandestine effort to undermine potentially "subversive" elements. (In November 1991 National

Press Books released *Who Killed Martin Luther King?,* authored by convicted killer James Earl Ray. Ray contends Hoover's FBI "ordered King killed and that he (Ray) was an unwitting pawn and didn't pull the trigger.")

Using the Freedom of Information Act to gain access to Bureau files, John Gittlesohn concluded that "Reading through the material…tells a different story of black history than any books." It was ghastly, in other words. Hoover's vendetta, according to one point of view, was analogous to the Confederate massacre of black Union soldiers at Fort Pillow, Tennessee. There Rebel soldiers went into an uncontrolled rage at even the thought of black men taking up arms against whites. It was simply unthinkable that blacks should ever square off on equal terms as *men.* In a *Treasury of Civil War Tales,* Webb Garrison reprints part of a letter from a Confederate soldier who, observing several of his comrades taunt, torture, then murder a captured black Union soldier at Petersburg, Virginia, wrote, "the Southerners all seemed infuriated at the idea of having to fight Negroes. Soon so many of them lay dead that it was difficult to make one's way along the trench without stepping on them."

Not content to spy on and harass black activists—many of whom were not "active" in fact, the Bureau developed a special program to track the activities of black elected officials. "Fruhmenschen," according to Congressman William Clay, was based on the premise of black inferiority, incapable of governing." The German name for this program suggests the contempt with which black elected officials were held for literally translated it means "primitive man or ape."

Congressman Clay notes that the FBI is joined by state and local law enforcement agencies in harassing black officials and gives as an example the fact that of the two hundred black elected officials in the State of Alabama, "one-third"… (were) under indictment or investigation. For any African American aspiring to "use political strength to enhance the economic stability of black communities," harassment has to be assumed. Writing in *The New York Times,* Lena Williams, quoting Mary Frances Berry, warns: "Every black official ought to assume that someone is after them because of racism, so they ought to behave the way anyone would if someone was out to get them."

(In a work that is a logical successor to Sam Greenlee's *The Spook Who Sat By the Door,* David Louis Whitehead (*Brains, Sex, & Racism in the C.I.A. and the Escape*) chronicles a first-hand account of how America's foremost external "law enforcement" agency handcuffs its few black professional employees. According to Whitehead, even after he left the Agency, its tentacles were so far stretched and powerful that he was denied job after job in the private sector.)

A Day in Court

In any society the administration of justice typically parallels the patterns exercised by other branches of government. In the United States, with some notable exceptions, the rule also applies. Police treatment of black citizens is reflected in actions of the court system. Regarding minority youth (black youth in particular), a report out of the Hubert H. Humphrey Institute of Public Affairs clearly documents institutionalized racism in the administration of justice:

> Minority youth are being incarcerated in U.S. public juvenile correctional facilities at rates three to four times that of whites. *Contrary to popular beliefs minority youth aren't committing a substantially disproportionate amount of this country's serious crimes.* (Emphasis added)...However, they are more likely to be arrested and charged with more serious offenses than equally delinquent white youth. ...(which) brings into question police arrest practices.

A disinterested observer would be inclined to think that if the objective of disproportionate arrests is to get black men into the police filing system and/or into the prison system, the law enforcers have been more than successful. Thus there would be little need to "prolong the agony" into the prison system itself. That this is not the case is asserted by former New York City Police Commissioner Benjamin Ward who points out that not only are African American males being incarcerated at the same rate as blacks in South Africa but that the "nation's prison system is plagued by 'institutional racism'." That the system itself is part of the historic "conspiracy" to deny equality of treatment to blacks is shown additionally in the fact that virtually all convicted black youth offenders go to public correctional facilities, many of them substandard, whereas about sixty-five percent of white youth are placed in private detention centers of much better quality Further, prisons have become prime recruitment ground for white supremacists.

A blatant example of systematic race discrimination is shown in federal sentencing of drug offenders. In a revealing report *USA Today's* Dennis Cauchon revealed wide differences in sentencing of *powdered* cocaine users and *crack* smokers. Powder abusers are sentenced to what amounts to a slap on the wrist while crack users are given mandatory sentences without parole. Possession of up to 5 grams of crack calls for a mandatory sentence of 5 years. Possession of the same amount of powder may bring one year, as only "crack has mandatory minimum sentences for mere possession."

The disparity in sentencing is reflected in who uses which variety of cocaine. Cauchon reports that 91 percent of those arrested for crack possession are black, and adds that in a given year "2000 black (and 60 whites) are sentenced under federal law." About 75 percent of powder cocaine is used by whites and Hispanics.

Americans are unanimous in believing we need a "war on illicit drugs; but the law that provides such manifest disparity has to be changed and Clinton's Attorney General Janet Reno has committed to an inquiry.

When asked about the drug problem in our communities, a minimally educated self employed craftsman said "when the white man realized his mistake in allowing blacks to get too much education, he figured he could get rid of us and control us by pouring drugs into the community to make us kill one another," as writer and activist James Weldon claims was done to Harlem at an earlier time by a massive and planned introduction of heroine. My streetwise friend is not alone in believing that drug dumping in black communities is politically motivated. The *Washington Afro-American* (July 3, 1993) editorialized that as Southeast Washington has become desirable property to whites who wish to live in a nice neighborhood nearer to downtown the sudden appearance of a massive drug problem and the accompanying crime problems is a deliberate attempt to drive blacks out, many of whose families have lived in the community for several generations. Louis Farrahkan has said of the black drug epidemic that "it stems from a calculated attempt by whites to force black self-destruction." A *New York Times*/CBS poll found that 60 percent of blacks (compared to 16 percent of whites) felt that the *government* might "deliberately be making sure drugs are available in poor black neighborhoods." The reader may recall the scene in the movie *The Godfather* where a decision was made to pump drugs into the ghetto.

> "We don't have the self-esteem or the common sense to stop it (buying and selling drugs). The white man is turning black people against one another so we'll just be erased off this earth."
>> Tiffany Bell, 18, at *Parade* (May 23, 1993) sponsored black teen discussion "Why Is There So Much Violence?"

It is black high school students like these, according to Stephanie Coontz, "not whites, who have spearheaded the steady decline in drug use in the school."

Cruel and unequal treatment by the court system is not confined to the young black offender. Numerous studies have confirmed the racial content in prosecutions and convictions. Warren Richey cites "widespread prejudice against blacks" in the death penalty, especially where the victim is white. Amnesty International reports that in a two-year period—1976 to 1978—black on white crimes accounted for 89 percent of executions. Liberal *New York Times* columnist Tom Wicker was so outraged over the killing of several black men who were "executed for dubious reasons" that he titled a column "Why Did We Kill These Men?"

Amnesty International has belatedly begun to realize that since racism is a big influence in capitol crimes sentencing, it's victims are as much political prisoners as are those who commit "crimes against the state" in Eastern Bloc nations. *Black News'* Marilyn Jai reported that the 1991 execution of South Carolina's "Pee Wee" Gaskins for murdering a black person was the first such execution in "nearly 50 years," a time span which had more than 1,000 executions. When blacks kill blacks few murderers are executed, accounting for only 1.5 percent of all executions during 1976-78. A phenomenal figure given that most black homicides are black-on-black.

Discriminatory treatment of blacks extend even to the selection of juries. The widespread use of peremptory challenges by defense attorneys and prosecutors to limit the number of blacks on juries, especially where a white person is involved and in cases where prosecutors so want a conviction they believe (mistakenly, it has been shown) black jurors will favor black defendants, is a cruel, however clever, circumvention of constitutional rights and protection.

Rounding out the indictment of the American court system is the unequal treatment of blacks even when they *win*. Studies have shown that not only do blacks lose more criminal and civil cases but that any damages they may be awarded are "only 74 percent as much as white plaintiffs received for the identical injury." Compounding the problem is a dearth of black lawyers. Of more than 600,000 attorneys in the country, only about six percent are minority. Blacks were not even admitted into membership in the American Bar Association until 1943 (although a president of that organization help found the National Association for the Advancement of Colored People!)

A Better Day

While the entire criminal justice system in this country reeks with a virulent racism nurtured over the entire history of the nation, that is by no means all of the story. And this is the important part of the tale, an aspect which bolsters and vindicates the enduring faith African Americans have in their country. Justice and fair treatment are reaching more of their number. However it might have been accomplished, the black engineer and Marine corporal *were* exonerated. Blacks have won critical cases of race discrimination and harassment in the workplace; (In 1990 an African American professor was awarded $1 million by a jury which decided he had been discriminated against by a prominent California university. It was a rare verdict.) Alleged rape of white women by black men is being more critically examined as in the widely publicized Brantley case in Houston; many police executives are looking for ways other than brute force to deal with public disorders (Philadelphia police bombing of a house was a case study in how *not* to respond).

Though still far short of fair representation of blacks and other minority Americans, both the FBI and local police (especially in cities where large numbers of minorities live) are hiring and promoting minorities. In the recent slaying of several police officers, officials in Dallas not only lamented the murders but made plans to increase the percentage of minority officers until their numbers match their particular group's proportion of the city's minority population. (This kind of "quota" hiring is not desirable or necessary. Of greater concern to blacks is the tremendous increase in white female officers who have far outdistanced blacks in law enforcement.) In America at the beginning of the last decade of the twentieth century, there were close to one hundred black police chiefs and public safety directors, a far cry from their meager presence only a decade ago. These police executives are joined by about thirty black fire chiefs of some of the nation's largest cities.

Among the obvious benefits African American police executives confer are, Lee May comments, "increased rapport between black communities and black officials, reduced reports of police brutality…and more officers on the streets."

(In Birmingham a white male cop marries a black female cop. They are the black mayor's bodyguards! While they are shunned by most whites they enjoy an active social life in the black community.) In truth few material benefits accrue to black city dwellers who elect a black mayor. One of those few has certainly been a decided reduction in police-community tensions. One would hope that the mutual fear traditionally undergirding police-black citizen relations gives way to respect and recognition of mutual need as appears to be the case in most *white* communities.

Mere presence of a black mayor and police chief does not guarantee better treatment, however, at the time of the Rodney King incident Los Angeles had a black mayor who had been in office more than twenty years.

Police brutality in Detroit occurred under Coleman Young and a black police chief; as did the mass murder of black children in Atlanta under two black mayors and a respected black chief. As police chief of the nation's largest city, New York, Benjamin Ward often expressed frustration with his inability to change an encrusted department. When New York City Mayor David Dinkins responded to complaints of police irresponsibility in 1993 and advanced the idea of establishing a civilian review board, 10,000 of New York's finest staged an angry demonstration resembling, in Ben Chavis' words, "a post-modern lynch mob full of bigotry and hate...where some shouted, Get the nigger out of City Hall."

Three big difficulties lie in the way of police reform. Powerful unions; a pro-police political culture dominated by a conservative posture, one wing of which is racist and applauds police maltreatment of blacks; and an internal police culture that establishes its own system of rules, rewards and punishment. An extreme of this culture as it relates to racism was believed by many to be reflected in the display of a Nazi Flag in the Berwyn, Illinois police headquarters. The flag was ordered removed in a settlement to a lawsuit brought by a Jamaican family after the firebombing of their home. The September 1993 Mollen Commission hearings into police corruption and criminal activity revealed widespread law violation —lying to grand juries, drug running, murder and assassination, all protected by a "Blue Wall of Silence." Former New York City cop Frank Serpico, himself once the alleged target of fellow cops gone bad, told *USA Today* reporter Lori Sharn that "you cannot have corruption in any police department or law enforcement unless you have it at the top."

While African Americans are making significant gains in the police executive ranks and will be able to exert *some* influence over the rank-and-file, perhaps the character Police Chief Stump in Robert Vaughan's *Hard Times* represents an old line racist blacks can live with. Though doubtful of black intelligence and ability, Stump is flexible enough to acknowledge the superior training of a Northern trained black medical doctor and is willing to "follow doctors orders" in matters outside medicine. More importantly, "in his treatment of Negroes, Stump had drawn a line that he thought was fair, and he never stepped across it." His subordinates had to toe that line or look for work elsewhere.

Perhaps what our cities and small towns need are not only more African

American police chiefs but more Stumps.

All citizens need to support their law enforcement agencies, but the agents of the "law" have to be true to their calling: brave, impartial enforcers. Occupying probably the most stress laden position in modern society, it is no surprise that they suffer such a high rate of physical and psychological indisposition. Police departments have begun to recognize the imperative need to develop better screening methodologies as well as offering more employee assistance programs and some departments, most notably Houston's, are recognizing the value of having officers working in and with neighborhoods.

> Nor, alas will the justice of one's cause suffice to ensure justice. Constitutional protection, and the judicial interpretations built on them, have real importance but, all too often, work out in practice in unanticipated, and destructive ways...too often we forget the seldom acknowledged self-interest of segments of the dominant society.
> Derrick Bell, *And We Are Not Saved: The Elusive Quest for Racial Justice*

One sees at least *some* progressive decisions from the current Supreme Court. The racial element in death penalty sentencing and the use of peremptory challenges to exclude blacks from juries have come under closer scrutiny. The appointment of blacks to the federal bench, particularly during Jimmy Carter's presidency, and George Bush's appointment of Clarence Thomas to the Supreme Court (over very outspoken opposition), is, it is to be hoped, a signal that the nation is beginning to recognize talent and merit irrespective of race. That former president Reagan did not appoint more than a few black federal judges is not necessarily a testament to his racism; rather he could have been playing out the logic of elective politics: You reward those who put you in office. How many blacks voted for Reagan? is the question, not how many might be qualified for the federal bench (or for a cabinet or diplomatic post).

Blacks cannot expect the current Supreme Court, even with the appointment of Clarence Thomas to replace the liberal Thurgood Marshall, to be anything other than conservative on matters of civil rights, whether in employment, housing, or other public welfare issues it should be noted. The winners of the court's decisions will be white females and males who claim victimization by reverse discrimination. As U.S. Civil Rights Commissioner Mary Berry told *USA Today's* Barbara Reynolds, the issue now (and for the foreseeable future) is not whether the Court will be against or in favor of a case dear to liberals but whether they "will lose 6-3 or 5-4." With this predictable outcome, Berry adds, blacks need to drop reliance on court decisions—they're "becoming irrelevant." She adds: "Anyone who has a bias complaint should stay away from the courts. But if you are a white male and you think you are subjected to reverse discrimination, run to the courts; you will win."

Equal enforcement of the law and judicial protection of civil rights across racial lines are two of the greatest challenges in race relations in the waning years of the twentieth century. With it's achievement so much else will become manageable and easy of accomplishment. Law enforcement agencies represent the massive external power imposed on African American communities. All too often they have been the worst offenders in denying humanity to black citizens. To the extent that illegitimate police behavior disrupt families, induce fear, thwart aspirations and ambition, black communities can be said to suffer Jack London's "Iron Heel."

When wealth, power (as exemplified by police agencies), and racial prejudice combine forces to thwart progress, the African American quagmire gains a clarity otherwise denied to the uninitiated.

The Face in the Mirror: Self-Images

The fundamental crisis in black America is twofold: too much poverty and too little self-love.
Cornel West

Unknown to most whites is the extreme deleterious effect white racist acts continue to have on how we blacks view ourselves. It is true, in the absolute sense, that fewer whites harbor the extreme prejudice of their forebears; it is also a fact that what researchers such as Charles Lightfoot, Michael Olivas, Derrick Bell, and others conclude as a widespread unconscious brand of racism is, in its effect, just as detrimental in how blacks and whites interrelate *and* in how blacks perceive themselves. Many blacks know that many American whites no longer share the South African Afrikaner's belief in the total debasement and "natural" degradation of blacks, but sense or see too many instances of behavior which can only be explained by a set of attitudes and beliefs which relegate them—blacks, *all* blacks, to a kind of subset of humanity. As New York City Deputy Mayor Stanley Grayson told a *Time* reporter, "No matter what I accomplish as an individual, I will always be judged by what people see first, my color."

Racism is like that local creeping kudzu vine that swallows whole forests and abandoned houses; if you don't keep pulling up the roots it will grow back faster than you can destroy it.
Alice Walker, *In Search of Our Mother's Gardens*

Every slight, every hostile stare, every demeaning gesture however slightly revealed, every *rejection,* felt by a black person becomes a part of that person's psychic baggage and subconsciously, if not consciously, contributes to the store of images and predispositions he or she brings to the next encounter with whites. Open and wanton racist acts such as those reported by the news media—the Howard Beaches, Cummings, Georgia, and Mobile, Alabama—are nothing compared to the almost daily "small" insults suffered by black individuals. The book *Black Rage,* authored by two black psychiatrists, was an effort to explain to white America how black anger, usually too dangerous to openly express against the object of its source, builds to a point where the black victim simply has to strike out at *someone...*or...*something* in some kind of way. Jesse

Jackson as a young waiter spitting in diners' food; maids committing any variety of retaliatory acts; blue collar workers sabotaging and stealing from employers; black white collar workers imagining how they can "get back" at colleagues and bosses who deny them equal access to perks and promotions; blacks of all backgrounds all too often striking out at other blacks, whether family, neighbors, or strangers, or engaging in other self-destructive and counter-productive behaviors. (A personal friend who is nationally recognized for her agency's role in promoting minority employment, wrote me early in 1990 from her midwestern city: "Ed, the black community...has exploded! There is not a day that passes that a murder/assault/violent act does not occur. Drugs have run rampant in our neighborhoods. Law-abiding citizens are afraid to take action. A few of them did a couple of times and they were murdered violently.")

Individuals who feel good about themselves do not engage, as a matter of practice, in some of the otherwise unexplainable behaviors found too often and consistently among many blacks. (It is of interest here that research done at the time found a dramatic decline in black-on-black crime during the height of the civil rights movement.)

No matter what some university presidents, federal presidential appointees, newspaper columnists, and neoconservative scholars, claim as a decline of race as a factor in black well-being, blacks know that the Kerner Commission was right when it laid the blame for the creation and maintenance of the black ghetto on white racism. What was true in 1968 will still pertain in much of the nation in 1998.

I define a ghetto as a place where a group of people, identifiable by a common characteristic—such as skin color or religion—are forced to live whether they wish to or not.

For the sake of readers less informed, Chicagoan Iola describes in a letter to me (7/2/93) the ghetto of her youth:

We (community age peers) are all over the world. Most of us had to leave the community (as adults) because there was no room for us to buy property in Woodlawn. We lived at the southern-most end of the "black belt." I'm told that the term "black belt" in the South referred to the area in which the soil was richest. In Chicago, it was a long area of segregated confinement which resembled a slim belt. The Jackson Park "L" (elevated train) from Downtown gave me a weekly view of the black belt. It began soon after I headed home from voice lessons at the American Conservatory...as the "L" came out of the subway, I looked at our people living in old housing where rent was cheap no doubt because the "L" rattled past rear doors every few minutes...Other (black communities) like Morgan Park developed near wealthy white communities. The reason was to have servants for the mansions in the Beverly community. Evanston has an established black community for the same reason...

...Many of the women of Woodlawn worked in homes in Hyde Park and Southshore (now black)—that was before WWII. My aunts...worked for rich Jews and other white families as domestics...the whites were very glad to hire (them) because they were fitted seamstresses. These "rich" women would bring home expensive dresses which…could look at and copy (no pattern necessary). The dresses went back to the store…

…Our Woodlawn was a "Joseph's Coat" of talented back people (then called Negroes). Looking back, I think that our elders were well educated. Some were self-trained, some were institutionally trained but most people either had superior common sense or had no nonsense extended family members.

Income was not a factor in where blacks lived. We lived in the black belt. We lived within racial boundaries. We lived in Morgan Park, Evanston, Englewood, Hyde Park (in servants quarters called coach houses) and on the North Side nearby what later became gentrified as "Old Town"…

…Chicago's viaducts became manmade territorial borders between antagonistic enclaves. Shopping areas were off limits or war. I'd shop along with my mother in the white area…but lack of money made this a moot question for the most part. Oh yes, movies were also safe haven until '46 when the white perverts began to bother black women. I was 12 years old by then.

In his seminal work *Black on Black Crime* Harvard psychiatrist Alvin Poussaint connected low self esteem, feelings of being forever locked in a cage with few escape hatches, and the high rates of violent crime in black communities. His work was in the tradition of the pioneering studies of E. Franklin Frazier, Albert Menni, Franz Fanon, and other social scientists who had earlier pinpointed racial oppression as the prime source of self-hate among blacks and other victims of racial oppression. Psychologist Kenneth Clark's monumental study of the link between low self-esteem among young black school children and legally imposed racial segregation led to the landmark U.S. Supreme Court decision in *Brown v. Board of Education.*

Even with increased desegregation (over the 1954 level of school segregation), America's black youngsters have not shown much overall gains in self-esteem. Research duplicating that of Dr. Clark's has found that in the 1980s low self-esteem was "still there" among black youth. The ABC-TV News Special, *Black in White America,*…run in mid-1989, clearly, and visually, demonstrated low self-esteem and self-loathing among African American youngsters. This writer's own son, who has attended some of the nation's better public schools, from Vermont to Alaska, where, in most instances, he was, if not the only black in his school, the only black in his class, almost in exact duplication of what black Louisiana children told the Clark research team, exclaimed "out of the blue" that he wished he were white. As he was only six or seven years old at the time, as a parent I can only marvel at the appearance of this low self-value, especially since I have always been careful to closely monitor his schools' programs, informal as well as formal. More puzzling is that he comes from parents who take visible pride in who they are. His mother could even be called a militant! If *my* son can be so infected it is no wonder that there is a continuing identity crisis for black youngsters.

The fact of the matter is that black children from an early age, perhaps even before birth, are "taught" in ways too numerous to list that they have less value by virtue of their skin color. This denial of value comes from white school and play mates, teachers and other school professionals (often in ways so subtle they don't realize it), non-professionals such as custodians and secretaries, and from other blacks, sometimes within their own families. That the oppressed as societal outcasts practice put-downs on themselves is a recurring observation of "identity" research. In a recent case in Atlanta a federal district judge acknowledged that blacks can discriminate among themselves", acknowledging what blacks have known for generations: if you're light, you're alright; if you're black get back. In the Atlanta case the reverse was true—a darker complexioned boss discriminated against a "high yellow" subordinate! The fact of intragroup discrimination is what is important.

So the black child grows up believing implicitly that he/she is less valued as a human being than the white child, and he or she might place their self-worth at a higher or lower rung in the pecking order within the group depending on skin coloration. So many—unnecessary—burdens at such an early age. Black children who rebel against the credo are likely to wind up on the wrong side of the law, whether of school, police, or black peer group. The lucky ones somehow manage to channel their rage into "proving" their worth through athletics or other non-threatening outlet. A few excel in academic work. By the time the lucky few reach college, most, not without some trepidation, are ready to "get into" this special experience, all the while anticipating, on a deeper, even unconscious level, the rejection that almost always comes. All the major studies conducted on black college students conclude that alienation and estrangement are major factors in black college student attrition, accounting for the recommendation by black researchers such as Jacqueline Fleming that many black youth of college age would have a better chance of succeeding at a traditionally black college. The luckiest child of all is one from a family of strivers and achievers who also have a highly developed sense of who they are and a realistic "fix" on the state of the world around them.

There is little in American society which affirms the black child's value as a person; little to make these "children of Africa" feel good about themselves. It's almost as if Robert Penn Warren's title, *Who Needs the Negro?* had the unintended purpose of declaring all blacks unwanted and unneeded. Whatever their public utterances or station in life all blacks know a sense of being trapped and constrained due to their color. And, for some, there is a certain security in this knowledge.

> Some soul-searching during the long nights in the cage convinced me that my go-slow reasoning was merely an excuse for not really wanting to escape. Whatever it's discomforts, the cage had become a kind of womb. Inside was shelter and food. The predictable behavior of the guards told me that they would not mistreat me. Outside was coldness, uncertainty, and a North Vietnamese jungle whose villages would be hostile. It was perfectly natural, I knew, this mental aversion to escape. I sensed that the worst error I could make would be to accept my present condition, and I told myself repeatedly that I must always think of my captivity as temporary.
> Ernest C. Brace, *A Code to Keep*

(The value)...lost to the community of what might have been accomplished by joint effort was staggering. Choirs would have been sweeter, taxes could have been kept lower if black incomes had been allowed to rise, baseball teams would have been more capable if black players had been accepted, and in almost any enterprise the results could have been more productive if black energies had been enlisted.

James A. Michener, *Chesapeake*

If any human life has value and it is a crime to destroy it, then the world is vastly more criminal today than it was at any other stage of history. There are millions more dying needlessly now in peace than ever died under the onslaught of the Huns or in the trenches of Belgium and France.

Ronald Segal, *The Race War*

Know the enemy and the battle is half won.
Know yourself and the battle is yours.

Sun Tzu, *The Art of War*

The African American family has received so much bad press in the last two decades (beginning with Daniel Moynihan's widely accepted "benign neglect" proposition) that it might appear redundant to add to the chorus of black voices responding to our detractors. But things are bad, incredibly bad, for many black families in the late twentieth century, much worse in some respects than they were during slavery and the bleakest years of *de jure* segregation. At least during slavery, the argument goes, where slave families were allowed to remain intact, which was the condition on most slaveholding plantations, the nuclear family was assured of some degree of security and certitude, no matter the undeniable harshness of their general treatment. Slaves could, and did, influence their young by setting examples of personal conduct (whether for "liberation" or "going with the flow"). They worked as integral family units, engaged in communal rituals and ceremonies, revered and provided tender care for the aged. Brutally enforced segregation meant dehumanization and often death, of course, and must never be permitted to resurface. But one does not have to wish for a return to legal separation to acknowledge that one of the outcomes of that social system was that it reinforced in-groupness, a sense of community, and strong bonding within families. The issue of segregation and desegregation will receive additional attention later in this chapter.

The Future's Family

Any system that deprives a people of its family structure, denies the humanity of that people...History has no equal to match the terrible ways in which White America treated and destroyed the black family. White America stole it, but Black America must return it.

Richard Williams, They Stole It, But You Must Return It

It is true that American families in general were not in the late 1980s what they were in the 1960s. In 1960, according to Spencer Rich, almost all white children were in two-parent homes, as were 75 percent of black children. By 1985, Pickney points out, not only were more than half of all black children living in single parent homes, these households are more often than not led by women stuck economically below the government's poverty line (this compares with only thirteen percent of black families below the poverty line when both spouses are present). With sixty percent of black children (compared to 34 percent of white children) born out of wedlock in 1986, it is not surprising that so many children reside in single parent homes. By 1993 the percentage had grown past 70 percent, according to a *Newsweek* special report; and only one-fifth of black children were growing up with two parents. (Depending on one's point of view, that black female teens opt to avoid abortion and have their babies at a higher rate than white cohorts, may or may not be a blessing!) Nor should Unger's prediction of 70 percent female headed black families by the year 2000 come as a surprise, given the state of black male existence, among other factors. Mehren believes that before reaching their sixteenth birthday, nine of ten black children "will live with a single parent at some time."

Whatever the arguments for hoping single parents can make successful families, there is general agreement that two parent families offer the most potential for nurturing black children in a threatening world. Photojournalist and author Gordon Parks, former presidential candidate Jesse Jackson, and former Armed Forces Joint Chief Chairman Colin Powell (among many other successful African Americans) speak of how no matter how harsh the racism of their childhood or the bleakness of economic opportunities, the parental love they received from *both* parents made their world one of brightness, of faith and hope. They glorify their childhoods in endearing terms like "trapped in a love triangle" (of home, church and school for Jackson), and "good fortune of being born to Sarah and Jackson Parks." This blanket of love, in Parks' words, "was enough to offset the misery of growing up black in America." Jackson says that "not even segregation and barbarism could break" his "love triangle." In the eulogy for his murdered father, super-athlete Michael Jordan spoke of the influence of his parents: From his father he got "my personality and my laughter," and his mother provided "my business and serious side."

Increasing numbers of black youngsters simply do not have such fortunate circumstances, with even the loving concern of church and school rapidly disappearing. The bitterness expressed in singer Billie Holiday's sad admonition to a young Maya Angelou is the more likely experience of black mothers and their offspring in these last years of the twentieth century:

> All crackers is bad and niggers ain't much better. Just take care of your son. Keep him with you and keep on telling him he's the smartest thing God made. Maybe he'll grow up without hating you.

Another consequence of single parent upbringing is in educational achievement. High achieving children overwhelmingly come from two parent homes. The disparity is so great—80 percent versus 7 percent—between students who received "A" grades and those who did not that the only plausible explanation for the 7 percent is that they were gifted as individuals and extraordinarily lucky to have a parent, and perhaps a grandparent or teacher, who was so inspirational and who made extreme sacrifices for the child's welfare.

Of course there are intact husband-wife black families. A great many of them. As columnist Carl Rowan warns, one can't speak as if there is a "stereotyped black family," adding that "black families in which the parents have good education and decent jobs are among the most stable in America." That's precisely the point: increasing numbers have neither of these necessary ingredients for success! African Americans are beginning to, perhaps belatedly, acknowledge the degree of damage the black family has undergone in just one generation. The heightened awareness is producing healthy results. Important leaders such as Coretta Scott King are publicly decrying black family disintegration noting that her own "top priority has always been my family."

Family reunions are of increasing importance, and black service organizations like Jack and Jill are redirecting resources to "family-related charities." Sociologist and black family scholar Andrew Billingsley reports that close to a quarter million blacks "of all classes and kinds of families" came to the nation's capitol to "debate the black family," giving birth to numerous local organizations. Sheila Rule reports a growing awareness of the additional stresses faced by black families simply because they are black (a fact that could never have eluded previous generations of blacks!), and how these factors exacerbate domestic tensions and contribute to the "soaring divorce rate" among African Americans.

Not overlooked in the new interest in the black family is the positive role which grandparents ought to again be playing in the rearing of children. *Washington Post* columnist William Raspberry remarks that Jewish grandparents are an important element in child nurturing, and urges black grandparents to "help inculcate good behavior in youth."

Proportionately, African American children tend to be represented at higher rates among homeless and parentless youth. For various reasons black adults do not adopt these youngsters in great numbers. Most whites wishing to adopt, and who fail to find eligible white children, seek out Indian reservations; many have used the services of white "baby breeders" in Brazil, and still others pursue Korean and other Asian children (CBS News reported in August 1991 that one of every nine adoptees is from Korea or South America.) By and large they ignore black children in their own country and the truly needy children of African countries like Ethiopia and Uganda.

A small number of white Americans have adopted African American children, however. (The December 1989 "adoption" of 28 Haitian children by an Indiana missionary couple was an aberration and hardly represents the attitudes or inclinations of most American whites.) Adopting black children is both a tribute to their courage and their personal conviction of what America ought to be. It is also an act around which much controversy has been generated, among blacks as well as whites, and in the courts. Whatever the merits or reservations about such adoptions, it is clear that adoption by white parents is preferred to abandonment to a life of social and physical pathology, and lack of love. Indeed, according to Rich, some studies have shown high degrees of self-esteem in trans-racially adopted black children, and "a positive experience for both white parents and for non-white children they adopt." And wouldn't adoption by white parents of the young black Gary, Indiana girl been preferred to losing her legs to frostbite brought on by abandonment by a mother who lived in the streets? And, yet, somehow I can't erase the memory of that two-or-three-year-old black child, a girl, obviously adopted by a white family, whose plaintive stare at a Burlington, Vermont, shopping mall, spoke volumes of her inner need to relate to me, to in some way connect. That my own hesitancy to interlope, to reach out to her even with a passing greeting, was a lost moment, is with me after almost ten years.

What the African American child needs more than anything else is to be reared in what Jackson called a "triangle of love" where parents or guardians, of whatever color or gender, have decent incomes affording the material, spiritual, and cultural underpinning and stability so necessary to a healthy childhood.

According to Iola adopting and *legal* foster parenting are recent to the black experience. Her own family history illustrates the point. Writing of a grand-niece she sometimes cares for, she says:

> Her mother is 17, single and into the awful trap of responsibility for a child. Now, Ed, is "Aunt Joan" distant, indifferent and too middle class to be involved? The hell you say. I'm aware that my family has had children whose parents never married...I don't know of any child of ours who was put up for adoption...Our family has found a way to raise our children. No child has been "fostered."

Perhaps gone forever are the warm, supportive black enclaves such as that described by Edward Smith in the January 1, 1992 *Washington Times* ("In Less Violent Times"). The District of Columbia, long thought of as the black "cultural capital" of America, Smith comments, was home to some of the great personalities in African American history—the likes of Frederick Douglass, Dr. Charles Drew, Nobel Peace Prize winner Ralph Bunche, and others. It was a community where even maids and ditch-diggers could achieve distinction in their communities through church, fraternal, or educational activities. Most importantly the young had numerous role models, surrogate parents, and mentors all of whom "encouraged the respect for adult authority and discipline, the application of proper manners and good grooming habits" and getting a good education. Love was effusive and pervasive. With today's television where violence, "sex-saturated, me-oriented" programs dominate and all the other already discussed changes in black communities and black families, only the church remains of a community once sitting at the pinnacle of black love, self-help, and sacrifice for the good of the community.

Getting Back to Basics, Beginning Again

Girls and boys,
Women and men,
It is time that we think—
About beginning again.

You say "beginning again,"
Again for what?
I say, to get our race,
Out of this terrible rut.

We have gone from bad to worse,
As a race that is you see,
We agree that anything goes,
Without much morality.

Our children have no scruples,
No discipline or restraint,
Ask them to do what is right,
Their answer is "I ain't."

Children used to say "hello,"
To their elders and their own,
The most that we hear from them now,
Is profanity and "leave me alone."

It does not matter anymore,
What our youth do or say,
As long as they are happy,
And can go from day to day.

Life is not all fun and play.
And laughter with a loud music box.
There is a serious side to life,
Now fun I will never knock.

Parents, it is your responsibility,
To rear up your child,
To see that he is being trained,
And is not growing up wild.

He might not like what you do now,
And your rules nor the restraint,
That is used when he is stopped
From making mistakes that stink.

Discipline your children, you will see,
As life goes on with them,
They will love you because,
You didn't give up on them.

We need to be role models,
For our children to see,
That all of the discipline we talk about,
Can be seen in you and me.

When they are grown you will hear
Words of appreciation—"thank you,"
For all of the love that they received,
As they grew up under you.

For they will say as they go on,
Work on me, Lord,
For I will not be defeated,
For I have your precious word.

Mrs. Artie Brown
Retired Tampa School Teacher
Used with permission and blessing.

Notes on African American Youth: Education and Segregation

At a time when other 18 year olds are getting ready to graduate from high school,...Clarita Frazier already had college behind her and is about to enter medical school.

Matthew Daly, *Washington Post*

You can't be what you ain't seen. And so many of our young boys ain't seen nothing but the gangs and the pimps and the brothers on the corner.

Black Inner City Minister to *Frontline's* Roger Wilkins

People become only what they can imagine themselves to be. If they can only imagine themselves working as menials, then they will probably subside into that fate...If they see other blacks become mayors of the largest cities, become astronauts, become presidential candidates, become Miss America, and, more to the point, become doctors and scientists and lawyers and pilots and corporate presidents...then young blacks will begin to comprehend their own possibilities....

Lance Morrow, *Newsweek*

Compared to 16 percent of whites, 47 percent of all black 17 year olds are functionally illiterate, and Jeannie Barry predicts that by the turn of the century that percentage will describe almost half of *all* black youth of high school age. In part due to the appalling teenage illiteracy rate, black college enrollment at all levels has declined over the past decade, in spite of a significant increase in high school graduation (some say "social promotion") rates. In the past the problem was not enough high school graduates and limited access to segregated white schools, thus low college participation. Today it's insufficient numbers of academically prepared youngsters.

In such a state of ignorance and ill-preparedness African American youth can function only at a minimal level of efficiency in the modern world.

Black female headed households and teenage illiteracy correlate closely with poverty. U.S. Census Bureau data indicate that more than half of all black children live in poverty, compared to 15 percent of white youth. Black teen employment is a disaster. In communities like Harlem the youth unemployment rate is as high as 86 percent. And surprisingly, as Tidwell reported, the unemployment rate for black suburban youth isn't much better, suggesting factors other than illiteracy at work, since black suburbanites have higher educational achievements than their inner city counterparts. The significance of the unemployment rate lies not only in lack of income and experience in the world of work, there is also the observation made by many prominent blacks that the very fact of *working* raises self-esteem and gives the individual a more positive, hopeful outlook on life. As Clifton Wharton has said of black youth, "Confidence in their ability to achieve would raise academic achievement." Black youth who work stay in school, and, compared to working white youth, stay on the job longer.

Youth On the Loose

Enjoying wide popularity in higher education circles is the idea that young African Americans need role models as part of their total educational program. "They can't be what they ain't seen." One brilliant black entrepreneur noted that a "dearth of male models" stymied and delayed for 20 years his realization that his "independent, precocious nature was the glimmering of an entrepreneurial spirit." With such early role models, he declared, "I'd be a Donald Trump by now." The minister correctly points to the paucity of desirable role models for black youth in inner city neighborhoods. (Army General Colin Powell has correctly noted that while *black* role models are needed, whites as well as blacks can be *mentors* to black youth.)

> "I first found the word 'love' in a gang. I learned how to love in a gang, not in a family atmosphere."
>
> Rap Singer ICE—T to *Parade*, 6/6/93

Actor Lou Gossett's encounter with a twelve year old gang leader and drug pusher in the neighborhood of his youth is not atypical. Gossett had "gone back" to see if he could help by rapping about positive things to the young brothers. The gang leader wasn't impressed, and told Gossett, while pulling a wad of large bills from his pocket: "This is $22,000. I make this every day and I take care of my mama, my grandmama and three aunts...If you can replace this, I'll listen to you." (Gossett later adopted this "child of the streets.") Thus, along with the Superfly attired ministers and (very) small business persons (the doctors, lawyers, and most other professionals having departed—hurriedly—with desegregation), young blacks have few "images" to believe themselves capable of becoming.

Even African American teachers are becoming a thing of the past in predominately black public schools. And because of this leadership vacuum in black underclass communities, black youth have no one to point them in constructive directions. When the few opportunities available to them are not *known to them*, it should not be a surprise that, contrary to news columnist Raspberry's observation, they are not ready when "jumps" are made possible.

There is another, more fundamental aspect to the "missing adult male" issue. Generally acknowledged as a critical ingredient lacking in the development of too many young black males (and young black females too), the father or male "significant other" has been widely discussed. Stretching the scope of the issue beyond the implications of race mythologist and poet Robert Bly, in *Iron John: A Book About Men*, contends that all young men suffer from the effects of industrialized society where men virtually disappeared from the household; even those who were married no longer had the time to invest in their son's "initiation" and development.

> ...the love unit most damaged by the Industrial Revolution has been the father – son bond.

If "the son's fear that the absent father is evil" is true of "stable" middle class families, the addition of "race" to the equation compounds the dilemma of young black males. The black mother no more than the white mother can replace the absent father.

> "If I had a daughter I could teach her how to be a woman. I can teach my son how to be a human being, but I can't teach him how to be a man. He has to learn that on his own."
>
> Maya Angelou to Bryant Gumble, Today Show, February 4, 1992

The absence of Bly's "Iron Man" from families in industrialized society has vast social and political implications. Twenty-six million young American men are raised in fatherless homes. Due to modern work demands, millions more get only fleeting glimpses of fathers on the run. When the highly mobile quality of twentieth-century American life is factored in (most of us move several times in a life span), depriving sons (and daughters too) of the traditional influence of other relatives—uncles, older brothers, grandfathers, and respected neighborhood leaders, the effeminazation of the American male becomes real. Bly's traditional male has a feminine side but in the New Man it is exaggerated.

> "Not since slavery has so much calamity and ongoing catastrophe been visited on the black male."
>
> Louis W. Sullivan, President Morehouse College, former Secretary U.S. Department of Health and Human Services

We Still Live Apart

The most important lesson we have to learn in education, is to live together, not calculus.
Ramsey Clark, Jr., former U.S. Attorney General

At this point in our history Americans should know that racial segregation between black and white is greater in 1990 than it was in 1970. Now as before 1970, ghettos are created by whites; as put by Nicholas Limann, "The single overriding factor in the creation of the American ghetto is racial prejudice." So long as whites as a body reject residential desegregation, "chocolate city-vanilla suburb" will continue to be the social-racial reality of America. (Interestingly, many older black activists and professionals speak nostalgically of how racially integrated New York City boroughs used to be. Except Harlem.) A *Newsweek* Special Report concluded that "housing is the single most segregated aspect of American life." Sociologist Karl Taeuber found that *all* American cities with 100,000 or more blacks are segregated cities. The fact of continued racial segregation of blacks is confirmed by a 1991 *USA Today* analysis of housing patterns turned up in the 1990 census. The report concluded that "the majority of the nation's 30 million black people are as segregated now as they were at the height of the civil rights movement in the '60s."

In only a handful of cities such as Park Forest, a suburb of Chicago, have there been concerted efforts to make residential integration a going concern. Columbia, Maryland, founder James Fouse wanted a "community of people of different races, religions, and income groups—not a homogeneous clique of all-white families in split-level dwellings with two-car garages."

Park Forest and Columbia are exceptions; and not really all that much to get excited about. Both are artificial communities. The former has to deny housing to many more blacks than to whites, all for the goal of not reaching the "tipping point," known in sociology as that level of black presence that would cause an avalanche of white flight. (Hacker points to research confirming that in residential integration, a black presence in excess of 8 to 10 percent sends whites fleeing.) Due to its proximity to the nation's capital with its large black middle class, Columbia can draw black government workers but must also keep a keen eye on numbers. With a population of only 60,000 it is at best simply a model.

America will continue to be a largely racially segregated society until much larger numbers of whites don't mind blacks living next door. So long as blacks are attacked for merely *passing through* certain sections of the country and in certain neighborhoods, as diverse as Toledo, Ohio and Cummings, Georgia, and Frontenac, Missouri (where a black university professor was stopped and questioned by police for simply "looking into store windows") there will be only token residential desegregation in America. The use by some suburban communities of ruses like a residency requirement to gain employment and the possession of a job to gain residency points to the resiliency of opposition to housing desegregation. The U.S. Justice Department reported in 1989 that a majority (actually over 75 percent) of the race violence cases it investigated were housing related. That figure was up from 25 percent in 1985.

An interesting development in residential patterns during the past two decades is the increasing acceptance of non-black minorities in racially prejudiced communities. The New York City borough of Queens, where Howard Beach is located, is more than 20 percent Spanish-speaking and has a large community of Asians. Studies reported by Ellen Coughlin revealed that "the segregation of Asians remained low everywhere. Cross burnings in Toledo, Ohio took place in a "predominately white and Hispanic neighborhood." Not surprisingly, the USA Today housing analysis disclosed that "Hispanics and Asians have largely surmounted those barriers (housing segregation), moving into white neighborhoods were blacks have never found a welcome, no matter what their wealth." The report further notes that the African Americans residency predates by many generations that of most of these late arrivals. Pauline Jelinek concluded that "integration is possible, even likely for all ethnic and racial groups except Blacks."

Racial segregation of African Americans will for the foreseeable future be the rule, despite Alice Walker's dream of being able to live "unafraid," anywhere, and "in the fashion and with whom" she pleases.

Like researchers Nancy Denton and Douglass Massey, most blacks believed that increased personal income would lead "to progressive integration in society." What we all understand by now is that the scenario works for all groups but blacks. Indeed, as Denton and Massey discovered, blacks "at all socioeconomic levels" are still "highly segregated" even as the "progress of integration and assimilation continues for Hispanics and Asians." In early 1992 the U.S. Department of Housing and Urban Development conducted "tests" that revealed wide-spread anti-black discrimination in the nation's housing industry, further promoting residential segregation. In all the cities and towns this writer has resided in (since the late 1960s all have been "college towns"), I have encountered race based prejudice when seeking housing accommodations. One owner of a duplex told me that "there was no way he would have rented" to me had his wife not "forced him to.") During the same period the Federal Reserve revealed that Atlanta's lending institutions were not alone in discriminatory mortgage practices; it was a national problem where blacks were concerned.

Yonkers, New York and Dubuque, Iowa are not alone in finding ways to limit African American access. A federal Department of Housing and Urban Development inquiry discovered gross discrimination against blacks in home financing, apartment rental, and employment, citing New York City, Chicago, and Los Angeles as the worst offenders.

"We have to be honest, we have to be truthful; and speak to the one dirty secret in American life, and that is racism."
Henry Cisneros, HUD Secretary

This one central fact of social reality simply must be understood by the African American community. For on it hinges the most important clue to how we will fare in the twenty-first century. Racial residential segregation will be the reality for most of us for the foreseeable future. That being the case we simply *must* plan to make our communities better where we are—"dropping our bucket where we are," in Booker T. Washington's words.

Beyond Segregated Education

The above comments regarding residential segregation serve to put school segregation in its proper context. Segregation in housing is almost as effective a factor as was the *de jure* segregation pre-*Brown* Supreme Court decision; and it is much more effective than the brick throwing anti-integration tactics used by opposition whites in Boston, New Orleans, and other American cities in the 1960s. As University of Michigan sociologist Reynolds Farley has concluded, "Integration of schools has been rare in larger cities," despite busing, magnet schools, and other efforts to implement *Brown* and subsequent court orders. And more black students are segregated in northern industrial states than in the South, according to studies conducted by Robert Pear.

For at least two reasons African Americans were for about two decades after *Brown* generally favorably disposed towards school desegregation efforts, even when *their* children had to travel long distances from their homes, sometimes braving open physical hostility, and even when, as frequently happened, many were bussed "intact," having little contact with white children during the school day. Blacks thought that since white students had higher achievement scores and their schools greater resources, their children would almost automatically benefit educationally, if not also socially, and be ready to take advantage of good colleges and later good jobs. The Good Life! Another, less publicly admitted, explanation has to do with a psychological inferiority characteristic, under-standably, of many blacks, leading to a feeling that "rubbing shoulders" with white children would somehow make their own offspring more acceptable, if not in skin color then in behavior and manners. (Former baseball great, Reggie Jackson, for some time an opponent of busing, feels that it's really the white children who need desegregation, and he hopes that through that means "white kids could find out that black children can be wonderful people.")

School desegregation, the experts say, has been a mixed bag for black children. Scholastic achievement has risen in some places and not in others. Black (and Hispanic) students in some desegregated schools receive "dispropor-tionate punishment," the *Dallas Morning News* reported in a major investigative story. On the one hand black commentators such as columnist Carl Rowan argues that "there is no way that a youngster who has never competed with whites in anything close to an equal basis can be more confident in suddenly competing with them than a person who has spent years in college in interracial competition." (Rowan apparently forgets the success of traditionally black colleges in producing leaders able to complete on equal footing anywhere with anybody.) On the other hand, other influential blacks such as *Washington Post* writer William Raspberry scores the NAACP for pushing desegregation litigation and wonders whether its efforts would have been better directed if it had looked "at such factors as teacher qualifications, school facilities and resources, and academic improvements, with a view to providing a better education for black children..." where they are, principally in black inner cities.

White public support for desegregation has decreased since the 1970s. Segregation in education has increased. Black parents no longer favor bussing *en masse*. While many still like to see students of different races and ethnic groups studying and playing together, they have begun to realize the high cost to their children and their communities. Outside of the relatively few black youth who live in integrated neighborhoods and who are therefore "naturally" integrated into predominately white schools, (and who do appear from the research to get a "jump" on their black peers from predominately black schools in adjusting to interracial college and work situations, at least in the initial contact), bussed black children have not made the dramatic gains in academic or social achievement many assumed would accompany desegregation.

Also on the "loss" side of the ledger, there are real economic losses. In "It's Not the Bus—It's Us," Jesse Jackson spoke of the loss of teachers and other academic jobs to thousands of blacks. One study done in the late 1960's estimated as many as 12,000 teaching jobs were lost in the South alone! Hooker estimated the number at about 20,000 when teachers "assigned out of their fields" were included. The millions in income that might have stayed in our communities, and the loss of black role models for black children since teachers and principals are among the few professionals African American children see on a daily basis. For these and other related reasons black parents in Prince George's County in Maryland, lobbied the NAACP to drop its lawsuit to increase bussing. They would prefer neighborhood schools even if they were predominately black.

Some education demographers predict that minority teachers will make up less than 5% of the nation's teaching corps by the turn of the century. In 1990 black teachers had already fallen below that mark. This "nearly endangered species," in Robert Marquand's words, are not only models of success but they also bring a level of motivation and interest in their students rarely matched by white teachers. In a society thoroughly tainted with racism, few white teachers can bring the level of dedication to the teaching of black children that former Congresswoman Barbara Jordan's black teachers, for instance, gave her in a segregated school. The black teacher influence on many of today's black leaders who attended segregated schools is enormous. And it's a story still, unfortunately, not known by the general public.

Even African Americans who disagreed with former Education Secretary William Bennett on almost every other issue, agreed that too many of our students have not been provided with "first class elementary and secondary education," directed by great teachers who are "architects of the soul." (No competency test can measure that combination of assets which go into the making of a great teacher.) When they teach black children black teachers know what is at stake!

Achievement Where: The Streets Or School?

Public school education of black youngsters is at a crossroads in the America of the last decades of the twentieth century. It is a far more complex issue than the experts and politicians would have us believe. While necessary, more money pumped into inner city schools will not alone bring about the academic improvement and behavior modifications most of us would like to see. Neither will more black role models, however essential they might be. Massive school desegregation by bussing or other means of "bringing the races together" has not produced desired results, and have been prohibitively expensive. *The Economist* of London suggests that "racial patterns in housing" is the underlying cause of many of black America's problems and that until desegregation is more widespread, "there seems little point in trying to deliver remedies for the other ills of inequality."

But housing segregation is not the *kernel* of the problem for if that were the case, other racial/ethnic groups who by force or choice have been segregated, could not have made the economic advances the public has come to know about in the past decade.

According to a poll commission by *Life* magazine (and confirmed by other pollsters), most white Americans no longer believe that blacks are inherently less intelligent than whites. Something blacks have always known, of course! Most Americans now know that blacks can achieve academically. Long before Marva Collins and her Westside (Chicago) Preparatory School, or the Piney Woods Day School in Mississippi, or Newark's embattled Eastside High, or the rise of a black inner city national championship chess team in Indianapolis, or numerous other programs and schools of achieving black children, many of us knew that under the right conditions black children could hold their own with children anywhere in the world. (I once worked as the only black—anything: teacher, counselor, administrator, chaperone—at an exclusive boys' Jesuit prep school. The school's black students were drawn from some of the roughest inner city neighborhoods in the upper Midwest (and a handful came from upper middle class professional families). They represented at their greatest number about ten percent of the student body. Whatever we—the total community—did for and with them, it worked (one of those being a black professional who was available 24 hours per day seven days a week and who expected achievement regardless of background). Unfortunately the school closed in 1975, but the black former students, with two exceptions (two kids from upper middle class homes) have "made it." At their 1983 Black Student Union reunion, I was greeted by success: physicians, attorneys, police and fire executives, businessmen on the rise including several bankers, and productive blue collar workers.) Detroit's black judge Jenkins knows that "go to jail or get your GED" works with black kids who land in his court because he understands that with proper motivation they succeed.

While deplorable, the declining presence of black teachers in predominately black public schools is a symptom not a complete answer. It's in the same category as Richard Lamm's observation that the highest achieving students—the "A" students-largely come from two-parent homes, which points not to a solution but to a symptom of a larger societal illness. Raspberry and Educational Testing Service's Nettles are correct when they suggest that too many black youth do not see the relationship between "a solid grounding in math and science"—which many consider "arcane knowledge"—and greater career options. But, once again, the finger is pointed at a symptom. The real issue is why do large numbers of black students fail to make that connection when all around them, particularly on television, they see the results of science at work?

Nettles pursues the question further than does Raspberry, and comes closer to the answer to the riddle of black under-achievement. *The single most important factor or predictor of performance, he discovered in testing college students, was the extent to which the students, felt discriminated against racially.* The generic issue is the quality of their value as persons felt or sensed by students. (An interesting discussion of caste and race influence on educational achievement can be found in John Ogbu's *Minority Education and Caste,* which confirms Nettles' observations.) Students who don't feel discriminated against do better. And in the public schools there is no question that black students know their inferior status in the world. What good teachers and other role models do is offer an alternative ("swimming against the tide," "succeeding against the odds") to an otherwise totally bleak landscape of despair and worthlessness, a situation where self-esteem is developed not in the home, school, or church but in the streets. Lou Gossett's young drug dealer and the thousands like him will not be reached by the schools. In the kid's mind he's already achieving the American Dream and without the benefit of sixteen years of "education." And from his vantage point who can argue with him? During a break at a conference on African American women, a chance acquaintance believes young blacks like this know more about how to actually run a business than many MBA's!

Edwin Delattre, philosopher and part-time observer of urban underclass gang activity, speaks passionately of this largely black youth group. The *Boston Globe's* Charles Radin, in an article entitled "Philosopher Hits Streets," gives Delattre credit for an insight rare among academic intellectuals; and what Delattre discovered about the pathology of hopelessness of "these mean streets" is worth quoting at length:

> Of their outlook on life Delattre discovered that "They say that, in the beginning of human history, nobody owned anything, nobody had anything and the only way to get anything was to take it. That sets the rule...Whether you have a right to possess a thing is simply a question of whether you have the strength to keep it...
>
> Of the sheer hopelessness of this situation Delattre contends that "For all that I've

said about the intolerability of their situation and the unfairness of it, it's not as if you could just go in and reverse it all… The consequences are more grim than that. In some of these youths, the savagery and contempt are so deep-seated that the chance for redemptory love and connections are negligible…You don't reverse attitudes like that except by getting there first…reaching those children before they are imbued with street values."

Delattre adds that these children number 26 million, and points out that of these millions raised in fatherless homes 63 percent are black, 18 percent white and 34 percent Hispanic. Of the living conditions of many of them Delattre notes that they "are thrown together in large numbers in living conditions so stark most people can't even imagine…where you can't walk to school in safety, where you can't sleep in a bed free of filth and roaches and rats—if you have a bed.

> "I asked (one gang member) what he was going to do for the rest of the night. He looked at me and said, 'I just live until I dies, man.' He was right. He will just live until the drugs kill him, or the competition will kill him or somebody he tries to mug will kill him. It was a moment of such prophetic hopelessness that I will not forget it."

"You can't be what you ain't seen." In an essay entitled "The Paradox of Desegregation," black academician Manning Marable scores the disappearance of the Buppies and other potential role models into white suburbia. Among this number are many inner city teachers and school administrators. Marable argues that a prerequisite for effective school learning is that the "overall environment reinforces their desire to excel." Moreover, if black youngsters sense, as many do, that blacks with MBA's, law and other professional degrees are still treated like "niggers" (See *Time,* cover story, "The Rage of Successful Blacks," November 15, 1993) in and out of the workplace, they may very well conclude, and many do, that education, in its formal sense, is so much wasted effort. A recent Gallup Poll found that more non-whites than whites see less value in a college education "in relation to what it can do for them." Louis Bedford quotes Harvard Law Professor Derrick Bell on this issue:

> Blacks who believe that hard work and education are all it takes to achieve are fooling themselves. Discrimination affects all minorities, including the well-educated, the highly talented, and the hard workers.

Teresa Wiltz's sad tale of self-destructive behavior by her black male peers, all of whom were high achievers who encountered ultimately debilitating racism, offers insight into a phenomenon too little discussed.

> "What integration meant for me and my peers was reinforcement of the notion that being black means being inferior."

Blacks in particular must begin raising new questions about the purpose of education: education towards what end, who should be educated and what should the content of the educational enterprise be? Answers to these questions cannot be forthcoming until the more seminal issue of not *who* we African Americans are but *where* do we stand in America, is discussed. Too many blacks still believe and teach their children to "get your education, nobody can take it away from you", and "education will get you over." These parents have not yet learned that formal education is certainly necessary but it is far from sufficient to ensure the good life for their children. There is simply too much evidence to the contrary. Yes, our children *must,* on the other hand, be prepared for what opportunities are or may become available.

Above the issues of declining numbers of black teachers, role models who are available to our children, and how best to design meaningful educational programs—above all of this is what Alice Walker called the "bond of black kinship" which has been severely undermined in the "cities of the North,"…has to be reestablished. Without it black public education cannot achieve its purpose for African American youth. The "fear of us" *for us* stymies all constructive and purposeful actions. Gordon Parks says only when we achieve true unity, beyond the "quick thumbgrip and a give-me-some skin handshake," will respect for one another lead to abandonment of the most destructive brand of racism—that practiced by blacks against blacks.

> Sometimes I think I am the only Negro living who would not prefer to be white.
> Paul Robeson, "Negroes—Don't Ape The Whites"

During the early 1990s (as in the late 1960s) there was much national debate about the efficacy and legality of schools run by blacks for the benefit of young black males in several large cities. Hoping to counter the absent father impact, have a focused curriculum and develop black-male survival skills, black adult males, many of them public school teachers, opted to provide their own brand of education. While many had to abandon use of public property and money, some managed to survive on shoe-string budgets and rented facilities. To the extent that young African American males are the most endangered of the human species in this country, and to the extent that black adults are in the most advantageous position to design relevant programs and must assume this responsibility, these programs should be supported. Given the fact that it is young black males who are most victimized by the absent father programs which provide such "role modeling and imprinting are essential for black male children (in order for them) to understand adult male role functioning," in the words of black psychiatrist Frances Cress Welsing. Robert Bly adds a salient observation from Detroit's Police Chief: "The young men he arrests not only don't have any responsible older man in the house, they have never met one." Like thousands of other black self help efforts these "points of light" represented by innovative educational programs should be encouraged.

Of course, black men do excel absent a father (or "father figure") in the home. A casual survey of black male achievers—athletes, entertainers, businessmen, academics—would probably reveal a high proportion who lacked the home bound father, although the nurturing benefits of Bly's Iron man could be lacking even in them.

In a 1980 publication (*Black Students in Interracial Schools*) this writer laid out a set of recommendations designed to guide black high school and college students to successful educational experiences. Emphasis was on what *individuals* could do for themselves. In the decade since publication of that work, it has become clear that what is now needed is a systematic assault on the entire structure of education, an extensive examination of the entire enterprise.

Does a Good Education = A Good Job?

Black Americans are paid less than whites for their work, are more often unemployed, and more of their families are below the poverty level—racial differences that will probably continue.
Black Issues in Higher Education, January 15, 1987

Economics hold the key to the future of Americans of African descent. For far too long too many blacks have divorced obtaining an education from jobs and economic well-being. Understandably, since slavery denied access to meaningful educational opportunity, blacks have historically put great store in education because they literally believed that the "pursuit of happiness", began at the completion of a formal education program, whether of Booker T. Washington's trade school or the classical education often associated with W.E.B. Du Bois. They were sold on the power of education to secure the good life even when they could see around them the racial limitations imposed on those—black lawyers, doctors, teachers, and other professionals—who had in fact met and achieved that standard.

Now, as then, achieving a quality education is necessary but it alone is far from sufficient to ensure equal employment opportunity. The statistics are chilling: Blacks with college degrees had a 13 percent unemployment rate in 1987 compared to five percent for whites. The unemployment rate for black college graduates rose 108 percent between 1981 and 1982. Indeed, Tidwell has shown that the "unemployment gap" between blacks and whites is highest among those who have higher education, which is almost like admitting that blacks who pursue college and university education are punished for doing so! And, according to Pinkney, the gap widened between 1970 and 1980, a time coming on the heels of the Civil Rights Movement when opportunities were supposedly more available. Even the conservative U.S. Commission on Civil Rights has had to admit that "lack of education is not the reason for high minority unemployment," concluding from it's own study that even when education levels are identical and the same area of the country is studied, blacks are more likely to be unemployed than white males. One report concluded that "a majority of cities with a population of at least 10,000 have no blacks in top jobs," and many have no black employees at all even when "most have large black labor pools." There is absolutely no way to explain these gross disparities without fingering race bias.

(It is true that declining availability of resources to support black college attendance and lack of interest after the 1970's in assisting black youth in gaining college admission explains some decrease in black enrollment. Just as valid as a reason to explain black male declining matriculation—falling from 4.3 percent in 1976 to 3.5 percent in 1986 (while black female enrollment held steady) may be the perception that college graduation does not in fact lead to the Pot of Gold at the end of the rainbow (good jobs). The evidence is all around them.)

African American males are hit hardest with unemployment. James Seaberry's investigation found that not only were black college educated males more likely to be unemployed but that this phenomenon "is not a result of past inequities, but of present practices." Black men without jobs are estimated to be well over 50 percent, and black male college graduates are four times more likely to be unemployed than white male college graduates, according to conclusions reached in studies by Margaret Wilkerson and Jewell Gresham. In Washington, D.C. more than 40 percent of the city's "discouraged workers" who are black males have college degrees or some college education. When an advertisement was placed in a Detroit paper for a van driver, at $5 per hour, more than 100 people—all black—showed up, many with college degrees or some college, along with the high school dropouts. This story is repeated in similar "rush to jobs" fashion by blacks around the country. In early 1992 a crowd of more than 9,000, largely blacks, stood in line in freezing temperatures in Chicago to apply for 1,000 jobs at a new hotel.

> We had great hopes that education was really going to do it. But education was an indoctrination. Both class and race survived education, and neither should.
> Actress Beah Richards to photo/journalist Brian Lanker, in *I Dream A World*

The fact of the matter is that blacks have been sold a bill of goods about the value of education and it's power to ensure the good life. And we have bought it hook, line and sinker. What we all have to understand is that ultimately he who controls the wealth controls the jobs. And in the late twentieth century gainful employment is the answer to any number of social ills. Until, and if, America legislates full employment for all Americans willing and able to work, the historical black-white disparities will persist, notwithstanding all the current rhetoric from black and white conservatives hyping self-help and group effort (which are good but insufficient).

The Health of Black Americans: An Overview

> I will tell you this, my friend, for every Sammy Davis, for every Jimmy Baldwin, for every black cat you have heard of in the history of this country, there are a hundred of us dead.
> James Baldwin to David Frost, in *The Americans*, 1970

As important as formal education may be to the economic viability of African America, without a healthy population base all else is for naught. And, as the reader might guess and the experts already know, black America is not now, nor has it ever been in an optimal health mode. (Neither has white America, for that matter.) The fundamental difference between the health status of black and white Americans is not one only of quality; it is an economic issue in the sense that money buys quality health care, like everything else in our kind of capitalist society; and it's a political issue in that distribution of that money—wealth—has never been fashioned in a way to benefit blacks as it does far more whites. Since racism permeates the society, it is a wonder that blacks have done as well as we have in health as in other areas of life.

Health As Wealth

This brief overview is intended for the reader who does not know or have access to publications such as the National Urban League's annual *State of Black America* or more scholarly studies. It adds black health status as a piece of the black American pie. Some facts: there is one doctor for every 700 white people, but only one for every 3,800 blacks. Three times as many black as white women die in childbirth; in parts of Detroit "babies die every year at the same rate they do in Honduras, the poorest country in Central America," television host Phil Donahue discovered. The National Cancer Society reports that African Americans have a greater incidence of cancer and die of it at greater rates than "for any other major social group." (But blacks don't *suffer* as long as whites. Due to lack of early detection practices, they are twice as likely as whites to die in the first year of the disease. Good or bad? Who can say.) The Society adds that 30 years ago the rate of cancer incidence between blacks and whites was virtually the same.

Hypertension, often associated with sustained abnormal levels of mental and physical stress, is twice as likely to hit blacks as whites. It is a primary cause of early death for blacks. Tobacco and alcohol, not cocaine and heroin, are the most abused drugs in black America, which does not necessarily give black abusers a greater edge on health or longevity but does dispel the notion that blacks somehow are the "evil ones" in the "coke" devastation, although the cocaine derivative "crack" is, in *Newsweek's* terms, "transforming the ghetto," and other communities too, one hastens to add. In a study of drugs and homicide in Detroit, 37 percent of murder victims had cocaine in their blood samples.

AIDS has become a household word throughout the world in the past decade. Much of the discussion, some of it emanating from white racists with evil purposes (as shown, for example, by the ex-Klan family who told viewers of the Oprah Winfrey Show that when they prayed, they "always prayed for AIDS" for blacks) and others who read their propaganda, or who simply don't know the facts, suggest blacks as the original carriers of the virus. For the record, AIDS spread from America *to* Africa, not the other way around, even though in parts of central Africa the disease has reached epidemic proportions, principally from contaminated blood and unsafe heterosexual practices, with 20,000 deaths expected by 1995. While some 25 percent of reported cases in America are black, it is white males who predominate in transmission by homosexual or bisexual lifestyles and use of blood and blood products. Black and Hispanic men contract the disease principally through sharing contaminated needles and heterosexual contact (the now dominant form of transmission), according to black physician Beny Primm. Since blacks are less likely to use prophylactic devices in sexual contact, and are least informed about sexually transmitted diseases, they, male and female and their offspring, are more likely to contract the disease.

In the last decade of the twentieth-century AIDS is taking its heaviest toll on African Americans. In one state (South Carolina) alone 93 percent of infants testing positive for the HIV virus were black in 1991. In December of that year the state's Department of Health and Environmental Control reported 22,400 persons had tested positive for the virus; most of these individuals were black. Given current trends a similar pattern can be expected to surface in other areas of large black population concentrations.

AIDS did not originate with blacks. There is much unpublished discussion about it's actual origin. Black poet and activist Haki Madhubuti (Don L. Lee) suggests a theory increasingly popular with blacks: the virus was invented as a deliberate act of genocide aimed principally at the world's darker, especially black, peoples. A CBS/*New York Times* poll disclosed that 29 percent of black New Yorkers felt the AIDS virus might have been "deliberately created in a laboratory in order to inflict black people." A young white female colleague, phlebotomist by training, feels that "when AIDS first came on the scene, it was man-made and designed to wipe out blacks and the poor!!" The Strecker brothers, physician (gastroenterologist, pathologist, pharmacologist) Robert and attorney Ted believe AIDS "is a man-made disease." Their video "The Strecker Memorandum" purports to identify the diseases' origin as well as the purposes toward which it was intended. According to a flyer ("Is Aids Man-made?") circulated by the brothers no major print or visual medium has permitted their side of the story to be told to the American people. With Ervin "Magic" Johnson's disclosure that he is HIV positive (through heterosexual intercourse), perhaps the Strecker brothers story will finally be aired.

In September 1991 public television's Roger Mudd narrated a series on public health. From the array of case data presented and the unanimous testimony of health care providers—policy makers as well as specialists who do hands on treatment—it is clear that a national health care crisis exists in the United States. *All* of America is at risk. And those most at risk are those at the bottom of the economic pyramid. Among those are the majority of African Americans. One segment of the show focused on a westside neighborhood in Chicago in which the author resided briefly in the 1950s. Depressingly, that community has not improved in any respects by any measure. With only one clinic, one doctor (whose income is lower than truck drivers'), and a physical plant reminiscent of those television has revealed prevails in the Soviet Union, one can only conclude that this and other communities like it are inherently doomed. There is simply no way that they will on their own become model places to live. That the Westside, like Selma, has not materially changed through all the civil rights progress is a testament to limitations of that progress.

The catalogue of health risks facing African Americans is long indeed. Michigan Congressman John Conyers has even discovered, from an obscure Government Accounting Study, that "75 percent of hazardous-waste sites…were situated in predominately black communities." An 80 mile strip of land between New Orleans and Baton Rouge, Louisiana, populated largely by blacks, has been dubbed "Cancer Alley" because of the death and disease resulting from petrochemical dumping. The First National People of Color Leadership Summit on the Environment discussed results of several studies which concluded, among other findings, that (1) race, not poverty, was the key factor in site location of hazardous waste dumping; (2) more than three out of five black and Hispanic Americans "live in areas with uncontrolled toxic-waste dumps." As with AIDS, in the view of some people of color, poisonous waste dumping in minority communities is another man-made killer of non-white people.

Our poor health is a symptom of our poverty. For sociologist William Wilson, the black underclass is here to stay. One-third live below the poverty line and will, he believes, remain there. Millions of others exist at or just above that line. Only about one in fifteen whites share our misery. We don't live as long as whites, black men have the shortest lifespan of any American social group, and many don't live long enough to collect Social Security, according to James Kilpatrick, which is derived from taxes they too paid. Thus black men are really paying taxes to support whites in *their* old age.

Not living to a "ripe old age" may be a blessing in disguise, however, when one considers the horrendous problems facing most elderly Americans. (Comedian Richard Pryor's wish not to be "old and alone" but "for it to be me and the old lady together" may be, under present conditions, reaching for a fantasy.)

The Economic Facts of Black Life

Since, as Glasgow warns, black poverty, gross ill health and neglect are no longer of concern to most Americans, who consider the black condition a "lost cause," black health has to become a high priority on the *black* agenda. Little progress can be made in any realm of social life by a group so lacking in basic health.

> *I tell black kids the truth. Don't look for pie in the sky when you die. Get something on the ground while you're around. In this society, your blackness is a shortcoming, and you better be able to deal with it, because you're going to run into prejudice, discrimination and*

segregation. But instead of getting bitter, angry and mad, get smart.
    Words of the Week, *Jet* (emphasis in original) *Black Economics, Buppies, Leadership*

"Blacks really only control two things in society, their churches and their colleges...(and the) latter were about to become dinosaurs.
    William A. Blakey quoted by John Custrik in *Black Issues in Higher Education*

"My friend, there is a Hell. It's when a man has a family to support, has his health, and is ready to work, and there is no work to do. When he stands with empty hands and sees his children going hungry, his wife without the things to do with..."
    Louis L'Amour in *Bendigo Shafter*

Without much exaggeration, the above three passages rather neatly sum up the historic black economic situation in the United States.

Often when such a sweeping pronouncement is offered, defenders of the "system" are quick to point to the success stories. They point to the Reginald Lewises, A.G. Gastons, John Johnsons, Berry Gordys, and Comer Cottrell, Jr., among others. And it is true that blacks own large and small firms and are among the nation's most active entrepreneurs. Yet when the facts are faced squarely, certain disconcerting conclusions have to be drawn. The example of John Johnson, one of America's wealthiest African Americans and a member of the exclusive Fortune 500 club, is revealing because he (and Motown's Gordy, hair products tycoon George Johnson, Birmingham's multi-millionaire Gaston, Bill Cosby, and others often named) in fact does not really control anything in the same way large white corporations do. Their combined incomes and jobs that they provide do not even come close to being essential to the economic well-being of black America, for instance. Furthermore, theirs are not mainstream enterprises occupying critical niches in the larger economic pie, and, except for music fans, would not be missed should they demise. I like *Ebony* and *Jet* but can survive without them. Many also like and use Cottrell's Pro-Line products but can do without *them*. Cottrell's Pro-Line Corporation is America's largest black owned company after Reginald Lewis's giant TLC Beatrice International Holdings.

By 1994 several major black owned corporations had transferred to white ownership, Motown and Johnson Products among them. Following Reginald Lewis's untimely death in 1993, Beatrice International Holdings, founded by Lewis, appeared to be a candidate for the same fate. Joshua Smith, chairman and CEO of the Maxima Corporation, sees tough times ahead for black-owned businesses. He points to a laggard growth rate (38 percent for blacks compared to 89.3 percent for Asian and 80.5 percent for Hispanic firms) and concludes that "black owned businesses will look dismal in the year 2000. A 1990 Census Bureau report identified white men as the most successful small business owners with an average $189,000 in profits, followed by Asian men ($107,000) and Hispanic men ($66,000). Blacks brought up the rear at $50,000.

117

While the heroic efforts of black men and women to build economic enterprises under extremely adverse conditions are indeed laudatory (and should be celebrated in "song and poem") and must be shown to black youngsters as models worthy of emulation, these same youngsters must not be misled into believing that those success stories are testimonials to what all, or at least many more, blacks could do if they would only develop the personal character qualities to "get over." There are simply too many ghoulish stories from the other side of the coin to justify that kind of faith.

So, while we must continue to struggle to become successful entrepreneurs, we must not forget that our struggle is far more complicated than that of the white boy or girl starting at the same relative position. And that awareness must inform our actions. Put another way, young African Americans must not assume that because a Michael Dukakis or a Madeline Kunin (ex-governor of Vermont), or a Lee Iaccoca, sons and daughter of immigrants, can rise to prominence, that surely a homegrown, aggressive, talented and resourceful black person can "make it big." For us, things simply do not happen that way. Even for those few blacks who have made it "big," wealth alone has not been accommodated by the social amenities—"perks"—often associated with it. For a revealing account of the limits imposed by race on even the wealthiest of blacks, the reader is directed to John H. Johnson's autobiography *Succeeding Against the Odds*.

The author does not wish to mislead the reader. Blacks have made gains in the business world. *Black Enterprise* magazine publicizes this progress, even devising it's own Top 100 *black* enterprises. The reader may be interested to know that one black firm, Beatrice International, had holdings in excess of $2 billion; a number of others had earnings in excess of $20 million in 1907.

A drop in the bucket is better than an empty pail!

A rung below the handful of successful large entrepreneurs are the high salaried black managers. These are individuals like the Dallas City Manager who earns more than $100,000 per year; and Barry Rand, corporate vice-president of Xerox (who in 1988 was the highest ranking, and probably the only, black super-executive in a private mainline corporation); or Clifton Wharton, Jr., who earns more than $500,000 per year as chief of one of the nation's largest pension plans. These men and the few women who are in the same "league" are the cream of the black middle class. (Alicia Johnson reports that in the nation's 1,000 largest companies, there are only four black senior executive officers, an "increase of only one since 1979.") Despite equal opportunity laws, federal government employment of black executives is no better. Of 29 million employees, only 20 blacks were in policy making positions in 1987, down more than 100% since 1980.) In Senate and House employment, African Americans are paid equally poorly. A Newhouse Survey revealed that of 8200 that "effect legislation and political divisions," blacks held about 300 positions. Of 2700 high level senate positions, blacks occupied only 68. Virtually all positions held by blacks were with black lawmakers.

The principal social (bread-and-butter) issue for most Americans in early

21st century will be jobs, who gets what and how. Already in the mid-1990s, economic downturns and a host of closely related problems have made the dream of securing a decent job, a problematic quest for many Americans. Grim statistics bear out the reality: Enormous layoffs by many *Fortune* 500 companies—Sears, General Motors, IBM, American Express, GE, in addition to Rust Belt industries going under in the 1970s and 1980s. *Modern Maturity's* Linda Stern reported the loss of more than 4 million *Fortune* 500 companies jobs after 1980. With more than 1 million defense-related jobs expected to disappear and the military downsizes ("rightsizes," in official jargon) an additional one and one-half million positions, the massive ripple effect amounts to uncountable millions of jobs lost by the turn of the century. Add this to jobs going out of country and, as Janice Costro reports, the fact that one-third (and growing) of all American workers hold less than full-time positions with "few benefits and no security," the prognosis is grim.

When *race* is factored into the equation the future is even bleaker for blacks. Some headlines suffice to make the point: "105 mil bias settlement against Shoney's Restaurant...more than 20,000 blacks denied jobs or promotions;" "Trying to Fly in the pace of discrimination...2 black pilots sued and got up to $1 million in back pay...Northwest Airlines settled agreeing to spend $3.5 million on affirmative action program;" "Young black males looking for entry-level jobs in Chicago or Washington are discriminated against 20% of the time," a new study by Urban Institute; Denny's accused—several times of job and accommodations discrimination.

To make corporate leaders more sensitive to our job needs, an important and effective tool (when organized properly) is the economic boycott. When whites and Hispanics in Miami refused to give Nelson Mandela an official welcome, the accumulated rage over the virtual exclusion of blacks from the booming economy, attorney Marilyn Holifield and others organized a successful boycott lasting three years. It resulted in an estimated loss of $5.0 million in convention business and forced Miami's leaders to negotiate a better deal for African Americans.

Anti-black employment discrimination is pandemic; not only are corporations of all sizes in all regions of the country limiting access to blacks but employment agencies and other "middle men" organizations are participating. Public institutions such as universities and local governments fare no better in most sections of the country.

The New Black Elite

The careers of most of these individuals pre-date the rise of the Buppies. Young, black, upwardly mobile individuals are a relatively new phenomenon on the American social scene. Generally holding the MBA, law, or other professional degree from some of America's most prestigious universities, they represent the cutting edge of the contemporary African American middle class, shuttling through occupational doors pried open by the Civil Rights Movement. Extremely bright, confident of their ability, and oriented towards achieving the upper rungs of the fabled corporate ladder, they, having not, for the most part been around and personally involved in the turmoil and pain of the 1960's, have not known harsh racial discrimination at first hand.

Exile physician David James seems to speak for the group when he opines how he grew up in an integrated neighborhood and never experienced racism ("although my brothers and sisters who came after me…" experienced it in direct ways), and adds in characteristic Buppy-Yuppy style, "I think they (blacks) forget that no matter how far you go, you always have to remember that no one owes you anything, and you don't owe anyone anything." It is of interest to note that Dr. James, having completed medical studies in Europe and married a European, returned with his family to the United States to practice, then made a hurried, it seems, about face, and went back to Europe to settle. He does not tell us what caused the hasty "retreat," but one can surmise that at least in part he had finally met his racial Waterloo!

Buppies were part of the 56 percent of blacks earning middle class wages in 1980, according to *Newsweek*. Two obstacles stand in their way as they attempt to scale America's formidable corporate ladder. One obstacle is a direct result of racism; the other is only indirectly related to race and is caused by economic factors affecting many Americans of all colors. Most Americans are acutely aware of the nation's worsening economic situation during the early and mid-1980s, and the frightful downturn of the early 1990s when many of the nation's largest corporations—IBM, Xerox, General Motors, etc.—laid off white collar workers in the tens of thousands. The oil "bust", fierce foreign competition for consumer markets traditionally aligned with American industries, jobs disappearing to foreign labor-intensive regions, and other factors all combined to put a heavy economic squeeze on several areas of the country and on certain industries. To cut costs and adjust to a changed financial configuration, top management made drastic cuts in middle management, where the great bulk of the Buppies work. *Black Enterprise* magazine editor Earl Graves observed that "since 1984, over half a million middle managers have been terminated, and a good number of these casualties have been black executives." And when they have fallen, it's been a long way down: "scores of black white-collar workers (have been sent) to the unemployment lines," many never to make it back up to their former status. This situation, to Graves, poses "a dilemma that threatens the well-being of the black middle class."

President Carter's unsuccessful re-election bid had already accounted for the ouster of dozens of black federal appointees, few of whom were retained by his successor. And few were picked up by the private sector. (Black retiring military officers, of whatever rank, face the same dilemma, many taking on menial jogs after distinguished careers. The Marine Corps highest ranking black officer, a Lt. General, currently works in the security department of a large corporation. He is not the department head!)

The other horn of the dilemma of the Buppy fast-trackers is the racism endemic to American life, whether corporate or public, economic or social. A 1984 study of Harvard MBA's by the American Jewish Committee found that while Jewish MBA's are "doing well...there is a deep seated prejudice and dislike for black "managers." Even women, who have experienced much historical discrimination, are moving ahead of blacks who have been knocking at the doors much longer. (In this context "women" means *white* women.) "The changes have been tremendous for women, but for blacks, it's harder now than it was a few years ago," the study concludes. A white male manager admitted that "if a white male had two comparable candidates in terms of ability, one black male and one white woman, consciously or unconsciously, he'd pick the white woman."

Numerous studies, including those cited in the book *Black Managers in White Corporations,* have confirmed the debilitating effects of corporate racism. Few black managers reach the corporate boardroom or executive suite. Opinion surveys of these black managers have consistently corroborated the AJC findings: in overwhelming numbers they say that "negative racial attitudes of white managers...(is) the number one impediment" to their progress. One Buppy told *Frontline's* Roger Wilkins:

> You play by the rules and you get an MBA from Harvard. You're being groomed to be a chief executive officer. Only you realize you're not going to be in that position. There will come a point at some...time when you have to realize (you're not going any further).

Another black manager told an interviewer:

> I was a good soldier...I figured that if you worked hard and did a good job you'd be rewarded, but that's not necessarily true.

His company had a different profile of what an ideal manager should look like: "You know, six feet tall, blond, blue eyes is the typical management type; and I'm short, black and four-eyed."

What Buppies fail to understand and can't intimately know about is the "good old boys club" so eloquently described by "corporate raider" T. Boone Pickens. The club is exclusive, with "membership confined to white males who run large, publicly owned corporations." It has no published governing policies or regulations and meets informally in a variety of settings, always plush. Membership is based on "wealth, power, or in a few cases, innovative leadership." But one can't *buy* his way in; a prospect receives a special invitation, often a mysterious and clandestine phone call. It is doubtful that any blacks will ever move in these circles no matter their wealth, power, or innovative leadership. They don't "fit" individually or collectively.

Race is the over-arching factor in determining who moves to the rarefied heights of corporate America. No other factor accounts for blacks being excluded from those "networks of friendship and support" so necessary for moving into corporate leadership. In all competitive situations there is room at the top for only a few; and the race doesn't necessarily go to the swift. More often than not it goes to the "fittest" in racial terms.

Buppies not only fail to move up the corporate ladder (penetrate the "glass ceiling"), their representation is fewer than many believe. Much of their advance is taking place not in the private sector where the "real" money is made and power wielded but in government employment. The U.S. Office of Personnel Management reported in early 1988 that almost 80 percent of the federal government workforce was female and minority. Pinkney, in his groundbreaking *The Myth of Black Progress,* found that 67 percent of all black managers and professionals and 42 percent of administrators, worked for the government.

Wilkins warns that this new African American middle class (Buppies) is disadvantaged in other ways. Not only is it "not rich and powerful enough to be totally free," capable of assuring that events move in ways beneficial to its members, but, unlike the smaller and more segregated black middle class of the past, it is "too far from the old black culture to be totally comfortable." It is rootless, in other words, and "moves across the thinnest psychic–ice."

Even with enormous problems, a segment of the Buppies is fighting back. Aware of their talent and training and confident in their abilities, they refuse to let racism beat them down. Many are leaving their stalemated positions in corporate America and becoming entrepreneurs in their own right. Others are active in the political arena in a way shunned by older blacks. *Washington Post* reporter Milton Coleman says of them that they are "de-aligning from the Democrats" and working to elect Republicans in several states. Melvin Bradley told *Christian Science Monitor* reporter Luix Overbea that these young professionals "will fight racism on every front, but they will not be consumed by the issue of white attitudes towards blacks."

The Buppies will create their own strategies and, despite obstacles, forge forward to achieve personal and career goals. Having to run a tougher gauntlet than their white counterparts (Yuppies) or blazing new trails altogether is a characteristic feature. It was a group of Buppy led blacks who, over the opposition of more traditional black community leadership, said to the City of Boston city fathers, "if you continue to shortchange our communities in resource allocation and public services, we will secede and form our own city, to be called Mandella (after the now freed black South African leader)." As Overbea reported "the referendum failed at the polls but stirred City Hall action."

The new black middle class is working on other fronts to assist African American communities. In Los Angeles the YBP's (Young Black Professionals) raised $250,000 for the "YOU COUNT" project, a public service campaign that encouraged blacks to participate in the 1990 census. Black social fraternity Alpha Kappa Alpha, among its numerous other programs, has joined Project 30,000 Homes, a South Memphis program designed to literally build 30,000 new homes for low and moderate income blacks. The Ravendale anti-crime, pro-jobs, pro-clean streets in Detroit is another Buppy initiative. In Philadelphia Buppies comprise the leadership of the city's "Blacks Educating Blacks

About Sexual Health Issues" project. Starting in Atlanta as a program run by young black professional men to address the problems of young African American males, the Buppy Black Men, Inc., by 1993 was a national organization supporting dozens of self help programs.

Politically, Buppies still grapple with finding an identity. Studies by the Joint Center for Political Studies have found them wavering between the two political parties with those in the 18-29 year old group "more likely to vote Republican." Given predictions of worse economic strife through the year 2000, this trend may be reversed. Wilkins idea of Buppy rootlessness spans the political as well as psychological arena.

Buppies have also joined with traditional self-help groups. How effective such clubs can be in serving their communities was described in a letter (Dec. 14, 1993) from my Chicago friend Iola. I quote from it in detail to give the reader an understanding that everyone can be useful even with limited funds.

The Duster Club was founded by a daughter of the late Ida B. Wells-Barnett, the famous civic leader who led the fight against lynching. After more than thirty years of existence and currently needing new members (as are many such mutual help groups across the country), Duster Club members are active in a broad range of community uplift projects. After noting that the annual Christmas party "was a fun event" though earning only a meager amount of money— not enough to "pay 90's rent" if it were a rent party—Iola enumerated member activities:

> Gwen — helped put together a consortium of not for profit organizations in order to better serve the young people within a large Southside area. Gwen's daughter Laura works with a wonderful theatre group called E.T.A. Linda — manages the entertainment programs for the New Regal Theatre ... June — works to develop literacy programs and works in all kinds of church programs along with her husband ...Barbara — teaches piano as an avocation and works (for bread and butter) for the city.

> Myra — raised all of her sister's children each of whom is now grown and self sufficient. Ira — is an active worker in my parish, since being in our group, she has earned her own bachelor's degree and her daughter...completed two degrees with honors...(My own daughter) works for the city...(and) says that club members boost her confidence...we do have other members who are special people (who also) rarely make news headlines. I like my association (with these women) because they carry the light of Christ and then pass it on.

Black Churches and Black Economics

In consequence of it's Buppy leadership, the modern black church is becoming much more *this* worldly and joining the parade of black institutions marching to the green of economic salvation. As Historian Mazuri might put it, black churches are moving from the old address where physical death was merely "changing your address", to a new residence of broad participation in American life. Spurning Zora Hurston's admonition to not tamper with God's "plan of the Universe," which presumably fated blacks to their lowly station, and moving beyond simply using religion as "an anecdote against bitterness," in Alice Walker's words, this Buppy led movement is transforming black religion.

An illustration of this new thrust is the formation in 1982 of the Congress of National Black Churches which from it's beginning devoted itself to looking at hard economic issues, such as which banks and other financial institutions best serve black interests and which ought to be denied black church deposits. This is precisely the weapon Julian Bond (quintessential Buppy, if somewhat older) called into action when a prestigious white newspaper discovered what appeared to be a conspiracy by several banks to deprive blacks, "whatever their income level" of home mortgage and repair loans. These same banks, when threatened with "direct action" made available $80 million in loans to blacks.

Under the circumstances one questions how another Buppy can call, in an *Essence* article, Atlanta "Our piece of the Pie," when blacks exercise so little control over economic and financial forces. Washington, D.C. minister Willie Wilson remarked that churches "must be involved in people's political, intellectual and economic lives as well as their spiritual lives." His church has invested $5 million in a housing development. Across the country, San Francisco's Rev. Cecil Williams is using his Glide Memorial Union Methodist Church as a base to wage war on the drug Crack and as a forum for addressing economic issues. U.S. Congressman Floyd Flakes' 6,000 member church in New York City "raises more than $3 million annually, to re-invest in our community, build affordable housing and try to develop our neighborhoods...(and) purchased about 30 million dollars worth of property." Nation of Islam's Minister Louis Farrahkan is "widening his support" and attempting to resurrect Elijah Muhammad's economic development programs. One of Farrahkan's chief economic concerns are the "businesses that might well have been ours...(but have been) taken over by Koreans, Indians, Pakistanis—the new Americans, who came to this country as immigrants and are achieving the American Dream...denied us."

As reported on Tony Brown's Journal, Bishop Luke Edwards' Meridian, Mississippi, economic empire (valued at $20 million) includes schools, farms, and numerous business enterprises. None of his followers need or are on welfare, all are well behaved, and all are receiving appropriate education emphasizing spiritual and character development. Bishop Edwards is giving meaning to life to hundreds in spite of having gone no further than fourth grade of formal schooling.

Chicago's late Dr. Morris Tynes, pastor of the huge Mt. Moriah Baptist Church and Yale classmate of George Bush, fluent in several languages, spurned tempting offers from mainstream institutions to work and inspire his own people. While spending much of her time working in predominantly white settings, Roman Catholic Sr. Thea Bowman (whom I got to know when we both worked in rural Wisconsin during the early 1970s) devoted her life to uplifting the downtrodden among her people and educating whites to the folly of race discrimination. Her huge likeness occupying a wall of the Jackson, Mississippi, African American museum is testament to her larger-than-life legacy. She should be sainted by her church.

The rate of black church participation in economic enterprise is a creative way, absence other avenues, to involve more community level citizens in improving their neighborhoods. This method of carving out a "piece of the pie", following the example set by Mormons, Rev. Moon, the Amish and other religious groups, will surely be adopted by increasing numbers of African American religious institutions.

Black church leaders would do well to study the success—religious and temporal—of the Mormons (the Church of Latter-Day Saints). In many respects, that success can be replicated. In particular, they should read the Ethics and Religion writing of nationally syndicated columnist Michael McManus.

White Unions and Black Workers

Another area of economic activity that blacks need to bring under closer scrutiny is American labor unions. For far too long we have bought the line that unions are "for the working man." The truth is that labor unions, like other areas of American life, have been, and still are in some occupational areas, guilty of overt historical racial discrimination. The twenty-year sheet metal union's discrimination case in New York City is a legacy of trade union treatment of blacks throughout the history of trade unionism. Similarly, the "blatant" discrimination practiced by the pipeline welder's union "barring blacks and women from membership" is reflective of a broader, ingrained racism and sexism. Until the very day of its trial the Pipe Fitters Union, with no women or blacks among its 5,200 members, claimed that "skilled blacks or females were not available or willing to work under pipeline construction conditions." A famous major league baseball player related how his father, learning of a special program to train black apprentices in a skilled crafts trade, took and successfully completed the course, only to have his certificate torn up in his face by a white union boss. The father never recovered from this rejection and died a broken man. Brian Lanker interviewed a famous black woman whose father had been similarly "broken". In this case, the father was fired when a newly hired white apprentice refused to "be handed a tool by a nigger." An acquaintance told me in 1993 that he drove a truck for a non-union shop for 15 years because the Teamsters denied membership to blacks. "They didn't want us on the road. Period." He retired in 1991.

Even when blacks have somehow squeezed into a union shop and found employment, all too often they are not called for work at the same rate as whites, or, when they do find work, they are racially harassed by fellow union members. Perhaps the most famous of this form of racist bias came to light in a 1986 case involving a black engine tester who was harassed for "exceeding his production quota" (doing his job well). His tools were hidden, whites "sabotaged engines he was testing, and posted racial epithets, threats, (and drew) derogatory cartoons about blacks."Neither supervisors or company executives would act on the black employee's plea for relief. In mid 1993 a friend and former high school student of mine was selected for an AFL-CIO filed internship. Though he completed the internship he was not selected for further organizer training. In a letter to me he explained: "I found out very quickly that they did not want a thinking person. They are looking for African Americans that they can mold and control. Although I have the verbal skills, charisma and ability to move folks to do things for themselves, I was told that my political and community concerns might hamper my commitment to the Union." Benevolently, he added that "the things that I learned from this group of 'liberal Jews' will benefit the work I am interested in completing."

A stark illustration of how this subterranean racism works with labor unions was revealed by Camile Cosby. In an introduction to photographer Howard Bingham's book of Ali photos, she notes that husband Bill wanted Bingham as still photographer on "The Cosby Show." This wasn't possible because in 1969 "membership in the motion picture and television photographer's union was restricted to white males." Having no choice but to go along with the union rule that a photographer could gain union membership if he worked with a union photographer for a minimum of thirty days, on a set (previous to this show, "African American photographers were never asked to work on any sets.") Cosby paid for two photographers in order to get Bingham in. Then he learned that another rule prohibited Bingham as a low ranking member from working the set. So, for "the duration of the show," Cosby had to pay for two photographers; Bingham took the photos while his white superior "just sat in his chair."

Exclusion from trade unions and harassment in union jobs can be traced to the leadership of the union movement. Sam Gompers is hailed as a "great American" and founder of the modern union movement. Yet Gompers, in the fashion of his time, turned his back on blacks and used some of the most racist language in his speeches about black workers. The historical exclusion of blacks from large segments of the American labor movement prompted the late James Baldwin to write in his perceptive essay "On Being 'White'...and Other Lies," that "there has never been a labor movement in this country." At a time when labor leader Eugene Debs warred against Big Business and "money interests" on behalf of the "little man," his own union refused membership to black Americans. Economist Walter Williams says labor has not been the friend of blacks that contemporary labor leaders claim it to be.

Over many decades, the most successful labor organization for African Americans was the Brotherhood of Sleeping Car Porters founded by A. Philip Randolph. Largely barred by other unions, but welcomed by the Pullman Company, even though their employment was limited to "whisking lint, shining shoes and otherwise keeping passengers happy...Politeness and servility were among the job qualifications." Kept out of the white collar jobs for which they had been trained, thousands of college graduates "rode the rails." Pullman Porters became glorified workers to black city dwellers. Indeed, the Sleeping

Car Porters' Union was so successful that a case should be made that it is a model on which other organizational efforts can be launched. My friend Iola states it well when she wrote that "I consider the good works of this union of men an example of what we could do (as a group) to help our people make a confident step into 2000."

In recent years, particularly during the Reagan Administration, labor unions lost much of their political and economic clout. Plagued by falling membership rolls, intensified government surveillance and prosecution, corruption and alleged ties to organized crime in some locals, trade unions have perhaps passed beyond the peak of their effectiveness. It is for black labor and political leaders to decide whether American labor unions, with the obvious exception of A. Phillip Randolph's Sleeping Car Porters, have materially assisted the cause of black economic advance. What is clear is that *all* American institutions, including labor, have fallen far short of equal opportunity to African Americans.

Blacks must make a broad, organized and sustained attack on all American economic institutions. If General Motors, a corporation sometimes thought of as liberal toward black employment, can be charged with systematic employment discrimination and made to enter into a multi-million dollar settlement; and if the U.S. Labor Department can force a settlement from United Airlines for race discrimination in hiring reservation sales representatives; and if the giant Northwest Airlines is induced to make a $40 million settlement in a race discrimination lawsuit brought by blacks; and if also in 1991 six prestigious New York City and Buffalo employment agencies can be charged with systematic deceptive employment practices to deny blacks and others equal opportunity; and if after twelve years of denying bias in employment against blacks, the Illinois Central Railroad makes a $10 million settlement, then certainly less endowed employers with fewer six-figure lawyers and public relations staffs can be sensibly approached about their hiring practices. (The reader should keep in mind that most American corporations, including giants like General Motors and Continental Can Company, had no black employees prior to World War II. Employment discrimination was not confined to industry, of course. If the U.S. Supreme Court discriminates against blacks, having only two black law clerks in its entire history (all the court's *messengers* are black however), the depth of the problem facing black job seekers is clear.) If the nation's ninth largest health insurance company can be brought to court for allegedly firing its best salesman when he exposed his employer's policy "of not selling life insurance to blacks," and if one of the nation's major universities—Louisiana State— is forced to settle a bias claim brought by black job applicants, who, federal investigators said, "met the job qualifications *better* than the white candidates who were hired," (emphasis added), the claim of little job discrimination remaining against blacks is ludicrous. While Professor William Wilson's "guaranteed employment" idea may not take hold in the American mind as "the key to combating urban poverty," it is clear that government efforts, meager as they may be, must be joined by a powerful organizational effort generating from blacks themselves.

Du Bois warned us almost a century ago, in *The Philadelphia Negro* (his first book length work), that "the bulk of the work of raising the Negro must be done by the Negro himself." Too many of our leaders have forgotten, or never knew this injunction, and seem to form lines to Washington and white philanthropists, when much of that effort could productively be redirected inward towards building viable economic and social institutions within black communities. After all, in America generally, 80 percent of us work for the 80 percent of American businesses that are small and that are located in communities (as opposed to business districts). They must get behind programs like those developed by the all black National Alliance of Postal and Federal Employees to assist a sinking Fisk University, invested in black business ventures like now defunct Air Atlanta and provided substantial support to the anti-apartheid campaign. Jesse Jackson has warned that "dependence and fear" are our greatest enemies. Only black leadership can refocus our attention away from perpetual dependence and the "enslavement and exploitation" which follows in it's wake.

A Proper View of Self Help

On the political front black leadership does not have to be in disarray. Disagreeing white political leaders can still come together when their collective constituencies stand to gain. A traditional problem with black leadership, whether in political, business, educational or social life, is a general inability to accept criticism, no matter its quality. The result is that in many black headed businesses and social institutions, managers are surrounded by people who are exact copies of their bosses; and it seems that black managers and leaders, far more than whites, are quick to take offense and discipline any subordinate who dares to disagree or offer criticism. If the "absence of criticism," as Nigerian Nobel Laureate Wole Solinka warns, is the "greatest threat to freedom" in the political sense, intolerance of criticism in black institutional life is a measure of stagnation, lack of creative expression, inertia, and eventual institutional death. It is no secret that more than a few black scholars and intellectuals refuse to work at black colleges and universities and business enterprises for that reason. Rev. Jesse Jackson's call to the Democratic Convention for "expansion and inclusion" could appropriately be applied to black leadership.

> To try to go it alone is to doom ourselves to failure. If I have a bowl of soup, you have a bowl of soup. If you die fighting for what is right, then I must die beside you—for I am your brother. You are a black man.
> Malcolm X explaining the Muslim philosophy to Gordon Parks, in *To Smile in Autumn*

General black progress will come with a higher degree of quality black unity (not unanimity), so many past and present leaders have proclaimed. It *can* (not necessarily *will*) come in the same way it has for other groups in American society, when, first, group members look out for the welfare of its own members. The Kiwanis Club, for instance, has as its purpose "the mutual exchange of preferred treatment in professional and business dealings." Some black political leaders, particularly mayors of large cities, have taken the hint and are using their leverage to see that blacks get "municipal jobs previously closed to them."

Small, community based independent efforts to enhance black welfare must be publicized and praised by national black leaders. The National Association for the Advancement of Colored People (NAACP) and the National Urban League should award medals and honors equivalent in stature to the Spingarn Medal to local leaders who are making a difference in African American life—people such as former All-Pro football player Mel Blount who paid for the family farm then turned into a successful youth home for "wayward" kids (so successfully that the Ku Klux Klan has threatened to destroy it!); Floyd Brown who studied under Booker T. Washington, took the ideas learned at Tuskegee to Fargo, Arkansas, and by 1949 had a school serving several hundred students; or the unnamed black teenager who challenged a group's decision to name yet another institution for "Dunbar, Carver, or Booker T. Washington," asking, "Why do we always let 'them' pick our heroes?…Will we ever be ready to decide for ourselves who our heroes are?" She wanted Paul Robeson chosen.

Black leaders should praise, rather than envy, idea generators such as television host Tony Brown whose "Buy Freedom" program is designed to use black "culture as a basis of (economic) competition" with other ethnic groups. Numerous other largely unheralded efforts go unreported to our disadvantage. A black heroes wax museum here, a Buffalo Soldiers museum there, a black oriented bookstore in yet another inner city, the personal commitment of black professionals like the psychiatrist Dr. Margaret Lawrence, schooled in the nations best medical faculties, yet devoting her life to the people of Harlem—all deserve our applause. Haki Madabutis (60s poet Don L. Lee) successful operation—book store, publishing company, independent school, is worthy of praise and emulation, as is Rita Smith's anti-drug crusade in Harlem about whom a book, *The Woman Who Took Back Her Streets,* was written, and to whom *Reader's Digest* referred in a special book section as the "Miracle on 143rd Street."

Not often thought of as *individualists* in the same sense some blacks use the term when speaking of whites, many blacks have shown a definite reservation about pooling money for the sake of financial advancement. In a major report, news columnist Claude Lewis scores blacks who, despite an estimated $282 billion annual spending output, save far fewer of their disposable dollars than do others. Even with less disposable income than most groups, pooling of available dollars could represent an important avenue of income generation. Blacks have not in any significant numbers (important exceptions are mentioned elsewhere in this book) done this. Rather the inclination has been to "do your own thing" regarding use of money.

If black communities are to be rid of crime, black leaders must join Jesse Jackson in active and overt self-help campaigns and use their considerable clout to help community and neighborhood generated efforts. Drugs are only one (and in the long term not the most devastating—alcohol abuse is) of the many ills disrupting and destroying our communities. In fact the horrendous black on black homicide rate (in 1985 40 percent of homicide victims were black; 94 percent of murderers were black; 605 blacks were killed by other blacks in Chicago in 1991) can be directly linked to the absence of an involved leadership. (Anyone who wishes to find out how deadly and disruptive homicide is in inner city black communities should read David Simon's *Homicide: A Year On the Killing Streets*. News reporter Simon spent a year with a Baltimore homicide detective unit.) Understanding the link between black crime and the "Black Condition" is one thing, but continuing to lay ultimate blame for crime on that condition; i.e. poverty, does little to restrain those with criminal intent.

There must be a moratorium on "blaming the system" and making excuses for black on black crime, as does Pinkney when he declares, "When they rebel...they strike at the most convenient targets, knowing that if they take their protests downtown they will simply be slaughtered!" Black leaders must get behind what *U.S. News and World Report* called "do-it-yourself drug busters" who are helping African American communities "reclaim their neighborhoods." And finally, we must all understand that despite the transient glitter sported by the petty pushers and dealers in our communities, we are by no means the "big money" profiteers in the drug business. Whites are. In late 1991, for instance, the U.S. Justice Department revealed that $500 million in drug trafficking had been laundered through Rhode Island banks and another $30 million in Florida. That kind of money simply does not circulate in the most drug-infested of black communities. We are the victims not the victors. Jill Jones, in an *American Heritage* article, identified Arnold Rothstein as the "founding father" of "big-time international narcotics trafficking," inventing this very lucrative "industry" in the 1920's.

> One cause of black-on-black crime is drugs, because people fight over drugs and turf. Black people don't make drugs, they don't run the country, and they don't control how cocaine gets into the country. White people do.
> Tiffany Bell, 18

> "It really gets on my nerves when, every time something doesn't go right, I hear people in my family say, "It's the white men's fault." Black people should stop using white people as an excuse for why they don't do right or why they do this or that.
> Devin Lawson, 17

Black leaders must be prepared to join this crusade against criminal activity even if it means confronting representatives of legal authority such as police officers who will not protect us or who, themselves, are involved in violations of law. Maulana Karenga has written that we have a constitutional right to defend our communities as well as our persons, and that "any action (to protect and defend ourselves) is better than sitting at home, looking at TV, talking bad, and doing nothing." Legitimate anger does not have to push us to irrational acts of violence or to the physical suicide of a Leonita McClain, the late *Chicago Tribune* editorial board member (who in response to hate mail generated by Harold

Washington's first mayoral campaign, wrote, "It would make me feel like machine-gunning every white face on the bus.")

Our weapons must be more constructive than the machine gun or the barbiturate overdose. Organized effort directed toward achieving common goals must be the method.

> If I were asked what I consider to be the most important way to address crime in America, I would cite jobs.
>> Lee Brown, Clinton Administration Drug Czar, former police chief of Atlanta, Houston and New York City

> Look, the Soviet Union is not the challenge to America. I am the challenge to America. I have no job. I and my family were born here. We're Americans. We live on food stamps in a rotting tenement. You offer me money to join a volunteer army, to defend the white society that lives like lords while I live on the poverty line. I don't want a uniform and a gun. I want work!
>> Herman Wouk, "A Choice for Freedom," *Parade*, October 19, 1980

> Who is your master? Whosoever controls those things which you seek or shun.
>> Epictetus

And yet, in all the hue and cry about "black crime," one is forced to ask: Why is it that if whites commit more than 70 percent of crime in this country— as they do—are they not convicted and imprisoned at that rate? Who is slated to occupy Bill Clinton's new prisons?

Blacks as Professional Soldiers and Athletes

With the exception of some areas of commercial entertainment, African Americans have known their greatest successes in professional sports and as members of the nation's armed services. From black race horse jockeys who were dominant at the turn of the century to champion boxer Jack Johnson (whom many consider the greatest pugilist of all time for his courage in and out of the ring) to ex-heavyweight champion Mike Tyson and the multi-million dollar salaried baseball and basketball players, blacks have become so dominant in some aspects of professional sports that some team owners, failing to find Great White Hopes in America, are vigorously recruiting European players "so a little more salt is fielded with all that pepper!" While at the same time many talented black athletes are *exporting* their skills to Europe and Canada!

For an even longer period of time (but particularly since President Truman issued Executive Order 9981 which demanded "equality of treatment and opportunity for all persons in the armed forces without regard to race, color, religion or national origin") military careers have been a popular way out of poverty and collective despair for many American blacks. (Interestingly, on the international scene, outcast groups in other countries constitute significant proportions of their nation's military services, eg, the so-called Oriental Jews in

Israel.) Whenever they have been allowed to enlist African Americans have volunteered in disproportionate numbers.

As professional sports and the armed services have played such a pivotal economic role in the general welfare of black Americans, this section offers a brief outline of these two areas and suggest their future importance to the black community.

Blacks and the Military: Evolution to Equality

Black soldiers ... served as common fodder in all America's wars to keep the country free.

U.S. Army Colonel David Hackworth (Ret.)

We look first at the military. Historian Lerone Bennett, Jr., among others, has reported on the five thousand blacks who participated in the nation's first war, the Revolutionary War. Beginning with the martyred Crispus Attucks, "the first to die in the cause of America's freedom," through Lt. Flipper, first black graduate of the U.S. Military Academy, to the fifteen Medal of Honor winners in Vietnam (virtually all of whom got the award posthumously), African Americans have served nobly and honorably in every theatre despite doubts from many whites both about their courage and their loyalty. In the long history of America's wars only one black has ever deserted or refused repatriation as a prisoner of war (this in Korea), compared to dozens of whites who have done so. No black American, Jesse Jackson reminds us, has ever been convicted of treason, and only one, a woman, has been tried and convicted of espionage. (This case, which occurred during the past ten years, would be ludicrous if not for its seriousness, for the offender had been, in a typical love-spy manner, divulging information to a national of a third rate, Third World country which in no way is, or is likely to ever be, a security threat to the United States.)

James Baldwin wrote an interesting commentary on treason: Responding to the "confusion and horror and heartbreak and contempt" black people felt over the treatment of Muhammad Ali when he refused to be inducted, he said, "The romance of treason never occurred to us for the brutally simple reason that you can't betray a country you don't have. (Think about it.) Treason draws its energy from the conscious, deliberate betrayal of a trust—as we were not trusted, we could not betray. And we did not wish to be traitors. We wished to be citizens."

So, despite the extreme obstacles imposed by individual and institutional racism in much of the armed services, blacks have been patriotic in the extreme, and largely without a display of public bitterness. The excerpt below, from Vietnam combat psychiatrist Ronald Glasser's *365 Days*, makes the point for both cases: the pent-up emotional feelings about prejudice experienced by black service people (black psychiatrists Cobb and Greer termed this suppressed emotion *rage*), and the rational basis for that rage (the legitimacy of which is usually denied by whites).

A doctor is treating a black battlefield hero who had suddenly "broke" under the pressure.

"I'm white," doc says, "but let me tell you what I think's bothering you. It's not that captain you cut down or the ward master or even me. It's that you go through all that shit, risking your life for white and black, for God and country, and then they take you out of it and it's the same shit that you left. If it was me, I'd be angry too, angry as hell…most of all angry at myself for being so fucken stupid as to think anything would change. Believing that if I did my job it wouldn't be the same."

This perspective is mirrored in an episode in the television series *Tour of Duty* where a black grunt, having left the streets of inner city Detroit for another tour in Vietnam, tells his platoon sergeant that black participation in the war had changed nothing in the black community, and that not only was he returning to combat but joining a LURP (long range reconnaissance patrol) unit, a virtually suicidal assignment. Indeed, things had not changed at home. Alice Walker recounts an episode in a black Mississippi woman's autobiography where during the same period when her son-in-law was fighting along the Cambodian border, being wounded three times, "the Klan was backing into our house to throw a bomb off." In an article about "Blacks in 'Nam," Basil Harde tells of how a black army officer, on his way to Vietnam, while phoning his wife from a phone booth, was shot in the back by a racist assailant in a Southern state. A black veteran of Desert Storm returned home to a hero's welcome by a fourth grade class in a school where his mother taught. He was later murdered by a white man on a street in Florida.

(In the Marine battalion the)…most volatile problem was race relations. If the blacks' anger could be honed down to one immediate concern, it was that they were being used as cannon fodder in a war that was of no concern to them.
Kenneth Nolan, *Death Valley: The Summer Offensive I Corps, August 1969*, 1987

Michael Norman's *These Good Men* offers sad poignancy to this state of affairs during the last years of the war and at U.S. bases after the downfall of Saigon. It was a time when black and white Marines lived almost total separate lives, when each Marine palled with a select group of white or black buddies, each daring not to fall asleep without a weapon close by, a time when "men openly challenged authority, refused orders, even assaulted their officers."

Given their historical treatment in the United States African Americans have shown an almost illogical and irrational degree of honor and courage in America's wars and "conflicts." Over objections that we would not fight or would prove to be dumb and cowardly, the nation's first general, Washington, was forced to recruit and admit blacks into the Continental Army when the British offered freedom and respect to black enlistees. Almost one hundred years later more than two hundred thousand blacks answered Lincoln's desperate call when the Union's fortunes of war were at low tide, "the supply of white manpower having slackened." According to Catton, one Union general, when learning of Lincoln's recruitment plans, was so incensed he declared, "I think it is a disgrace to the army to make soldiers of them." While visiting the Petersburg battleground where black soldiers "took six of the sixteen guns captured," Lincoln confided to Grant that he "was opposed on nearly every side when I first favored the raising of colored regiments." He was happy that he had done so because "they have proved their efficiency." In the account of Lincoln's visit to the front by General Horace Porter, Lincoln was "mobbed and worshipped" by black troops.

In the view of many commentators, these black volunteers of the 54th Massachusetts and other units made the difference in the war. In spite of atrocities committed by Confederate forces against black Union troopers such as the Fort Pillow Massacre, even a Confederate (Robert E. Lee) general wanted to enlist blacks, "guaranteeing in return freedom to every slave who gave his support to the Confederacy." (According to historian Webb Garrison, a proposal supported by Jefferson Davis and Judah Benjamin—a powerful, and only, Jew to serve in Davis' cabinet—was passed by Confederate lawmakers only a month before the end of the war. Ironically, it called for the enlistment of 20,000 slaves, since the Confederacy was out of manpower except for "old men, boys, and political leaders," and did not guarantee freedom or manumission while they served. The war's end made of this "death gasp" a moot gesture.) Free African American Henry Brown's service in a Southern Carolina regiment as a drummer is the only documented case of a black serving as a "genuine" Confederate soldier. Curiously, at the rededication of his monument in his hometown of Darlington, South Carolina, in February, 1990, "a host of state and local dignitaries, as well as retired United States Army General William Westmorland and the Honorable Michael P.W. Stone, U.S. Secretary of the Army," were in attendance. Few Medal of Honor winners receive this kind of special attention!

From the Apache to the Sioux, black soldiers (Plains Indians called them Buffalo Soldiers because their "wooly" hair resembled that of the plains bison and out of respect for their fighting ability) were the key element in the subjugation of the Western Native American, a fact which even today evokes in some African Americans knowledgeable of that period, contradictory emotions. There is not necessarily any emotion of pride induced when Sioux chief and medicine man Black Elk could say that after a particular skirmish against Gen. Miles (a contest won by the Indians), that "the fourth one (slain American Soldier we exhumed looking for souvenirs) "was a black Wasichu," literally, a black white man.

On the other hand, whites employed Indians to kill Indians. William Hafford found that of thirteen native American Medal of Honor Winners from Arizona, eleven were Apache "who had been hired by General George Crook to find and subdue other Apaches." Crook was said to understand that "only an Apache could successfully fight Apaches."

Blacks have excelled in all theaters of war. Blacks *saved* Teddy Roosevelt's Rough Riders at San Juan Hill (for which they have never been properly appreciated). Like other military leaders before him who had experience with black soldiers, Roosevelt respected their fighting ability but denied their humanity. President Roosevelt declared that interracial marriage would be suicidal to the white race. Because of their reputation as fighters, according to Ron Tuch, black military units were chosen by the French to "lead the March on the Rhine" in World War I. The black 369th Infantry Regiment, respectfully nicknamed "Hell Fighters" by the French and the German enemy, led by nineteen officers, one black among them (the band director), demonstrated their toughness during the Meuse-Argonne offensive, never losing "a man captured, a trench or a foot of ground." This in spite of the extremely bigoted behavior of white soldiers and officers and a policy of official segregation.

Little discussed are the numerous instances of blacks fighting with Indians against whites; from the Seminole Wars to the battle on the Plains. Writer Terry Johnston discovered that a black army deserter, a bugler, fought with the Commanches at the famous battle at Adobe Walls in 1874.

Most Europeans, Germany excepted, have not harbored the extreme prejudice of their New World descendants. Frenchman (and Richard Wright son-in-law) Michel Fabre points out that by 1917 the French Army's black contingent consisted of "2 generals, four colonels, 150 captains, and countless lieutenants." This at a time when high American military and political leaders were proclaiming "this is a white man's war" or re-debating the fighting ability and courage of black men.

An all-black Corp of Engineers built the Alaska Highway to meet the Japanese threat in that territory. They were employed for this massive task over the strenuous objections of Alaska Army Commander General Simon Bolivar Buckner (whose Confederate general father had surrendered to Grant at Ft. Donnelson), whose antipathy toward blacks was well known. With no white troops available in 1942, Buckner had to use blacks, even as he doubted their ability to operate heavy equipment. Black troops constructed the highway in record time under some of the most extreme conditions in the world. Buckner forbade them from visiting any Native town or village believing they would "intermingle" sexually with Native women thereby causing the "inferior strain" carried by blacks to "infect" natives, producing, in his words, "an astonishingly objectionable race of mongrels." A veteran of this road-building epic said to me on a 1992 visit to Alaska that when he first heard of Buckner's characterization of blacks he didn't know what a "mongrel" was.

It was not until 50 years later—in 1992—that this remarkable accomplishment by black soldiers (it has been compared to construction of the Panama Canal) was given its due by historians and other scholars; i.e. the highway has long been applauded as an engineering wonder, only recently was the world allowed to know it was *black* soldiers (and their white officers) who built it!

Despite continuing segregation and official hesitation to use blacks in combat in World War II, the war Dover called "two wars" because it was both ideological, between Germany and the Allies, and racial, because whites defined it that way against the Japanese, African Americans continued to be proud

135

and effective fighters. Du Bois and other civil rights activists had to cajole and threaten demonstrations to get the United States government to train black airmen. Eventually, almost one thousand flight crewman were trained at Tuskegee Institute in Alabama. (There would have been more if the government had not set a quota wherein no more than 10 percent blacks could graduate of the total white pilots completing a training course in nearby Montgomery, which caused one black officer to quip that some of the blacks "flunking" the course could fly circles around graduate white pilots.) Close to five hundred of these Tuskegee trained airmen saw combat, and were so effective that the Germans called them "Black Birdmen" due to their daring skills and the fear they invoked. Black fighter pilots flying cover for bombers "never lost a bomber."

By war's end more than one million black Americans were in the nation's armed services.

Little publicized is the fact that black American troops were first to arrive at Dachau and Buchenwald concentration camps. (The all Japanese 442nd combat Infantry Regiment liberated another camp.) While Jews of the postwar years and the American press have all but ignored this contribution, the black liberators "were recognized by the concentration camp victims as playing that role."

Also little acknowledged is the generally pliable manners and personal conduct of the African American soldier during all the nation's wars. Already noted is the absence of treason and desertion in their ranks. Little publicized is the fact that until Vietnam, blacks, while recognizing and discussing among themselves the glaring contradictions in fighting wars "to save the world for democracy" while being denied democratic rights at home, have made better soldiers, they have taken orders better and brought to the military environment a more pleasant manner and attitude. What artist Frederick Remington observed on "A Scout with the Buffalo Soldiers," during the Indian campaigns has been the black soldier's general manner through the years:

> They may be tired and they may be hungry but they do not see fit to augment their misery by finding fault with everybody and everything...officers have often confessed to me that when they are on long and monotonous field service and are troubled with a depression of spirits, they have only to go about the campfires of the Negro soldier in order to be amused and cheered by the clever absurdities of the men.

The closing years of the Vietnam conflict ushered in dynamic changes in attitudes among black soldiers, particularly the draftees. But even with resentment over conditions "back home," black soldiers continued to show exemplary conduct on the battlefield, however. North Vietnamese prisoners said they always knew when black soldiers were in action against them. "Bloods" would "throw everything they could get their hands on—grenades, tear gas, anything...," and "they (NVA) feared the black soldier more than the white, because the black soldier fought more fiercely, with more abandonment."

The black draftee in Vietnam was a new phenomenon and changed the social scenario between the races. Muhammad Ali's dramatic declaration that he would not be drafted for religious reasons and that, anyway, the Vietcong never called him nigger (implying that his fight was in America not Vietnam); the Black Power Movement, which affected large numbers of young streetwise blacks who would make up the bulk of black combat draftees; and a generally heightened political awareness of a new black G.I. Combined with the dissension within the entire American citizenry over participation in Vietnam (some Americans never forgave Jane Fonda for going to North Vietnam—"giving aid and comfort to the enemy", others still praise her), and the representation within the ranks of white servicemen of a group already disdainful of blacks in general and the Civil Rights Movement in particular, a potentially explosive racial situation was at hand. One black grunt was quoted as saying, "Hey, I got a M-16 too, so I know ain't nobody gonna call me nigger." Incidents such as the documented case of a black grunt risking his life to pull a wounded comrade out of the line of fire only to be taunted repeatedly by the rescued "Put me down, nigger," did much to intensify an already bad state of affairs.

More than the generally negative portrayal of blacks in the highly acclaimed and successful film *Platoon,* episodes in *Tour of Duty* clearly show the tension and stress induced by the race issue. The black led *Anderson Platoon* was almost forgotten in the rush to praise Stone's production. Further, black vets from the unit on which the movie is based roundly criticized its many distortions and racism. Interestingly, the "racist right" represented by the tabloid *The Thunderbolt: The White Man's View,* also did not like it claiming that the film's chief villain "is not the Red Viet Cong" but white Southerners like Sgt. Barnes. In this writer's view, though a bigot Barnes was a fair and effective platoon NCO. The acting in this role should have won an Academy Award.

Black journalist Wallace Terry's *Bloods* poignantly captures the spirit of black combat fighters who were not only disturbed about having to fight a war against other people of color but who, unlike Remington's Buffalo Soldiers, were not so pliable and accepting of racist acts as were so (too) many of previous generations. As one black grunt summed up the shared sentiment of many others, "It was depressing to be several thousand miles from home and getting blowed up fighting communism when maybe I shouldn't have been here." Army unit Commander Lanning relates how one black trooper, even in the face of being labeled a coward by other blacks, absolutely refused to return to the field, saying, simply, "It ain't my war." Another contributing factor to the discontent among black and white troops when compared to World War II was that in Vietnam the average age of combat soldiers was nineteen; in the "Big War" it was twenty-six.

In Vietnam as in the civilian sector back home some whites in positions of authority practiced racial exclusion. Rear echelon assignments were rare for blacks. Some elite unit commanders didn't want African Americans in their commands. Mangold and Penycate tell the story of a white sergeant who, out of prejudice against blacks, "would allow none to be appointed as tunnel rats." In the same way that Randolph Hearst closed his newspaper empire to black employment (not readership!), here in Vietnam they were denied the (dubious) opportunity to take part in an important field of military work. (That SGT. Batten accepted Hispanics as tunnel rats is instructive and may well point to the direction of future white/black/Hispanic relations in America.) As noted previously, no blacks were awarded the Medal of Honor during WW I or II. Blacks have never in fact been awarded medals in proportion to their deeds of valor and courage. New York Congressman Dioguardi has introduced legislation to "correct this longstanding oversight."

On the other side of the coin, blacks were sometimes picked for certain duty assignments because they *were* most hazardous. Point men in *Tour of Duty* are almost always black. Famed photojournalist Gordon Park's son noted how during his 'Nam tour "Negroes and Puerto Ricans" were handpicked to serve as Forward Observers (FO's), a "hairy business". That blacks were exposed to life threatening situations at a greater rate than whites is reflected in casualty rates. While only ten percent of total Americans involved in the war, *Frontline* reported in a 1987 program that blacks constituted 23 percent of total casualties.

As already noted, reservations about the "justice" of the war, concern about conditions at home, and racism in the ranks did not alter the tradition of black courage and patriotism. One black marine said he fought because though he "knew Americans were prejudiced, were racist, and all that, but, basically, I believed in America 'cause I was an American." The psychiatrist Glasser saw them in his hospital wards, the ones who came in physically or mentally scarred but who wanted to get back to their units. William Pelfrey, author of *Hamburger Hill,* called them "that proud group who had an even tougher time trying to rationalize being where they were than did the other grunts." One black Marine told Mark Baker that he was proud of his blackness "but I also had pride in being a marine." Baker told the story of how a former black Muslim had fought to stay out of the "white man's war" but once inducted and sent to 'Nam "became the most ruthless and vicious killer." The grunt reported that "all of a sudden I wasn't the black Muslim revolutionary anymore. I became one of the group." Like the NVA prisoners, Glasser captures the fighting spirit of black Vietnam combatants. In a "diagnosis" of a casualty:

> Fighting, for him, was a part of living. The strong won out, and the weak went under. That was all there was to it. Of course there was suffering, but that was the price you paid.

High spirits as a fighting man *and* as a black man brought mixed consequences to African American G.I.s. A sense of one's blackness often meant a willingness to challenge conventional military decorum which historically has consisted of large amounts of racism. Such blacks, in and out of service, are seen as "militants" or "radicals" with "chips on their shoulders." One consequence for many black G.I.s is "bad paper," dishonorable or bad conduct discharges. As in World War II, according to Christian Science Monitor correspondent Harvey, "minority servicemen were often punished for standing up for the very rights they were fighting to preserve."

A more positive assessment suggests that blacks no longer felt compelled to suppress their cultural heritage in the presence of whites. Indeed, in *Platoon* and *Tour of Duty* the Motown Sound was prominent. Black use of the denigrating self-deprecating "nigger" when referring to other blacks began to be used in the presence of whites by some black grunts. One told a companion from a middle class upbringing, who had criticized such usage, that what blacks said to each other around whites mattered not in the least in white thinking about blacks. "These chucks," he said, "man, it don' matter you sound white on white like they want. They still gone think you a nigger." And reassuring whites that you have no design on "their women" and have no desire to move into "their neighborhoods" would not matter either.

Yet this same streetwise black grunt saw military service as a good life for blacks. To him such duty was the "best years of life for a Bro. Man. Here you be fed. You carry the biggest gun on the block. All you be asked is be ready to be the baddest nigger on the block. What be better than that?" Lest the young man's thinking be deemed simplistic and inconsequential, authors Bunch and Cole add that he had a way of viewing whites, learned from his dope dealing mentor, that was as sane as the white major's, who "was a born paranoiac," the authors adding that "In combat, believing that someone is hunting you with intent to kill is very, very sane." And that is precisely the thinking of the young grunt. He further instructs the middle class grunt "every one of these Charlies want to kill us…So the rule I learn, and I be trying to teach you, is live yo' life like you be a big black submarine. Submarines only end up fucked when they come up for air." (The informed among us are aware that with modern electronic warfare equipment, submerged subs are indeed vulnerable to sub-surface attack as well as traditional depth charges. Yet the grunt's point of understanding one's position in relation to a clear and present danger and developing a strategy for dealing with it is well taken.)

Relations between black and white service people have never been perfect, in any period of our history. Black writers such as the late John O. Killens (*And Then We Heard The Thunder*) and John A. Williams (*Captain Blackman*) have explored the divisiveness and counterproductive racism within the ranks of the military. Much of the violence that occurred between black and white soldiers in both World Wars has been officially suppressed and the files sealed by official Washington. Suffice it to say that many pitched battles were fought, sometimes with so many dead and wounded that entire units had to be disbanded or reorganized. The attrition of officers due to "friendly fire" in Vietnam was greater than in all other wars combined.

Whatever the state of relations between black and white service persons, no one questions the fact that military service is one of the few non-sports, non-entertainment areas of American life where blacks, men and increasingly women, have been able to advance. And as Joint Chiefs of Staff head Colin Powell told a *Black Issues in Higher Education* interviewer in 1990, opportunities in military services will continue to outstrip it's civilian competition for the simple reason that the modern military establishment has a system that denies to the racially biased opportunity and leverage. Powell adds that "I think if you compare us against any other segment in American society we would come in number one, and it will get better over time."

Over strenuous objections from most segments of the white community, Truman's reluctant order abolishing segregation spawned a vast arena of opportunities. It was a blockbuster decision. Near the mid-point of World War II American government and military leaders were agonizing over black demands for equality. And not knowing how to handle the situation. Secretary of War Stimson called it the "explosive" race problem; John Dover reported that General Marshall, in a confidential report to news reporters, said he "would rather handle everything that the Germans, Italians and Japanese can throw at me, than to face the trouble I see in the Negro Question." In this light, Truman's 1948 executive order is even more courageous.

Blacks have taken advantage of the opportunities desegregation opened up. Numerous studies and the comments of black service people attest to this progress. One study concluded that "moving up the career ladder" had been for blacks phenomenally successful in the armed services, far surpassing anything "in any other major sector of American society." Gen. Marshall himself would, hopefully, be proud to know that a black has served as National Security Advisor to a president and later became Chairman of the Joint Chiefs of Staff. He would probably also like Gen. Powell's credo"

> Success is the result of perfection, hard work, learning from failure, loyalty to those for whom you work, and persistence.

He might also be proud that numerous black enlisted men serve as command sergeants major, one of whom said on his retirement, "Anybody with any desire and determination at all can be a success in America...You just got to go out and get it."

Like other groups in American society, African Americans know a good thing when they see it, and, like water in physics, follow the line of least resistance (or greater reward). Black enlistment and re-enlistment far exceed their proportion in the general population. Moskos reports that as of fall 1985 blacks constituted 13 percent of Navy enlisted personnel, 17 percent of Air Force, 20 percent Marine Corps, and 30 percent Army. In 1982 almost half of "qualified" black youngsters enlisted in the armed forces compared to 14 percent of white youths. It is instructive that the Navy continues to lag behind other services, even the Marine Corps, it's "sister" branch and a traditional nemesis of blacks. So much so that in 1988 the Department of the Navy launched a two year study to find out why there are so few black officers and why blacks are more subject to courts martial and other disciplinary action than whites. Forty years after Truman's executive order. The answer, as any objective survey would have to show, is the continuing use of race within the Navy as a criterion for much that involves blacks. The Navy's 1933 order barring blacks from all but menial steward positions birthed a bitter legacy.

Black youth realize their options in civilian life for development and advancement are much more circumscribed than those of their white counterparts, and they have been quick to seize military opportunities. They are aware, from recruiting posters and hand-me-down knowledge, that the new GI Bill opens up educational opportunities they would not otherwise have access to, particularly at a time when the nation's colleges and universities are de-emphasizing minority, certainly black enrollment. They know there are four star generals like Bernard Randolph and Colin Powell and that a black woman heads the Army Nurse Corps and that a black man served as commandant of West Point. So it is possible, they imagine, to go all the way to the top!

Black women have not taken a back seat in this development. The Nurses Corp is not the only service unit to have black female representation. *Black Enterprise* magazine reports that between 1974 and 1984 black female representation rose from 16.9 percent to 28.9 percent with the Army leading at 42 percent. Black female Brigadier General Sherron Cadorva of the Provost Marshall Corps, told *Christian Science Monitor's* Luix Overbea that "Black women can succeed beyond expectations in the military services." What they do is reflected in the fact that in 1980 more than half of the white female service personnel did not complete their three year enlistment while only 34 percent of black women terminated early. In the Persian Gulf War (Operation Desert Storm), a black female officer commanded a Patriot missile platoon that destroyed two Iraqi Scuds; another won a Bronze Star for heroism.

Amy Merkel makes a strong case when in a letter to the editor of the Burlington, Vermont, *Free Press,* she stated that "the military is fast becoming the only means of survival for an increasing number of minorities in this country."

> "…we as soldiers in a foreign country especially during wartime get along like brothers. We fight in another country and be buddy-buddy, and come back here and cut each other's throat."
> *And Brave Men Too,* 1985

The Military Takes on Racial Prejudice

Racism has always been a problem in the military services. Long before integration, as was noted previously in Dover's comments, our war with Nazi Germany was over ideology, while with Japan we made it a racial war. Dover further noted that "It is virtually inconceivable…that teeth, ears, and skulls could have been collected from German or Italian war dead (as they were from Japanese)" and later, Vietnamese, "without provoking an uproar." That the same racism was present in Vietnam showed in collecting ears and other "souvenirs" from enemy dead and from how most white soldiers viewed *all* Vietnamese. A young grunt, in a letter to his parents:

"A Vietnamese remains a 'gook' no matter whose side he's on even if they have clean towns, nice cars, TV sets, and western clothes."

The strong prejudice for other non-white peoples by white Americans may have been, and certainly will be in an increasingly interdependent world where non-whites, especially the Japanese, are able to play economic and political kingmakers, of concern to some military brass. Of far greater immediate import was the potentially woeful consequences evolving from internal racial dissension. If Vietnam proved unwise militarily and politically, the experience, what Basil Heard called our first "integrated war," moved Pentagon officials, however belatedly, to address the Race Question for the first time in a systematic, aboveboard manner. A major step was the institution of mandatory human relations training and compulsory attendance for officers at observances such as those put on for the Martin Luther King, Jr. holiday. As a resident of Alaska, which has more military personnel per capita than any other state, the writer has on occasion visited military installations and witnessed the high level of participation of white as well as black officers (and black enlisted personnel, of course) in several of those observances.

Responding to my puzzlement at the presence of the highest ranking white officers, black officer friends have said "they have to be here; they've been ordered to." Moskos reports that more than a decade ago officer and non-commissioned officer efficiency reports were modified to include a section on "race relations skills." Those who did not pass muster on this "test" were mustered out, with many white officers "relived of command." Moskos adds that "today one is more likely to hear racial jokes in a faculty club than in an officer's club. And in an officer's club one will surely see more blacks." Perhaps the most effective tool of insuring greater fairness and equity in the Armed Forces was adoption of "EEO" as one of three principal criteria (the others being loyalty and honesty) for evaluating officer effectiveness.

Part of the military's human relations thrust is the use of black role models. Television commercials and other recruiting mediums always show blacks along with other minorities and whites, many of the blacks in positions of authority or high interest fields such as aircraft pilots. Vietnam psychiatrist Glasser recognized the "healing" effect of black role models when he demurred at giving his black ward master permission to return to his old combat unit. Glasser asks, "What if you get lit up?...You know how important you are to the ward, Harold. The blacks need you there. They need to see a black face in charge." The Air Force's permission for an all black crew of twenty to fly a C-5A Galaxy mission acknowledges the influence of role models. According to the aircraft commander, "the purpose is to symbolize and commemorate the continuing commitment of black Americans to meeting our nation's worldwide defense commitment and the role blacks are playing in the international arena."

With all the progress the armed services have made in the utilization of African Americans, all is not well even here. Black sociologist Andrew Billingsly, while acknowledging progress made, points out that blacks are "grossly under-represented in the officer ranks." The National urban League's 1987 *State of*

Black America underscored this observation by noting that few blacks "hold policy-making positions in either civilian or military sector."

While there is much evidence to support the contention that continuing racial discrimination inhibits the advancement of blacks, other factors also play a role. One such factor, according to a black army officer friend, is that far too many black officers simply do not have the motivation to strive for the positions which are known to be jumping off points for higher rank. In infantry units for instance, it is the officer who commands field platoons and companies who later become higher grades. Supply, entertainment, education, maintenance, and other support functions are necessary but are of low value in the promotional scheme of things. Moreover, she adds, too many blacks want the nine-to-five work routine and disdain the long hours and difficult personnel situations with which line officers have to contend. She also has found too many young black officers "cocky" and "heady" and unwilling to listen to old-timers and develop mentoring relationships that are needed no less in the armed services than in other sectors of the work world. Another senior black officer remarked that young "brown bars" (2nd Lt.) tell him he "can't do anything for them"! Because of these self-imposed limitations and the downturn in interest across the nation in civil rights issues, her long term prediction is that at some point in the not too distant future America will have an armed service with few black officers and a predominately minority enlisted complement. Like the 54th Massachusetts and the 369th Infantry Regiment, it will be a white led though black (and Hispanic) dominated military.

Whatever the eventual makeup of the military services, all of American society would do well to heed Gen. Patton's comments on receiving his first contingent of black troops:

> "Well, men, I'm happy to have you here. I don't care what color you are as long as you kill those s.o.b.'s in the green suits."

So long as the door of opportunity for good careers remain more accessible in the military services than in other sectors of American life, African Americans will continue to be represented in large numbers. General Marshall's "Negro question" has not been resolved, however, and in any future war involving large numbers of draftees there is great likelihood that black and white American service people will again engage in pitched, often armed struggles among themselves. And it is very likely that the battles will be far more serious than anything we have seen to date.

While Marshall's "Negro question" awaits final resolution, there is simply no way to overstate the advances blacks have made in military service. Any reader of retired Air Force General Benjamin O. Davis, Jr.'s autobiography (*Benjamin O. Davis, Jr.: American*) has to be astounded at the progress made. West Point cadet Davis suffered through four years of the "silence treatment" where no other cadet would speak to him, he had to room alone, was shunned at the dining table, and denied all the social perks occurring to this select group of young men. That he could survive at all, only speaking to the superintendent and other managers of the academy as they called him in from time to time to ask of his progress (more accurately to see if he were breaking under the pressure) is a testament to the strength of human will. His story, too, should be celebrated in song and poem.

"Rightsizing" the military during the 1990's, post—Desert Storm, ushered in a new era of relations. The blatant fraud committed by the Army against Lt. Flipper, the despicable treatment of Johnson Whittaker, another early black West Point Cadet (who "was found beaten, mutilated, and tied to his bed," then charged with "staging the beating in an attempt to get out of an exam"), the unforgivable inhumanity meted out to Benjamin O. Davis, Jr. (and his father for that matter), along with other racist acts too numerous to count, will not, probably, be the principal stratagem this time around. Rather, what individuals like Willie Hightower (who heads a private investigation company) hears as he travels the U.S. military installations around the world responding to cries of "help" from black military personnel, are situations—only a few of which are publicized—where blacks are being harassed to the point of forced retirement or resignation, or "bad paper" discharges. No rank is safe: a military friend tells me how a general rank black officer is hounded "in a thousand little ways by military and civilian subordinates," so much so that the Inspector General had to step in; at Ft. Rucker, Alabama, *Jet* reported, a black doctor thought white by other soldiers, is harassed by whites up and down the ranks when a marries a black woman—also an officer—even when he issues disclaimers that he is not white. *His* job was threatened.

Despite Colin Powell's appointment and other advancement, that the military services is far from having achieved equal opportunity for African Americans was reflected in comments made by the Marine Corps Commandant when asked about allegations of discrimination against blacks (and other minorities) in selection for flight training and promotion. Minorities were not well represented, the general told *CBS 60 Minutes* in January 1994, because they couldn't swim as well, read a compass as well, or see as well, as whites. This in contradiction to statements by more than a dozen witnesses who claimed first-hand experience or knowledge of the discrimination.

The litany goes on. Many black military personnel, seeing no resource within the service and acknowledging the predictable damage to their careers, have taken their cases to civil rights groups and congress and the Willie Hightowers. Without strong interventionist tactics from military leaders, the American public should expect increased physical bloodletting around *race,* in particular white attempts to drive blacks out and the latter's reactions.

After attending the June 14, 1992 Pentagon ceremony belatedly—very—honoring black soldiers, one of the vets, during a post-ceremony briefing at the hotel, noted that the Military Hall of Heroes had permanent displays of all groups save African Americans. There were large sealed cases for Hispanic Medal of Honor Winners, Women (white), and Asians. The oversight, if that it be, is unforgiveable. Also noted by a veteran looking on, who had served with Patton was, the Army's acquiescence to movie makers showing white troops in

The Red Ball Express when those support troops were in fact black. Same with Ted Turner's 1994 film *Geronimo*.

Without internal policing and external vigilance, the military of the early 21st century will have reverted back to a same racial battleground.

The Black Professional Athlete

"White people have to have white heroes…I, myself, can't relate to black heroes. I'll be truthful—I respect them, but I need white people. It's in me."
National Basketball Association Team Owner.

This chapter is dedicated to all the black men who, through sports and through ballgames in particular, symbolically are recapturing "the balls"—for that is also a part of the struggle. They are forcing the oppressors of black people up against the psychological wall and, thereby, heightening the contradiction.
Dr. Frances Cress Welsing, "Ball Games as Symbols: The War of the Balls" (August 1976) in the *ISIS Papers: The Key to the Colors,* 1991 Edition

Certain professional sports—namely, baseball, boxing, football, and basketball—have been good *to* blacks. Whether they have been bad *for* blacks is one of the questions explored in this section.

As with careers in the armed services blacks have sought out professional athletics both as a way of circumventing the barriers often found in other career paths and because big dollars and personal glory await those who reach the top. It is well to remember, however, as fitness expert and professor of physical education Tom Wells has written in response to Jimmy "The Greek" Snyder's remarks about the "laziness" of white athletes accounting for their poor showing in the pros, whites don't have to see sports as *the* solution to personal ambition because "Our culture just offers them more attractive motivators outside of sports than it offers to the black athlete."

Why Sports?

The lure of glory and big money for little apparent effort (an erroneous belief shared by many whites) has made certain sports almost a way of life in black communities. Basketball, for example, has become so popular that, unlike white suburban neighborhoods where in homes with sons a backboard over the garage door is as common as the two cars in the driveway (John Paxson, hero of the final game in the 1993 NBA Championship series, told reporters that his winning 3-point shot was a shot he had "practiced hundreds of thousands of times in my driveway growing up." 6/20/93), the sport virtually permeates *all* aspects of living. In large cities the school playground substitutes for the driveway (producing better *team* players in the process). Black youngsters "eat

145

and sleep" the game often to the tragic neglect of other areas of their lives such as school work. Nor can they be convinced that only a handful out of those hundreds of thousands aspirants will reach the level of a Magic Johnson or an Isaiah Thomas. (The late Arthur Ashe told CBS 60 Minutes that the country has only 3000 total professional athletes of which only 300 are black.) Black teens have fought, and sometimes killed, over a pair of prized tennis shoes.

The attraction of certain professional sports is more complicated than the hypothetical racism of other fields of work. That racism exists is unquestioned; but drawing a line between its existence and the decisions isolated inner city youth appear to make is an unclear proposition. Put another way, black young-sters hear about racism all the time but it is questionable whether that form of knowledge or information impacts on their inclination towards certain activities. A more plausible explanation may be that since most of their life's activity centers around physical activity, principally athletics but also simply moving around the neighborhood—hanging out, and since few black role models pursuing other careers are seen in the home, community or on television, it logically follows that many would be lured towards big-time professional athletics.

What Do (or Can) They Give Back?

The issue of black professional athletes' contribution to the black community is an interesting one. And the perspective I take is probably an unpopular one. Because professional athletics have acted as lures (illusions) to too many young impressionable black youngsters who wind up with broken lives partly as a result of following, like fish, the "shiny bait," professional athletes cannot, in my opinion, be judged as good for the black community. Moreover, even while public excellence justifiably induces a sense of pride in being black and in individual black athletes, even here, as we shall see, white backlash (reminis-cent of the disappearance of the black jockey) is again beginning to close the door of opportunity to blacks looking for careers in professional sports. Finally, only in a minority of cases do black athletes earning big dollars come out on top when their professional careers are over. Poor education and lack of budget management skills, unscrupulous and charlatan business agents, and living in the "fast lane" all contribute to the rapid economic decline of many black professional athletes, ending where they began, poor and black. Black young-sters should remember the star Miami Dolphin running back, the gold tooth-pick pitcher for the then New York Giants, the Giant Hands basketball player, and on and on. These are only the more celebrated of the many rags-to-riches back-to-rags cases. The Wilt Chamberlains, Jim Browns, and Muhammad Alis are the exceptions.

Even those who beat the odds are often snared by other forces which limit their ability to transfer athletic achievement to success in the "larger" world. The career of Jesse Owens and Joe Louis illustrate the point. As a twenty-two year old, Ohio State University student, Owens won four gold medals in track and field at the 1936 Olympics in Berlin. Adolph Hitler, in attendance at the games and hoping for an "Aryan" sweep of medals, after witnessing Owens' record breaking feats, made a hasty and deliberate exit from the stadium shunning the customary personal congratulations extended to winners. Owens, a devoted family man who walked the straight and narrow and who had hoped to parley his athletic conquests into post-track success (as did white champions), met with insurmountable odds. Chris Mead writes that "to convert his fame and popularity into money, Owens had to sell more than his time and energy. He tap-danced...on tour with Eddie Cantor...and raced...against horses and trains."

The rags-to-riches-back-to-rags phenomenon is seen in the career of Joe Louis. Raised in an Alabama sharecropper family, Louis rose to prominence as an adored heavyweight boxing champion. As the twentieth-century's second black champion he eschewed the role played by predecessor Jack Johnson: brash; flashy dresser; unapologetic in refusing to observe racial ethics including consorting publicly with white women; outspoken. Nevertheless, Louis' career ended no better than Johnson's as he wound up, during the last years of his life, using his head as a rubbing post (he greeted patrons) at a Las Vegas Casino.

A further question is the quality of the contribution professional black athletes make to the larger black community. From the evidence, it appears that only a minority can really afford to make significant financial contributions to black economic and social organizations. Business owned by black athletes and located in black communities tend to make no profound impact in the life of those communities. Pride of achievement in professional sports, without similar results from the broad spectrum of careers, is a hollow achievement. Few black pros have formed joint ventures in such a way that their combined resources can be put to use in mainstream corporate America. It must be admitted at the same time that the business successes of football Hall of Fame's Willie Davis, basketball's Julius "Dr. J." Erving, Michael Jordan and Wilt Chamberlain, and baseball's Joe Morgan, while representative of an insignificant minority, do offer hope that post-career success is possible. (In 1994 Joe Morgan won a substantial settlement in a brutality suit against white L.A. police officers.)

Actor and ex-football star Jim Brown's National Negro Industrial and Economic Union (N.N.I.E.U.) was the most serious effort in African American history to use the talent and financial resources of black (and other) professional athletes as a means of capitalizing small black business. At one point as many as one hundred black athletes—including stellar names like Lew Alcindor (late Kareem Abdul-Jabbar) were actively involved. The demise of such groups, as of the economic arm of the Nation of Islam and Garvey's various business enterprises, were dim stars never reaching their potential, and raising serious questions about prospects, for viable self-help economics.

Will the Dominance End?

There is reason to believe that even in those sports where blacks dominate on the court or playing field, that very dominance may be by mid twenty-first century a thing of the past—again! Chris Mead has pointed out that blacks were in professional sports shortly after the mid-nineteenth century, in baseball by 1872, and dominated the jockey ranks, winning thirteen Kentucky Derbys between 1875 and 1904. After 1887 there were no black professional baseball players in the major leagues until Jackie Robinson; and black jockeys literally disappeared from horse racing after 1911 "when the old-timers left."

The modern day version of the demise of the professional black athlete is premised on two sets of facts, both of which are grounded in America's continuing racial hostility to its African American citizens. The first concerns the college scene from which some (in baseball) and almost all (in football and basketball) professional athletes matriculate. Although dominated by blacks, boxing involves a small fraction of athletes, none of whom come from the college ranks.

Most American colleges and universities that have significant athletic programs belong to the National Collegiate Athletic Association. The NCAA issues rules and guidelines under which its various member sports can be accredited and remain in good standing. To violate a rule, such as those governing recruiting, is to face censure and possible probation. In 1984 the NCAA promulgated a new rule—Proposition 48—which defined the conditions under which a college athlete could participate in a sport. Essentially what the new rule did was to redefine academic performance for athletes such that if they performed below a "cutoff" score on standardized tests, they were ineligible to participate in NCAA approved athletic competition.

Predictably, this proposal was met with outrage by many white athletic coaches and administrators and virtually all segments of the black community. White coaches Holtz and Osborne said the new requirements were "culturally biased and will affect blacks far more than whites." The president of the Educational Testing Service, which administers the test (SAT) said it would discriminate against blacks, and added, "if the requirement had been in effect in 1981, 51 percent of all black freshmen would not have qualified for athletic competition at NCAA Division I institutions." Black college president Joseph Johnson called the rule "racist" and remarked that it was "instituted by racist people intent on denying black kids an education." As a group black college presidents termed the proposition "potentially racist" designed to "reduce the number of blacks on teams of institutions with major sports programs." Writing in the *Crisis* magazine, well known activist and World Council of Churches leader Charles Cobb called it "racially motivated" and will "effectively remove large numbers of superior black athletes from collegiate...competition."

Despite the objections of all the historically black colleges and the protests of several major college white coaches, the proposition passed. And it achieved the intended aim: Of athletes signing letters of intent in 1986, 175 blacks were ineligible compared to only 25 whites. *Black Issues in Higher Education* labeled these "*Proposition 48 casualties.*" In 1987 the *Washington Post* reported that of the 30 athletes selected for its all-metropolitan football and boy's basketball teams, nine did not qualify for collegiate athletics under Proposition 48. All nine were black.

In 1989 another restrictive proposal—Proposition 42—was announced by the NCAA. It would go even further in reducing black participation. This proposition was adopted by the NCAA in early 1992. Black basketball coaches boycotted a 1993 NCAA meeting, taking their grievances to the Congressional Black Caucus in 1994 and threatening to boycott a game.

The point here is not to condemn "stricter academic standards," for surely most Americans agree that too many of our schools sorely need them. (When only 25 percent of black male college athletes were graduating by 1991, there is serious trouble for the 75 percent who didn't graduate at all levels of the educational enterprise.) Indeed, some public school systems, including the city of Los Angeles, have opted for tougher academic standards for students wishing to participate in *any* extracurricular activity. No matter the public explanation for Proposition 48 (and 42), however, fewer black professional athletes will be seen in coming years. Whether racially motivated or not, the result is the same. Douglas Lederman reported in July 1992 that blacks were getting a greater proportion of scholarships though their "overall enrollment lags at Division I colleges," which is to say fewer students, with aid to more of their number. By 1993 Proposition 48 resulting in more than half (56 percent) of white athletes graduated followed far behind (32 percent) by blacks, according to Steve Wieberg in a report for *USA Today.*

The other factor in the equation of black demise in professional athletics is the intense recruitment presently underway to bring "international" players into big-time American sports. That racism, at least in part, accounts for the greatness of a Larry Bird or Kevin McHale (white sports writer Rob Ryan believes that "It is naive to contend that Bird and McHale, as great as their athletic skills may be, possess a market value based solely on their basketball ability") now compels team owners to seek them—White Hopes—abroad since it is clear that the home grown crop is neither interested in or has the ability to provide the "heroes white people need." (That even young whites feel this "need" was dramatically illustrated at a college basketball game when a youthful, possibly seven or eight year old, white fan seated next to the author on one side, turned to ask his parents "Why doesn't our team have white players like the other team?") One must ask why, if, as Atlanta Hawk general manager Stan Kasten claimed, professional basketball is becoming international, (thus his recruitment abroad) are only European countries—Italy, Greece, Spain—the favored recruiting areas? It does not take a genius to decipher that one! So, as in many other walks of life where the "tipping" point has been reached in black numbers, ability or merit is out and color is in again. In July 1993, coming off three (3-Peat) consecutive NBA championships, and after "a three-year court-ship," the Chicago Bulls signed Toni Kuboc (the 'Magic of Europe') to a long-term multi-million dollar contract. Political Correctness wins again!

Thus, as Feinsilber argues, blacks hoping to enter professional athletics have obstacles beyond skill to contend with. Even though "certain positions are reserved for whites," and blacks who do make it "must be better than white players to succeed; for many race, not merit will determine whether they get in at all. The author recalls watching a professional basketball game with a white couple (friends) when, as if on cue, the wife exclaimed "I wish there was another league for smaller players." This echoed a comment by another white friend who said he thought hockey was "rougher" than football! My middle school age son has often remarked how his white classmates say to him that "hockey is rougher than football." The racism in these comments is so subtle that even their owners would deny it if confronted. This unconscious racism is no less real than that of the white club owner who said he *needed* players who looked like him, or for the white amateur basketball referee who responded to a high ranking black Army officer's (and former coach) insistent complaint that his son was being unfairly called for fouls, that he treated his son different because he had more talent than the other—predominately white—players.

Time magazine, in a cover story, reported on Mets pitcher Dwight Gooden: "In a bountiful pitching crop, there is good, very good, and Gooden," but white fans in Massachusetts still rioted and attacked black fans when their favored Boston Red Sox, known for hiring few black players, were the losers.

Blacks have to understand that the issue of the White Hope is more compli-cated than simply a matter of race. There is also economics. Dwindling atten-dance by loyal white fans will make the most liberal owner look for drastic measures. What Bob Ryan called "racism among (white) fans" has moved teams to concoct all kinds of schemes: leaving downtown; recruiting white "interna-tional" players; maintaining a certain percentage of white players in the lineup; and, according to Pirates Chief Scout Howie Hoak, tacitly permitting racist fans, as in Boston Garden, to literally hound black fans away with racial slurs and even violence. Ryan comments that Boston fans even direct racial slurs at their *own* black players. And anyone, black or white, who's ever attended a Celtic or Red Sox game can attest to the shameful racial intolerance of many white fans.

Racial tolerance is not promoted when leaders of the sports world add their own bigoted comments to the atmosphere. One can perhaps understand early sportswriters casting racial stereotypes. Joe Louis' biographer Chris Mead writes of what one had to say about Louis:

> There isn't an ounce of killer in him. Not the slightest zest for fighting. He's a big, superbly built Negro youth who was born to listen to jazz music, eat a lot of fried chicken, play ball with the gang on the corner, and never do a lick of heavy work he could escape. The chances are he came by all those inclinations quite naturally.

What that sportswriter apparently did not understand was that, following

Jack Johnson, who "had openly flouted the conventions of segregated America," and "confirmed the worst stereotypes of black behavior," and at a time when even pairing a black and white boxer "was a venture into the unknown, a social gamble and a financial risk," Louis had been carefully coached about proper conduct in and out of the ring... Above all, he was to refrain from liaisons with white women, most certainly in public (although it was reported that a white woman had *private* lessons and furnished Louis with a new automobile each of the seven years they saw each other), and he must never publicly savor victory over a white opponent.

In an era when science has irrefutably debunked theories of inherent racial superiority, comments by sports leaders such as Kentucky's A.B. "Happy" Chandler, the ex-Dodger Vice President Campinas, and ex-CBS sports Commentator Jimmy "the Greek" Snyder, are almost unforgivable, in the opinion of many African Americans. But there is a flipside in defense of all three: Knowledgeable blacks are aware of the contributions all have made in helping integrate American athletics, and, in Chandler's case, higher education. Which simply goes to show that there is such a thing as innocent bias and that sometimes racist attitudes do not prevent a person from doing "good works." One is reminded of Spencer Tracy's role in the film *Guess Whose Coming to Dinner*? Famous blacks such as Bill Cosby and Harry Edwards have come to the defense of Campinas and Snyder. Under the circumstances their defense is appropriate.

There is no defense for Cincinnati Reds managing owner Marge Schott. Her reported comments that "I'd rather have a trained monkey working for me than a nigger," and the reference to Dave Parker and Eric Davis as "million dollar niggers," had to be challenged, censored, and punished.

In collegiate and professional athletics there is still the problem of racial attitudes within the ranks of participants, as well as low representation of blacks in management positions. A famous coach of a past top ranked professional football player was rumored to have always called his black players aside the first day of practice to read the "racial code" to them: leave white women alone, stay in your room when not on the field, go to the big city for entertainment. At a college whose best players were black, the entire contingent of fourteen black players were kicked off the team because they "wanted to wear arm bands to protest the Mormon Church's rule against having black priests." Lone black professional hockey player Ritchie Herbert is so hounded by racist players on opposing teams that his white coach "really feels for him and some of the things that have been done to him." For Herbert it's 1947 and Jackie Robinson all over again. But the coach is happy that Herbert is hanging tough and is not hearing so many "direct racial comments...anymore because he is so good."

Frank Robinson was for many years the lone black manager in professional baseball. Football is even further behind. (It is interesting that no racial connection at all was made when a Hispanic coached a major pro football team for several years.) Other sports are just as bleak. To his credit former baseball commissioner Peter Uberhoff moved swiftly to change the front office situation. Over a one year period the 20 blacks on his staff became 150, reported McNeil-Lehr. The lesson in Uberhoff's action is clear: where there is an active commitment, the job can be done. In 1992 professional sports had two black football head coaches and one baseball manager, the latter getting a "C" on Jesse Jackson's group's annual "Racial Report Card."

There is vast ignorance of the influence of race in athletics. Jackie Robinson's widow Rachel remarked about overhearing wealthy whites on her commuter train genuinely disclaiming knowledge of the "extent of racism" as they discuss various newspaper reports. Beyond the massive ignorance off the court and field, relations between black and white players are probably as bad now as they ever were. Reggie Jackson said there is an "invisible wall" and suggests it's due to social segregation where children of different racial and ethnic groups have little opportunity to interact. Closer to the truth, according to other commentators and Jackson's own subsequent statements, there is both massive fear of blacks and massive prejudice against them. Jackson's ultimate solution is to bus or otherwise integrate the races at an early age "so white kids could find out that black children can be wonderful people." Jackson and Atlanta humorist Lewis Grizzard are equally wrong in feeling that the mere presence of a common task or objective such as schooling or making music, will in itself reduce racial friction (actually, what they don't say but hope is that whites will become less bigoted).

In "One Who Was There, recalls Branch Rickey's fight for civil rights," Red Barber recounts the story of how Rickey (the man who, with rare courage, brought Jackie Robinson into big league baseball) first committed himself to civil rights.

As a college coach in 1904 Rickey encountered a talented young black player whom he took on a road trip to South Bend. Refused hotel accommodations, the player could stay in the coach's room "as long as he didn't register." When he went to check on the player -

> this fine young man was sitting on a chair, tearing at his hands, and sobbing as though his heart would break. 'It's my skin, Mr. Rickey, it's my skin...If I could just pull it off I'd be like everybody else...It's my skin, Mr. Rickey...It's my skin.

While Rickey is due enormous credit for bringing blacks into professional baseball, most Americans don't realize that it was actually Kentucky's Happy Chandler who really caused integration to happen in professional baseball. As baseball commissioner he overruled the baseball owners, all 16 of whom, except for Rickey, voted against integration. For this action Chandler lost his job. His intemperate remarks regarding blacks at the University of Kentucky should be placed in the context of his pioneering work in getting blacks into professional sports and school desegregation in the Blue Grass state.

Notes on Black Women (and Black Men)

"Oh, you women…You are always ready to go with the conquerors. You recognize nothing but power. If it is a woman, a cow, a ewe, a doe or whatever female it is—let the male fight and die for her, and the moment that he is thoroughly beaten or killed, she gives herself to his conqueror."
Zora Neal Hurston, *Moses: Man of the Mountain,* 1939

The challenge to black womanhood in the twenty-first century is to go beyond cultural prescriptions. We need to discover how we can function in an oppressive culture, change it, and live beyond mere survival. How do we make up a culture to empower ourselves as we go along? Survival is not enough. Liberation is the next step. Choice is the key to liberation. Choice is how we emancipate ourselves.
Kesho Yvonne Scott, *The Habit of Surviving*

The story of the trials and tribulations of African American women is an old one, and it has been told well by black scholars and writers and by whites such as Gerda Lerner. Over the past two decades black women writers such as Toni Morrison, Alice Walker, Toni Cade Bambara, Maya Angelou, June Jordan, the poet Nikki Giovanni, and others have given the reading public informed glimpses into the world of the black woman in a way never before witnessed. Black female poets as well as female political and business leaders have all added to the public fund of knowledge about African American women.

The purpose of this section is not to burden the reader with information already available but to offer a perspective which will shed additional light on the continuing dialogue and debate about the status of black women.

Some Good News

There is general agreement that black women are progressing in the business and professional segments of American society. Making up some 22 percent of all black elected officials by 1986, and occupying prestigious positions in many public institutions, black women have progressed far beyond the time when the bulk of their numbers (the author's mother included) were confined to cotton fields and white women's kitchens, being barred, along with black men, "from good jobs…(by) racial discrimination," according to Sara Rix. (Rix adds that in the early twentieth century married urban black women were the only group of American women "who pursued a lifetime of work outside the home.") The National Urban League's Glasgow reports that though still bedeviled in large numbers by poverty, African American female-headed households have moved from a 70 percent poverty rate in 1959 to a 53 percent rate in 1985. While that still leaves more than half in poverty, progress out of poverty has been meaningful.

An estimated one-half of black women were in the labor market in 1970; close to 60 percent were by 1985. Unfortunately, too many are still confined to low paying service jobs. Since "women will fill an estimated two-thirds of the nation's new jobs by the year 2000," Wisconsin's Project Equality reports, it is clear that employment prospects can be, but don't necessarily have to be, promising for African American women.

Glasgow also reports an interesting decline in birthrates among single and married black women, 13 percent and 38 percent respectively between 1959 and 1985; and while the general birthrate for white women continues to decline the "birth rate of unmarried white women *rose* by 27 percent" in the decade of the 1970s.

Black female progress is reflected in the success stories of women like talk show host Oprah Winfrey, called "Chicago's Television Millionairess" by *Sun Times* writer Robert Feder; Spelman College's first black female president after four white women and two black men; and eighteen of the nations 300 hundred other female college presidents; business leaders like Dorothy Brunson who owns three radio stations, and Dorothy Terrell who is Digital's Boston plant manager; Georgia's pioneering attorney Mabel Booker, "the only black lawyer with a practice in the Toombs Judicial Circuit"; and Mississippi's first black "Miss Mississippi" *and* "Mrs. Mississippi" (both in 1987).

In economics, the most promising contemporary trend among African American women is the investment club. Atlanta's Women's Investment Club, chartered in 1989, has averaged 35 percent on investments. New Jersey's Family, Inc. announced a 1991 portfolio of $2.3 million after only five years. Such self-help groups led by black women are becoming popular throughout the nation.

And Some News Not So Good

But to point to black female progress with pride is not to deny their relative lack of general progress when measured against the status of white women. Single and married black women have always worked outside the home—and not largely by choice during the generations when wives and mothers were told their "place was in the home." At the turn of the century, reports Rix, only about 20 percent of American women worked outside the home, and most of these were black women. Since 1980 that number has grown to more than half of all women. This massive movement of white women into the labor market has exacerbated the employment scene for both black women and men (which is not to *blame* white women).

Even though black women are attending college in record numbers (keeping in mind that one-half of all post-secondary black students are in two year institutions) "black women still are more likely than white women to be unemployed, underemployed, in low paying jobs, and to account for a larger proportion of those living in poverty." Glasgow says the "differential earning power of black females and white females is not only historical but continues currently," and it parallels the differential in earning power of black and white *families,* even where both parents are present, and even where black family members have more years of schooling than their white counterparts. What Darlene Hine calls the "myth that black women have it made" because they are counted twice—the "twofer myth" has blinded many to the real problems in the job market facing black women. Not one of *Black Enterprise's* "America's Hottest Black Managers" was a woman.

On the job, black women are more likely to be sexually harassed by white and black men than white women. One black woman was awarded $3.5 million by an all-white jury in a sexual harassment action. (The outcome in this case was an exception. In a significant study, McMillen discovered that when blacks sue, "they lost every case but one," compared to a 50% victory rate for white women plaintiffs.) Black women are also more likely to get the "silent treatment" from white women colleagues and be subjected to jeers and uncomplimentary comments about their intelligence and race.

Writing in the *Chronicle of Higher Education,* Karen Winkler noted that the feminist movement has forged important advances in the past two decades, so much so that by 1986 great strides had been made in "integrating the story of women into American history." Yet, "women of color" have been largely ignored, meriting only "one chapter in a women's studies book devoted to them," for instance. There is racism in the feminist movement.

As they have always done black women are fighting back, they are not obeisant to exclusion and put-downs, and they employ a variety of weapons. Barbara Gamarekian points to their emergence "from history's neglect," largely through their own scholarship. In 1944 Pauli Murray was awarded a Rosenwald scholarship to attend Harvard Law School. An admissions officer told her "your picture and the salutation on your college transcript indicate you are not of the sex entitled to be admitted to Harvard." She went on to become an important poet, lawyer, and an ordained Episcopal priest (the first woman) and Methodist bishop. Largely unappreciated by white, and oftentimes by black, public and the media, black women, from those who drowned their babies at sea rather than see them live in slavery, through Harriet Tubman and Sojourner Truth and Fannie Lou Hamer, to today's black women leaders, have been the warriors as well as the leaders. When some blacks accused her of being soft on racism in the South, novelist Zora Neale Hurston wrote, in 1942:

> I am ready for anything to overthrow Anglo-Saxon supremacy, however desperate. I have become what I never wished to be, a good hater. I no longer even value my life if by losing it, I can do something to destroy this Anglo-Saxon monstrosity.

Continuing that legacy of outrage and activism, June Jordan, writing in 1977, said:

> I think it is necessary to form or join a well-defined organization that can and will work to destroy the status quo as ruthlessly, as zealously, as nonstop in its momentum, as are the enemy's forces...

Many whites do not realize the intensity of this black rage. Those few who do marvel that blacks have not been more violently anti-white. Actor Eddie Murphy put it well in a February 1990 *Playboy* interview:

"My people are the most forgiving people on the face of the earth. To be here in this country and to be subjected to as much shit as we've been subjected to and not to have had a black revolution!...."

Having overviewed the general status of African American women, the contribution this section hopes to make to the discussion of black women revolves around two issues: the meaning of physical beauty and its social implications; and the nature of black female-black male relations. These two much discussed but little understood psycho-social issues comprise a cornerstone in the fate of the entire black community.

The Social Utility of Physical Appearance

Throughout American social history "looks", or the "appearance of things," have played a crucial role in determining how rewards are parceled out and relationships formed. However much the topic is underplayed and the notion of "merit" publicized as the prevailing standard, an individual's physical appearance—race, facial features, especially nose, eyes, and lips, hair texture, weight, etc., very often means the difference between getting what one is after and being left out in the waiting line. A story in the December 4, 1991 Fairbanks, Alaska *Daily News-Miner* is illustrative. This white welfare mother (itself rarely publicized though a majority of public assistance cases) is stranded in the bush without means of transportation though she lives in a paid for "four-bedroom comfortable log home." Interestingly, the reporter noted that "two of her blue-eyed, blond-haired toddlers crawled around in her lap", as if to suggest that these physical characteristics somehow were incongruent with the mother's plight or that some special recompense was due this family.

The reality of this informal yet powerful criterion of selection is manifested throughout the fabric of American society. Man wants the blue-eyed blond with slightly less than Dolly Parton breasts. Woman wants the tall, dark (but not Negroid dark!), handsome man. On her Christmas scroll wish list a white female branch bank manager had written "a tall, tanned, handsome man" for 1989. Secretaries are still often hired for their looks rather than their competence; and government agencies such as the FBI and CIA were long believed to favor white males of the James Bond variety.

Even though, as a black female friend pointed out, black Americans no longer as a group conform to traditional black African features—nappy hair, broad, flat noses, and thick lips (most African Americans who visit black Africa are immediately struck at the differences in physical features between themselves and their hosts), there is enough of Africa left in most of us to set us quite apart in physical appearance, even though "most of us can find a white

Southerner in (our) family tree." Interracial marriage, while relatively insignificant in proportion to all black marriages, was given impetus by the Supreme Court's 1967 decision outlawing miscegenation laws in the fourteen states that still had them. Marriage and a more significant level of interracial sexual liaison outside of matrimony account for the change in black appearance. Slavery played the larger role, with leaders like George Washington and Thomas Jefferson beginning the long parade of white men favoring black concubines. As Miles Davis told *Playboy* interviewer Alex Haley, all African Americans were originally black, very dark complexioned, "so every time you see one who is not dark there has been white gene infusion somewhere along the line."

Census Bureau found almost 2 million interracially married couples in 1990; and while such couplings involve virtually every "race" represented in America it is white female—black male relationships that get the limelight. The fact that in all but one year during the decade of the 1980s white males mated with Alaska Native females at a higher rate than these women did with Alaska Native *males* draws little attention. A popular saying in some Native cultures goes: Wherever white men have ventured the availability of Native men has dramatically decreased. The interesting and significant increase in white males and women of color matings is a story waiting to be told.

An Alaska Native leader related to me how her white father was incredulous when she informed him that she wanted to return to her people in Alaska. "I made you white," he replied, "why do you want to go back up there and live with savages." Abandoning his Native wife, he had taken the children to his own hometown when they were young. Needless to say, she did return.

Making others "white" appears to have been pursued with missionary zeal by some white males. W.E.B. DuBois biographer David Lewis noted that his subject had, in the novel *The Quest for the Silver Fleece*, targeted this phenomenon "with pistol-shot accuracy." Foreshadowing by decades the gender debates of the late twentieth century, DuBois said it was about power: "at bottom simply a matter of the ownership of women; white men want the right to own and use all women, colored and white, and they resent any intrusion of colored men into this domain."

It is an illogical irony that while white men are the most vigorous objectors to interracial sex, it is they alone who have done the most mixing, changing the color complexion of people everywhere they have gone. A college student whose trip to an Atlanta Black Men, Inc. conference in summer 1993, returned with applause for what Black Atlantans are achieving and to excitedly tell me about one workshop where the lecturer showed photos of native Hawaiians at the turn of the century. His point was the color change they had undergone from very dark to light. The same change can be found in Alaska and anywhere else white men have ventured, I assured the student.

While in America as little as 1/32 percent of "Negro blood" (the "one-drop"rule) can get one labeled black, the black population has been losing and the white group gaining thousands of "blacks" for generations. Louisiana's Susie Guillory Phipps was one of the estimated 25,000 "light-complexioned blacks (who) secretly (crossed) over into the white world every year." She simply got "caught" despite her protestations that "I'm not light...I'm white." Black novelist Ernest Gaines explored the Phipps phenomenon in his *Catherine Carmier.* A "black" woman who had been passing for white in the north returns to her family in rural Louisiana. The family, very light mulattoes except for the mother, exists in a world neither black nor white. This daughter explains to her sister why she has to take the white road:

> "That other way—I've thought about it. I've thought about it over and over. I'm not in love with it. I can't ever be. But I have no other choice. I'm not black, Cathy. I hate black. I hate black worse than the whites hate it. I have black friends, but only at a distance. I feel for my mother, but only at a distance. I don't let my black friends come close to me. I don't let her come close to me. I don't say get away. I've never said that. I just can't open my heart out to them.
>
> "I haven't opened my heart out to that white world either, but I'm going there because I must go somewhere. I can't stand in the middle of the road any longer. Neither can you, and neither can you let Nelson. Daddy and his sisters can't understand this. They want us to be Creoles. Creoles. What a joke. Today you're one way or the other; you're white or you're black. There is no in-between."

In an article entitled "A National Scandal No one Will Touch," Pulley comments that "reliable statistics" indicate that one of every five whites have "some black blood." Whites don't dare admit this genetic heritage even though they will "speak proudly of Indian ancestry," when it's convenient. Hacker notes with interest that over the two decades spanning 1970 to 1990 Americans identifying themselves as Native American rose sharply which he attributed to "a lot of people who had concealed their native origins." In my own experience in university personnel matters, at least part of this sharp increase, usually from *white* to Native American, is generated by a hope to take advantage of affirmative action programs. A university president confided as much when he said to me, "some of these (white) people claiming to be Indian have about as much right as I do to that tag." He was white and "one-eighth Indian."

Who Defines Physical Beauty?

> ...a black American with a lighter complexion has, on average, a 50 percent higher income than one with a dark complexion, even when both have similar education and occupational status and family backgrounds.
> Verna Keith and Cedric Herring, *American Journal of Sociology*, reported in *Chronicle of Higher Education*, Jan. 8, 1992

Historically (and to a significant degree today), it has been America's "light and damn near white" blacks who have reaped the greater benefits of society's perks to blacks. Today, many African Americans believe, it is the Lisa Bonets, Troy Beyers, Mario Van Peebles, and the Belafonte children—who are most attractive to white audiences and who get the plum roles not only in films and television but in many other occupations. Former Miss America Vanessa Williams as well as virtually all of the prominent black female models, like the Somali, Iman, are light of complexion and/or conform to European facial features.

So are the wives of many prominent black men. Alice Walker remarked that "the wives of virtually all black leaders...appear to have been chosen for the nearness of their complexions to white" women. Or they are white women. Malcolm X and Jesse Jackson are two prominent exceptions.

> The ideals of white beauty, when it comes to women, are so deeply inscribed in every male psyche, Black and White, that many brothers do have problems acknowledging Black beauty.
>> Cornell West to bell hooks

> Oh de white gal rides in a Cadillac,
> De yaller gal rides de same,
> Black gal rides in a rusty Ford,
> But she gets dere just de same.
>> Zora Neale Hurston, *The Sanctified Church*, 1983

The fact of the matter is that without physical characteristics acceptable to white America, and by extension to much of black America, the black female, whether in business or entertainment, will continue to be at a decided disadvantage. (Obviously there are exceptions such as Oprah Winfrey.) Prolific western fiction writer Louis L'Amour defines probably better than any contemporary American writer what physical beauty in a woman attracts the Euromale of the species:

> She had a kind of pale blond hair and skin like it never saw daylight, and blue eyes that made a man think she was the prettiest thing he ever did see.
>> *The Daybreakers*, 1960

> Laura Sackett was a strikingly pretty young woman, blonde and fragile...she seemed a pale, delicate flower, aloof, serene, untouchable.
>> *The Lonely Men*, 1969

The L'Amour definition of feminine beauty was not fictional nor confined to earlier generations or geography. Actor Kirk Douglas echoes his sentiments. Writing of one of the beautiful women in his life, Douglas opines:

> She was tall, slim, with ebony hair and ivory skin, beautiful blue eyes, and an Irish turned-up nose.
>> *The Ragman's Son*, 1988

Black women as a group can never attain the status associated with L'Amour's standard of feminine beauty. (For the same reasons most black men can never aspire to become "the sexiest man alive," a label applied to John F. Kennedy, Jr. by *People* magazine.) And since L'Amour's millions of books not only entertain but inform and teach (indeed, millions of his foreign readers get much of their misinformation about America from L'Amour, as he "reasserts old values," in social scientist's Matthew Holden's words), it is no surprise that the *black* black female, while the object of lust, does not enjoy the quality of attention bestowed on white and "high yellow" black women. The *black* black woman can never be a Marilyn Monroe or television's Diane Sawyer. (It should be noted that black women were barred from competing in the Miss American Pageant for more than thirty years after its inception in 1921.) The poet Robert Bly calls them Women with Golden Hair. Of Monroe's tragic role, he wrote: "A generation ago millions of American men gave their longing for the Gold-haired Woman to Marilyn Monroe. She offered to take it and she died from it." Illusions can kill; and yet they rule much of humankind's dreams.

(This fanciful gold-haired woman has spawned an important stake in what Ralph Ellison called "unwritten folk lore"—and in *real* fear and murder of black men. Ellison shares a bit of lore with John Hersey: A black man steals a look of admiration at a white woman that is seen by a white man:

Black—Oh man, will I ever, ever!
White—No nigger, you will never, never!
Black—As long as there's life there's hope!
White—Yeah nigger, and as long as there's trees there's rope.)

An avid reader of L'Amour, though cringing at his racial biases, this writer has for years been a bitter critic of the famous author's propagandizing on behalf of white female beauty. Lately, however, it has occurred to me that L'Amour is entitled to *his* view of feminine beauty no matter how few black *or* white women actually conform to it, or that in its educational function it is doing a disservice to women in general. I think most women, white as well as black, would prefer a less frequently appearing version of L'Amour's feminine beauty:

She was quietly beautiful moving with an easy grace and confidence. She was tolerant, understanding, and intelligent, a good listener ready with apt comment.

Unfortunately, it is L'Amour's predominating idea of beauty that continues to pervade American thinking, and that accounts for so many shattered dreams and hopes for those women who don't "measure up." One is reminded of the young ball player who had to use Branch Rickey's hotel room because of his "skin" color. Yet one black woman confided to the author that if the blond white woman co-host of a popular evening television game show represents the "highest standards" (both by physical anatomy and her TV role), the worlds women of color need have no envy!

I just think there's nothing we can't do. I never considered it to be a disadvantage to be a Black woman. I never wanted to be anything else. We have brains! We're beautiful! We should be able to do anything we set our minds to.
            Diana Ross

The Black Male Dilemma: A Black Female Disadvantage

In a book much praised for its contribution to the African historical record, African historian Ali Mazuri notes that in traditional African societies, women had two principal functions: perpetuating the group; i.e., makers of babies; and "economic producers," generating in many societies a large percentage of the real income derived, largely, from agricultural and business enterprises. While women may be subordinate to men in most aspects of life, the very fact of their economic significance would suggest an importance not enjoyed by their American sisters. It is true that in some cases, within the black underclass at least, women have earning power (including welfare) that exceeds that of their men. But this access to money bestows upon them little of the status of African women who are critical economic linchpins in the total well being of their nations.

Black African countries are not alone in providing more opportunities for women. Former Communist nations (some say because of the horrendous loss of men in WW II) have long bragged about the prominent role women play in the life of their societies. Not only are they represented to a greater degree in the professions-physicians, lawyers, professors, scientists and engineers, in some countries they have important positions in the armed services. A woman was deputy commander of all communist military forces in South Vietnam during that war. Of course women also assumed the traditional roles of nurses and entertainers.

If African American women bring home a lot of the bacon yet enjoy no real, lasting personal status because of it, they are even more vulnerable to the "thing" image associated with being used simply as objects of lust and the makers of babies. For various reasons of history and sociology, black men, to some extent in imitation of their value-setting white counterparts, have treated black women as if they were objects to be manipulated and possessed instead of the "quietly beautiful, moving with an easy grace...tolerant, understanding, and intelligent" human being many of us know them to be. Indeed, too many of us act as if we accept whole-hog Zora Hurston's depiction as expressed through her Hebrew characters. And popular black magazines have periodically carried commentary from black men confirming their suspicions that black women are selfish, aggressive, and "only out for what a man can give them."

Far more than any other group of women, African American women are insecure, and will likely remain so because black men are insecure. Increases in white male-black female marriages notwithstanding to the contrary, black women, unlike, say, Alaska Native women, Latino, and immigrant Asian and South American women, will continue to find mates in the black male population, and will continue to enjoy whatever degree of respect, love, support, and appreciation they can obtain from them. (In Alaska, the rate of black female— white male marriage exceeds that of black male—white female marriages.

White males also marry or are romantically linked to other nonwhite females in Alaska at a rate higher than the national average.)

The continuing precarious position of African American men in American society is that spoke around which much of Black American life will hinge. And the prognosis is not good. In his 1968 *Letters to a Black Boy* (his son), television personality Bob Teague wrote that "All black men are insane...and that includes your daddy." Teague further noted that "Almost any living thing would quickly go mad under the unrelenting exposure to the climate created and reserved for black men in a white racist society." Twenty years later avant-garde novelist Ishmael Reed was to say that "Being a black man in America is like being a spectator at your own lynching." Arthur Ashe said being black was tougher than having AIDS.

> I think black men are pariahs in society. A black boxer's career is the perfect metaphor for the career of a black male. Everyday is like being in a gym, sparring with impersonal opponents as one faces the rudeness and hostility that a black male must confront in the United States, where he is the object of both fear and fascination.
>
> Ishmael Reed, *Writin' is Fightin': Thirty-Seven Years of Boxin on Paper*, 1988

Black ex-Harvard Law School professor Derrick Bell sums up the black male dilemma:

> The dilemma...from slavery until now is the same: we must either accommodate to white domination and live, or challenge it as males should, unceasingly and without compromise, and be ground down to dust.
>
> *And We Are Not Saved: The Elusive Quest for Racial Justice*, 1987

Being "ground down to dust" is precisely what is happening to vast numbers of African American men, whether their work is corporate America or elite university (at a recent conference an older black scholar from a prestigious western university confided that his "every day is like walking through an uncharted mine field)." A psychologist who treats black corporate managers has observed that black men and women are "suffering severe pain." Black men are especially vulnerable because they want to be accepted "without being castrated." Those like Bell's uncompromising black male see themselves as fitting the "American model of being brave, strong, and courageous in order to be a man." Nonetheless, these men have a "low psychological survival rate." No one ever told them that the model applies only to white men, except, perhaps, in combat in a foreign land. In any event, given their attrition rates, including higher rates of layoff (Edward Jones reported that "Of non-traditional managers...black men suffered the greatest decline—almost 60 percent—between 1981 and 1984"), fewer black men in the higher income group are available as potential marriage partners or as peers and colleagues to black women, "a bad omen for families," according to Valita Sellers.

Newsweek's Special Report asked "why black men in America seem almost to be an endangered species." It is because, wrote black Congressman Augustus

Hawkins, they have "the highest death rates by accident and violence," have the lowest educational achievement, occupy 60 percent of prison cells in the country (70 percent in New York), have the second highest rates of unemployment and underemployment (the disabled have the dubious distinction of being first), while making up only 12 percent of the general population; and they die younger than any other segment of the population, with the possible exception of American Indians and Alaska Native men.

"...Our warriors are no longer allowed (in 1874) to be men who can hunt and raid— so they drink to fill that hole inside them where their spirit used to be. And when a man is no longer a man, he no longer feels the need to feed his family."
Terry C. Johnston, *Dying Thunder*, 1992

"The greatest struggle of any oppressed people is against their own weaknesses ... Our greatest struggle is not against our enemy. Our struggle is an internal one; 12,000 Black men will be killed by other Black men this year."
Manning Marable

"Our madness (may be) proof of (black men's) humanness," wrote Teague, and there are signs that for the first time in our history black men may be expressing their rage outward towards the white objects of their opprobrium even while continuing to practice fratricide upon one another. The case of an angry black man killing his ex-boss, a white man, on a commercial airline and taking 37 others with him; the black sailor who knifed a white officer who had allegedly continually harassed him; and the Texas truck drive who, in a fit of anger over a pay dispute, shot up his boss's office, killing six people (the police chief concluded "this was not a random shooting...the man...had a mission to accomplish.")–that this "on edge" rage is not confined to members of the underclass or to those aggrieved by job discrimination, is revealed in *Washington Post* reporter Nathan McCall's autobiographical novel *Makes Me Wanna Holler: A Young Black Man in America*. McCall didn't grow up in poverty and was raised by middle class parents. His rage, in childhood, is announced in the first chapter. A white youth is riding his bike through a black neighborhood. McCall and his buddies beat him senseless, without provocation, *"just cause your white"* (emphasis in original), adding retrospectively, "and it felt so good...it made me feel like we were beating all white people on behalf of all blacks. We called it 'getting' some get-back; securing revenge for all that shit they'd heaped on blacks all these years." These incidents could be powerful portents of a different future. Zora Hurston's comment about the oppressed having nothing yet are "scared to die" may be giving way to a new era where blacks are beginning to eschew dependence on "somebody else's gods."

It is sometimes difficult for even the black woman to comprehend the extreme emotional turmoil experienced by the black male who, trying to be a man—live the traditional American model of manhood—and survive, appears ultimately either as an emotional cripple or as one who can't stay out of trouble with "The Man," on the job or in the streets; or who is forever at odds with other blacks. Indeed, one view of the African American male is that *he is*

163

essentially a dead man. Unneeded, unappreciated and lacking the respect of almost everyone in his world, the American black man cannot, in the poet's words, choose to live or die; his only leverage is try to influence the time, place and manner of his dying.

Black social scientists such as Nathan Hare trace black male political and social impotence to a source ultimately beyond race. In patriarchal societies, he contends, males "predominate among the rulers," thus making them the immediate targets of rulers of other groups who would conquer and subjugate."...it is the oppressed male that must be derailed."

> If the male of the group is weakened or eliminated, this automatically impacts upon the women and children, the family, and the social stability of the group or race. There can be no viable race without a viable patriarch in a patriarchal society.

Viewed from Hare's perspective, the plight of black males (and certainly Native American males) becomes understandable and available to remedial action.

Whatever the reasons for black male problems the net result is fewer males available for black females, most of whom want a traditional home with a black man present. The problem is so acute that one prominent black woman, leader of a 125,000 member black women's organization, suggested that "polygamy could be a possible solution." *Jet* magazine reported the findings of a survey which concluded that most professional black women would rather remain single than marry "outside the race." An extreme situation sometimes requires an extreme solution. The shortage of black males is so acute that black sociologist Larry Davis wrote a book (*Black and Single: Meeting and Choosing a Partner Who's Right For You*) to address the problem.

When the general availability of African American male partners (itself the creator of a disruptive competitive situation) is coupled with the disdain and disrespect some black men have for what Alice Walker called the *black* black woman, and the tendency of a growing number of black men to seek mates outside the "race," the black female faces a unique dilemma.

Furthermore, black men are said not to favor assertive black women and have been known to even bar them from assuming roles as church ministers. Few black churchgoers would disagree with *Washington Post* columnist Dorothy Gilliam's statement that "verbal and physical harassment of black women churchgoers by a few black ministers is an everyday fact of life" in some black churches. If black women are not respected in the church, the most influential institution in the black community, where can they find genuine respect and appreciation?

Regarding the insecurity of black men and their less than full respect for the black woman (individual black men always set their own mothers apart in a special category!), Coretta Scott King was lucky in finding a black man who was secure enough in his person to make her "feel like a woman," who "was such a strong man that" she could "feel like a woman" and, in fact, "*be* a woman" and "let him be a man." Few black women have that luxury, and the likelihood is that the dilemma will continue until white America's treatment of black men changes.

The general public seems to have almost forgotten or tend to ignore the significant level of black female-white male liaisons: Lena Horne, Myrlie Evers, Diane Sands, Tina Turner, Charlene Hunter Gault, Dorothy Dandridge, Lorraine Hansberry, Johnnetta Cole, Marian Wright-Edleman, Maya Angelou, Whoppi Goldberg, Carol Mosely Braun, Faye Wattleton, Eartha Kitt, Pearl Bailey, Ruth Pointer (of the Pointer Sisters), to name a few of the more prominent. At the time Leslie Uggums married the white Australian his country legally denied citizenship to blacks and made obtaining a visitor's visa extremely difficult. Diana Ross married a wealthy European.

Before joining the Black Panther Party, Elaine Brown was mistress of a wealthy white show business liberal who refused to leave his wife for her. After serving as party chair in succession to Huey Newton, Ms. Brown, in 1993, was married to a wealthy Frenchman and living in a 135-room chateau, as reported by Ishmael Reed. In supreme irony, in a February 28, 1994 public address at the University of Alaska Fairbanks, Ms. Brown, reciting thinly veiled socialist rhetoric, noted how she had been appalled to hear a jubilant graduating senior of Atlanta's Morehouse College proclaim his appointment to a junior executive position at Coca Cola in that city. To her, Coca Cola was part of the problem and had "never done anything for black people." That the young man wore a kente scarf as part of his graduation regalia gave insult to injury, though she admitted that she had "no job to offer the young man." She engaged in further self-indictment by indignantly refusing to autograph a copy of her hook, *A Taste of Power: A Black Woman's Story,* for a white student who asked how she could be critical of Coca Cola when her publisher, Random House, was not known as a contributor to black "or any other civic rights cause."

A black Harvard professor who studied medicine in Sweden said he was surprised to discover a large colony of African American women married to Swedes, some of whom expressed no wish to ever return to America. Actress Halle Berry, wife of baseball star David Justice, was sued for $90,000 by her former white lover for what he called breach of contract. She said he was simply jealous. (*Jet* Dec. 93). Rita Dove, the nation's first black poet laureate, is apparently happily married to a WASP.

Celebrated TV film critic Roger Ebert took as bride "his longtime companion," Chaz Hammelsmith, a black Chicago attorney, in 1993. The former black head of the Army's Nursing Corps married a wealthy industrialist. *Jet* reported that the white husband of the black female mayor of Tallahassee, Florida, threatened to "kick the black ass" of her black male challenger in her 1994 bid for reelection. The husband later apologized.

> Does being a black woman mean I have to save the world?
> Kesho Yvonne Scott, *The Habit of Surviving*

Black women will not be, and cannot be, saved by the largely powerless black man. In the final analysis, black *women* will have to save black people and through that salvation save America from its path of ultimate self-destruction. Indeed DuBois was prophetic when he wrote in 1903 that the problem of the twentieth century is the problem of the color line; and racism will continue to be "the nation's number one mental health problem" into the twenty-first century. Racism, coupled with unbridled greed, are the only internal forces that have the capacity to bring destruction to the social order. For the most part, black men have been rendered ineffectual spectators in the struggle.

Black women must look to each other and to sympathetic whites, however few in number, to take them where they want to go. They must network among themselves and interact with the few black males who will be willing and able to work with them as partners in the struggle. As in the 1960s they must define for themselves what personal beauty is, whether it's wearing the Afro or using the hot comb. They have only their own selves as models. Television and print media will not promote a healthy black female self image, nor will most black popular magazines. This writer is reminded of the response the editor of a popular magazine directed to black females, gave to a letter questioning the rag's selection of light complexioned models in its ads. The editor replied that inasmuch as "black" covered a broad range of skin tones, they were all beautiful and equally valued. Even knowing that ad agencies actually select models, this writer disagreed in a letter to the editor (which went unpublished) and scored the paucity of *black* black models.

African American women must abandon the tinge of self-hate in their own ranks, a self-hate reflected by even Alice Walker's otherwise "perfect" mother and woman, who once asked her daughter "if I didn't think that (white people) were 'jest naturally smarter, prettier, better'." Walker notes that self-denigration extends to the revolutionary black women of Cuba who "paint their faces and process their hair" making one wonder whether "if a revolution fails to make one comfortable with what one is…can one assume that, on a personal level, it is a success at all?" Lerone Bennett answers no to that question saying that the black person "who accepts the ideal of blondness must, and inevitably, hate himself."

"My skin-folks, but not my kin-folks; my race but not my taste."

Hurston's "Negro Prayer" perfectly exemplifies the self-hate too many blacks—men and women—harbor.

"Lawd, you know I ain't nothing. My wife, she ain't nothing. My chillun ain't nothing, and if you fool 'round us, Lawd, you won't be nothing neither."

Black women have to continue also to define the nature of their—and their people's—struggle in America and in the world. That definition, born of study, observation and struggle, will lead to an understanding of the nature of the strategies one can employ to wage the war—and war it surely is. In the view of many black men, and not a few women, *The Color Purple* does not advance the struggle; rather, through its directed denigration of black men, it retards the march to justice and equality. (Too many often forget, however, that a very strong black woman—played by Oprah Winfrey—was literally broken in the movie version.) Poet Haki Madubuti was correct in saying that no poem (or book) ever won a revolution, yet we know the power of the printed word and visual media. Martinez wrote that the racist *Birth of a Nation,* for instance, was almost singularly responsible for the surge in Klan membership in the 1920s. Black women, more than black men, one surmises, understand that no matter their college degrees and prestigious positions, they are still black. An African American Ivy League student said it well:

> I know (now) that if I get caught in the "wrong" place, as Michael Griffin did that night in Howard Beach, my degrees and my education will mean nothing.... There is no real reason why it couldn't have been me, and that's what terrifies me and gives a lie to much of my education. It could have been me. It could always have been me.

Decades ago Malcolm X explained, in eloquent simplicity, why it wasn't "me." She, the student, was *not* there. Period. Probably not even realizing it, this young black women understands Zora Hurston's 1929 warning: college degrees and "losing black dialect" and "aping (whites') every move" may appear to be "marks of intelligence" but they amount to little more than psychological captivity and unproductive, even unsafe, actions.

> (By accepting European standards) we closeout of the circle of beauty forever the vast majority of black women...(We) must become deprogrammed from the blind acceptance of a single standard of beauty.
> Laurence Young, "Isn't She Pretty?...

Black psychiatrist Frances Welsing believes there can be no group salvation without black male-female joint effort. At the same time she concedes that "global white supremacy" is focused on totally eliminating the black man (and other men of color). It is for the black woman to decide to what extent she buys into this seemingly compelling argument and what steps to take to save the black man and black people.

Blacks and the Media

> Maine was relatively free of race prejudice but...Thomas Dixon's novel, *The Klansman,* had been made into a motion picture and released under the title of *Birth of a Nation.*
>
> Along with other Negro students at Bates, I went to see it. It was a vicious, cynical, and completely perverted characterization of Negroes. Even in Maine, the picture aroused violent emotions and stirred up racial prejudice.
> Certain parts of it evoked violent words and threats from the audience. My fellow Negro students and I were not sure that we would be able to get back to the campus unmolested, but we did.
> Benjamin Mays, *Lord, the People Have Driven Me On,* 1981

So much for the point of view that claims little psychological influence of visual and print media.

Flowers Bloom Again in 1960s

With "liberals" dominating print and visual communications media in America (former Maryland governor and U.S. Vice President Agnew called them "effete snobs"), an observer would assume that African Americans and other racial minorities would be more fairly represented among producers, directors, film-makers, and the dozens of other specialized groups who manage the massive communications industry. It simply ain't so. After the terrific and wonderful outpouring of black authored books and black produced films dealing with black themes during the late 1960s and early 1970s, the industry is not much further along than it was prior to the civil rights movement. To be sure, many of the films produced during that period were justifiably labeled "blackploitation" works and some of the written works were of such poor quality they should never have reached the printer's ink. Most observers, however, point out that the period represented a flowering of black talent, like the earlier Harlem Renaissance, of the best in black intellectual and artistic life. That period indeed demonstrated to America that given a chance blacks would *put themselves* on front stage.

The Flowers Wither—Again

But instead of that period evolving into a mature, genuinely authentic artistic movement, it was virtually stillborn and its direction seized once again by those who do not necessarily have the best interests of blacks at heart. And, as in the Peoples Republic of China when the "thousand blossoms" were allowed to flower and a "thousand voices" could be heard from intellectuals, something of a cultural revolution has occurred that stymied almost all creative black expression. By the mid-1980s black faces were "again almost completely absent from the (television and feature length) screen." According to David Sterritt, even when black themes are explored, as in *The Color Purple,* whites control virtually every aspect of the production from deciding whether it will be filmed at all to who will cut, direct, etc., to how it will be made, with or without the wishes of the creator. Through the 1980s positive portrayals of black life, as in *The Homecoming,* were rare occurrences.

This state of affairs is due in part to the absence of a visible black presence at virtually all levels of the industry. In 1977, for instance, only one black executive could be counted among the 133 at the three major television networks. To illuminate this state of affairs in the filming of *Roots,* Jesse Jackson raised the rhetorical question of whether one "could imagine NBC's *Holocaust* with all black producers, assistant producers, writers, and directors, and none who was Jewish or white?" Of course not, it would be unthinkable!

The newspaper industry fares no better. An American Society of Newspaper Editors report concluded that blacks are nowhere to be found in two-thirds of the nation's newspaper staffs, and only four percent of news writers, editors and reporters, are minority group members.

The absence of blacks from the front side of the camera is especially important for it sends misinformed and uninformed messages to the nation about African America. The absence and mis-depiction of blacks is what esteemed scholar Matthew Holden termed "the most pervasive form of insult" by the media. And he agrees with *Brotherhood of Murder* author Martinez that films have "always been not merely a means of relief from boredom, but a means as well of reasserting old values or establishing new ones." (That was Mays' reference to *Birth of a Nation*). Certainly the selection of mostly light-complexioned ("high yellow") black persons to portray us devalues the full spectrum of our coloration. It especially devalues Alice Walker's *black* black woman who is *never* shown as a physically beautiful female. Indeed, few black performers are shown in other than one dimensional roles. Few have male headed families (*Cosby* is the exception), even fewer kiss and show deep affection. Rick DuBrow points to "statistical racism" in the industry as evidence of exclusionary practices. And never, ever, even in *Guess Who's Coming to Dinner*, is the racial line crossed in interracial sexual relationships, certainly not black man/white woman. Rarely is there even any *touching* across this invisible barrier. The one exception to this state of affairs was Spike Lee's 1991 *Jungle Fever*, the importance of which lies not in the film but in the fact that a gutsy *black* moviemaker had to do it.

Since critics have said that many of the film scripts "out there" could be played by "any American", the only plausible answer to the question of why so few blacks is "the problem stems from nepotism, greed and racism." Even the black exploitation films benefitted few blacks, according to Sterritt, for they were "white-generated and white-controlled products to make money for whites."

There are two answers to the question of what blacks must do to change the deplorable representation issue. On one level black political leaders must understand that "them that's got" are extremely reluctant to give up any share of their enormous advantage, naturally. Yet they must, our leaders, that is, confront at every opportunity the racism practiced in the communications industry. In this regard positive actions already taken by some blacks come to mind. Novelist Toni Morrison's failure to be selected for two coveted literary awards for her highly praised novel *Beloved* energized some of the nation's other leading black writers to take a full page ad in the *New York Times*. Ms. Morrison later won the Pulitzer, then the Noble Prize in 1993.

In the second instance, Jesse Jackson confronted the leadership of CBS and the other major networks and demanded a change in hiring practices in the same way he had successfully done at Kentucky Fried Chicken, Coco-Cola, and Coors Beer Company. The third success story involves National Black Media Coalitions Chairman Pluris Marshall who has, through the use of threatening to "petition to deny" licenses to broadcasters who do not improve their hiring, accounted for a "110 percent increase in minority hiring in the industry." Marshall is also credited with the dramatic increase in FCC (Federal Communications Commission) licensing of black broadcasters.

For many African American observers of the black literary scene, a distressing pattern appears to be developing. Over the past two decades many literary winners of major awards have contained definite, and apparently deliberate, references to blacks that promoted negative racial stereotypes. Ntozake Shange's *For Colored Girls...* comes to mind, while Alice Walker's *The Color Purple* is the most prominent example. With its thinly veiled suggestion that incest was rife in black America and it's general unheroic portrayal of black males, this work, both because almost from it's first page was anti-black male and the food it gave to white racists, probably more than any book—length work during the past fifty years, *black* sanction to racial stereotyping. In a similar way if not so profoundly Charles Johnson's *Middle Passage*, winner of the National Book Award for 1990, puts down blacks even as he, on the lecture circuit, claims celebration of blacks. As in the Walker book, his negative appears early: on page 30 of the 209 page work, he has the evil Captain Falcon denigrate affirmative action by claiming black illiterates are given degrees by whites who "feel too guilty to fail them, then employers giving the same boy a place in the firm since he's got the degree in hand and saying no will bring a gang of abolitionists down on their necks." The evil but brilliant captain continues: "and all because everyone's ready to lower standards of excellence to make up for slavery, or discrimination, and the problem..."

Joining Johnson's *Middle Passage* as a major prize winner in 1990 was Reginald McKnights *I Get On The Bus*. Also praised (and bought) by whites, it makes the obligatory, it appears, anti-black statement.

A young disaffected black male college graduate journeys to Africa as a Peace Corps volunteer. His selection of Africa as well as his choice of voluntary over a paid position seem to be motivated more by curiosity then a search for roots or a desire to serve the world's needy. In fact he is not militant but aware of his "racial" heritage in an intellectual way. After dropping out of the Peace Corps and moving from Senegal's capital city Dakar to a village to escape big city problems, he encounters a black American expatriate of some years experience in-country.

So on page 58 of a 296 page work author McKnight gives the reader his anti-black message. The expatriate tells the neophyte:

"But let me tell you something, brother. The majority of these niggers out here don't give a walking fuck for you or me or any other black American. Shit, most of the ancestors of them niggers in N'Gor, Ouakam, Yoff, and so forth, the better-off ones, anyway, made a great deal of their money selling folks into slavery.

"Think about it, man. You might be shacking with some family that got fat off selling your great-great-grands to some European slavers. Can you relate to that? I mean they grin and smile at you and shit, but brother, let me tell. If slavery existed today they'd do the same goddamn thing to you in a heartbeat. They play a lot of mind games, try anything to take your money. I've lived here twelve years and have never even set foot in a village. Nothing but a bunch of trifling fools out there. I can't tell you what to do, man, but "if I were you, I'd get my ass out of N'Gor."

Belatedly joining the clutch of black writers who find glee in finding faults is former screenwriter Eddy Harris. Two of his three works published to date—mid 1993—not only tell little, and nothing new about his subjects, they join the parade of black put-downs gracing best seller lists.

Native Stranger: A Black American's Journey Into the Hearth of Africa transgresses every tenet of good journalism as well as good travel reporting. In short, virtually everything Harris witnessed or experienced on his one-year trek through much of black Africa (after starting out in northwest Africa) is negative. Corruption, inefficiency, climate, terrain, animal pests and, most of all, the people do not stand up to what he apparently needed to make him feel good about his black relationship to Africa.

From "jump street" Harris wants the reader to know that he explicitly distances himself from anything African, beginning his first paragraph with:

"Because my skin is black you will say I traveled Africa to find the roots of my race. I did not—unless that race is the human race, for except in the color of my skin, I am not African." In Soweto, in South Africa, he found what any white American or European apologist would find: "it is indeed a ghetto, but not the horror I had imagined. I've seen worse neighborhoods in Chicago. And compared to other blacks in Africa, these blacks are doing very well."

After the widespread corruption, useless transportation facilities, endemic disease and other discomforts, Harris at last finds one redeeming "something" worthy of value. In a small Catholic church in Cameroon (he tells us on p 281 of a 315 page book), Africa finally makes sense. "Behind heavy wooden doors, the church was ablaze with warmth—not the heat of the day but the golden warmth of music and hope. The church rocked with singing. The church responded with hope.

"...I tried to resist but found myself caught in the tempo and the melodies, swaying in my seat and upon my feet dancing..."

"...they sang the joyful laments that breathe in the souls of black people and fill their hearts to overflowing, music that runs in their veins and lives in their genes, linking generation to generation to generation."

In preparation for this journey, there are so many African Americans with African experience Harris could have consulted, and so many books he could have read, by Africans, African Americans and others. He could have read, as beginners, works like Basil Davidson's *The African Slave Trade* and *The Black Man's Burden: Africa and the Curse of the Nation-State;* Walter Rodney's *How Europe Underdeveloped Africa* along with works by Leo Hansberry, John H. Clarke and other scholars to inform himself about African history, particularly about the devastating impact—into modern times—of the slave trade and the Berlin Conference of 1885-86 which balkanized Africa into nonsensical enclaves. To get a sense of how other "returnees" experienced Africa, he might have read Kofi Awoonor *Comes the Voyager at Last: A Tale of Return to Africa,* in this authors own (*Where to Black Man: An American Negro's African Diary*) and numerous works by African American visitors. For good information about conditions in particular nations he could have taken the time to read, for example, Doris Lessing's *African Laughter: Four Visits to Zimbabwe;* and to get some idea of the continuing impact of the West on Africa (devastating in some places, as in Angola), he might have read Bellants' works.

The reader may wish to contrast Harris's sentiments about Africa with others of African descent recognizable for their larger achievements:

> In my music, my plays, my films I want to carry always the idea: to be African.
> Paul Robeson

> The drums of Africa still beat in my heart. They will not let me rest as long a there is a single Negro boy or girl without a chance to prove his (or her) worth.
> Mary McLeod Bethune

> I must see (Africa), get close to it, because I never lose the sense of being a displaced person here in American because of my color.
> Paula Marshall

> Molded on Africa's anvil, tempered down home.
> Julian Bond

Malcolm X's retort to a person in the audience who proclaimed he "haven't left anything in Africa" was "you left your brains in Africa." Not well publicized is that an estimated 5000 African Americans went to work in Nkrumah's Ghana; a good many are still there. Also little known is that Louis "Satchmo" Armstrong was reported to be making plans to move to Africa when he died, having finally given up on America.

When Harris traveled to the South (*South of Haunted Dreams*) "to confront the source of my anger," which he failed to identify, if he found it, the reader comes away having learned little of note about Southern racial dynamics. Indeed, since his expectation "that before this trip ends someone will have died" did not materialize and he somehow escaped the South's harder racial edges, moving across the land rather quickly on the BMW motorcycle. Unfortunately, he didn't talk to people like Charles Tisdale, publisher of the black *Jackson Advocate* who railed about the "suicide" hangings of black inmates: "Things are not better than they were in the '60s. Things are worse." He didn't talk to another Jackson, Mississippi resident, a friend of this author who, born and reared in Mississippi, had gone North to school and marriage, then returned after twenty years to care for an ailing mother. She told me on my visit in 1991 that "nothing has really changed down here in any kind of significant way," as we discussed the Problem. Another friend, a white female originally from Milwaukee, could have told Harris that the two white cops who tailed us into town, even stopping for gas when we stopped, were not out there as our protectors!

It is to be hoped that his forthcoming book about Harlem will not reflect the

172

same personal distancing from his subjects as he did with Africans and Southerers, and that he won't have to inform the world that he is not connected: "If I didn't know it then, I know it now."

The politics of "political correctness" so hotly debated during the 1990s spawned additional restrictions and exclusions. University of Florida Sociologist Joe Feagin noted in the November 27, 1991 *Chronicle of Higher Education* that major New York publishers eagerly publish works of black neoconservatives such as Sowell, Walter Williams, Glen Loury, et al but refuse to handle works by black scholars "who focus on the massive racial discrimination that confronts black Americans today…" In Ishmael Reed's view, according to Joyce Mercer, black women fiction writes, especially those with little genuine writing talent, occupy the same rung on the black male bashing ladder. Their works "do little more…than vilify black men. Reed further believes that the "use" of Anita Hill to "perpetrate the worst beliefs about black men" in alleging sexual wrongdoing by Clarence Thomas was a deliberate effort by whites to put-down black men. What better instrument than an educated black woman.

Indeed, it would appear that many non-fiction works authored by blacks in the last two decades of the twentieth century are at some point decidedly antiblack. Some of the works most praised by white critics contain strikingly antiblack segments that, in some cases, seem incongruent with the thrust of the work's main theme. Among those which appear to have gotten the publishing nod on the basis of their "dirty laundry content" are long-time Martin Luther King aide, "friend", and confident Ralph David Abernathy's *The Walls Came Tumbling Down* and columnist Carl Rowan's *Breaking Barriers*. Abernathy's supposed revelations of King's "secret" sex life and Rowan's disclosure of the FBI's alleged finding of homosexual liaisons of King, are unconscionable acts in the view of many blacks. Tony Brown wrote of Rowan's work that "the bad guy is Hoover and the FBI. The good guy is Carl Rowan for digging it up and spreading dirt they (the FBI) manufactured to destroy Martin Luther King." Many blacks doubt that either book would have been published without the "dirt" they contained and their obvious appeal to many whites.

In a scathing review of Alice Walker's *Possessing the Secret of Joy* Terrence Cooper wrote that the work not only condemns the practice of female circumcision it also "does much to condemn the customs, the cultures, and the peoples of Africa itself," and adds that it probably "fuels existing fears and prejudices directed towards people of African descent." Apparently because he views such work by black authors as "get over" pieces he titled the review of Walker's work *Possessing the Secret of Fame*. Historian John Henrick Clarke noted that had Walker done her homework she would have known that it was Arabs who brought the practice into black Africa; it was not indigenous to black people.

In his final published work, *Days of Grace,* Arthur Ashe, while clearly a person of high integrity and commitment to racial justice, offers several views that ultimately serve the same ends as others more blatantly hostile to blacks. Ashe is anti-affirmative action even though he is obviously ignorant of how people actually get jobs and other advantages. He criticizes some blacks for harboring or voicing anti-Semitic sentiments in a manner that indicts all blacks, and like noted writer Henry Louis Gates, he is silent on anti-black Jewish prejudice.

For a scathing damnation of the new breed of self destructive, black on black, put-downs, see emeritus professor James Alsbrook's critique appended at the conclusion of this book.

The other front on which blacks must do battle is in the filmmaking arena, a financial empire unto itself. *Jet* managing editor Robert Johnson has told of how when Bill Cosby could not find conventional financing for his film *Man and Boy,* he used his own money to fund the project. Spike Lee's shoestring production of *She's Gotta Have It,* the commercial success of which permitted the higher budgeted *School Daze,* is another example of successful black filmmaking. Earlier black produced films such as *Buck and the Preacher, Uptown Saturday Night,* and even *Super Fly* made important, though largely ignored, statements about black America. That blacks must do their own thing in this area of the communications industry is reflected in the experience of Ali Mazuri's PBS series *The Africans,* a highly acclaimed work funded by the National Endowment for the Humanities (then criticized by that body's chairwoman as being "anti-Western.") Whites are reluctant to support authentic black works. But blacks do. Indeed, most of the 19 black directed films released in 1991 returned good profits, according to *Newsweek.*

In a review of the Tina Turner film *What's Love Got To Do With It?* for the *Washington Afro-American,* Samuel Banks echoed Reed's comments about *The Color Purple,* saying, "In the egregious and reprehensible failure to portray both Tina and Ike in human and believable human terms in a racist, hostile and inflexible body politic which governed and shaped their lives…(the film) is an ABYSMAL FAILURE." The reviewer's emphasis. Unfortunately, Oprah Winfrey's made-for-television film *There are no Children Here* (aired November 1993), while avoiding some of the technical shortcomings of *Purple,* still leaves the viewer feeling that the entire onus of responsibility for a fragmented family rests on the intermittently present wino husband. He is *the* cause of the family's plight, of having to live in one of Chicago's worst public housing projects. By extension he, the absent black man, is *creator* of public housing, and perpetuates it! There are no redeeming black male roles in this film. Having taken the lead female role, and accepted the script, it perhaps should come as no surprise that black men do not fare well in her latest film quest.

Works done about blacks, or on any topic, for that matter, have little benefit of black public opinion. *The Color Purple,* of which Reed said "has inspired the worst campaign of group libel against black men since the days of the Confederate writers," is an example of the kind of work about blacks that many whites *enjoy,* (just as whites prefer "primitive" art pieces to contemporary realistic works by black artists, according to a friend who owns an Atlanta art shop specializing in African and African American art.) They are in sharp contrast to works like Eddie Murphy's *Coming to America* which black readers of *Ebony* (September '88 letters) praised and white critics such as Lloyd Shearer called

"Trite Tripe." Sherer was kind enough to note that Murphy's films are "self-produced"! Independent filmmaker Robert Townsend told *Jet*:

> "Blacks must make their own films if they want to accurately portray black life: 'Nothing about black subject matter gets done until a filmmaker with clout…comes along and insists on telling."

Further, as *Los Angeles Times* writer David Shaw concluded in his Pulitzer Prize winning series, press coverage of black communities tends to be distorted, images that "perpetuate ethnic stereotypes and feeds (white) prejudices and ethnic conflict. Not only are middle class blacks rarely featured but stories are reported/written that fail to show that most violent criminals, drug users, or jobless and poor people are white." Movies such as *The Last Mafia Marriage* (aired May 1993), *The Godfather*, and the popular television series *Top Cops* are in that tradition. The question is asked among discerning black movie-goers: why is black gang activity portrayed as such vile, murderous, fratricidal, warfare when movie treatment of Mafia activity is presented in a mild, even sympathetic manner?

While Steven Spielberg's 1994 film about the Holocaust, *Schindler's List* (nominated for twelve Oscars) is only the latest in a long line of films dealing with some aspect of Jewish suffering, except for Alex Haley's *Roots*, there has never been a comprehensive commercial film on any aspect of the black ordeal: slavery, resistance, white terror. *Schindler's List* approached the viewer from the victim's point of view and was conceived and executed by descendants of the victim's of that terrible blot on history. Blacks need such epic works beyond *Roots* and Spike Lee's *Malcolm X*.

During a trip to the nation's capitol, I noticed a billboard near the Howard University campus which features Michael Fox and his black female co-star promoting the movie *Life With Mickey*. The caption read: "He's a talent agent. She's a thief." The thief reclined in a chair while Fox looned over her in an authoritative posture. Why couldn't those roles have been reversed? Fox could have retained the lead.

Formerly progressive and sympathetic to the struggle for civil rights for African Americans, large segments of the mainstream press have joined hands with neoconservative intellectuals and academics. Because such organs as *The New York Times*, *New Yorker*, *Progressive*, *Los Angeles Times*, *New Republic* and *Atlantic* have essentially joined the ranks of publications either ignoring or redefining reality, or attributing blame to society's victims, many literate blacks no longer look to them for balanced coverages or accurate reporting. The author recalls, during a Peace Corps tour in Africa in the early 1960s, going to great expense to pay for a personal subscription to *The New York Times*, but having by 1994 become only an occasional reader.

Of course, racism in the communications industry is not newly arrived on the scene. Like other aspects of American life its roots are buried deep in American history. Some of our most prestigious journals have joined forces with traditional southern racist tabloids to print "white lies" about blacks.

175

Pinkney reports that even such respected journals as *Atlantic Monthly, Harpers Weekly* and the *Nation*, which had provided the intellectual case for the abolitionist struggle and which advocated for black rights, made a dramatic shift after Reconstruction and began carrying articles "charging that blacks were innately inferior to whites…and that they were incapable of participating in the white people's civilization." Also accused, by Joe Louis biographer Chris Mead, are newspapers "from the *New York Times* to the *New Orleans-Picayune*" for excluding blacks from any coverage "except as perpetrators or victims of crime." The absurd lengths to which some news organizations would go to exclude and debase blacks is demonstrated by an incident reported by Geoffrey Ward. Visiting a collection of photographs from the 1920's made by a man for a news agency Ward was struck by the absence of blacks even "in any of the busy street scenes." The old photographer's quite simple answer was that every "image" in which a black appeared cost him five dollars in docked pay by his boss. "Nobody wanted them" (photos with blacks in them), the old gentlemen explained.

That same "distortion of history" continues today and blacks have to lead the struggle to put an end to it.

> But I didn't even have to carry a pass to leave my own place (slave plantation), like the other niggers. I had a cap with a sign on it: 'Don't bother this nigger, or there will be hell to pay'.
> "The Case of Cato," in David Oliver and Fred Newmans, *Black Views of America*

> They (African Americans) have been awakened rudely to the fact that white Americans will only accede to black Americans those rights which we can negotiate through pressure or take by force.
> Congressman William L. Clay

In the publishing field one of the tragedies of the Civil Rights Era was the break-up of the publishing arm of the Nation of Islam upon the death of its founder the Honorable Elijah Muhammad. *Muhammad Speaks* was one of the better black newspapers, and while Johnson Publishing Company does a creditable job of keeping blacks informed about success stories, few papers bested *Muhammad Speaks* in telling "the rest of the story." The *Afro-American* newspapers are excellent sources of local news. On the book front Johnson publishes a few works by authors it employs but there is no national black publishing company that prints more than a handful of the hundreds of manuscripts submitted each year by black writers which mainline publishers refuse to print. Reed says he is "one of the few black male writers being published." This is in part due to the observation that prominent literary agent Bill Alder made: only the rare black can be found above the "mailroom, stockrooms, and warehouses of publishing houses," and blacks are found in those places in abundance.

Finally, little reported or discussed are the implications for blacks of the thaw in U.S.—Soviet relations. As an antagonist, the Soviet Union looked for, and publicized, every embarrassing facet of American life, including race discrimination. Often shrill and laden with half-truths, this Soviet propaganda did serve to remind America of her own shortcomings on human rights. In that respect, American blacks had an unintended and uninvited ally. Another source of external finger-pointing which at one time worked to our advantage was sharp criticism of American racial practices by black African leaders during the early independence period. Many of these leaders had been students in American universities. Now that black Africa has all but disappeared from world attention, that independent voice has been essentially silenced.

CHAPTER III

The Hump and Beyond

TOWARDS ENLIGHTENMENT?

"People say that black folks ought to pull themselves up by their bootstraps. They forget that most black folks didn't get boots, and white folks did. We have to make our own boots, straps and all. With a little more help from the other side, black people would have, you know, respected ourselves more. Of course, some white people did their share to help. But a whole lot of them tried to stop us every step of the way. I think that's changing now. I hope so. I'd like to see the day when our young people have the same chance that everybody else has. Everybody will be better off, black folks and white folks. That's my dream now."

Mother to James Comer, M.D., *Maggies American Dream: The Life and Times of a Black Family*

I think God is both black and white, because the Bible says He created man in his image. Why would there be black people if God was not part black? Why did God make us black? All over the world people hate blacks. Since we saw the light of God, we Africans have clean hearts and we welcome everyone to our land. But whites never welcome blacks. We don't understand why God made it like this...

In heaven, everybody will be happy and everybody will be equal. There will be no rich and no poor. We will be married and have children, because this is how God started it. We will live in houses and drive cars, but everybody will be one color. I think everybody will be black.

Eighteen year old Ghanian housemaid living in Beirut, from *Life* Special Issue, "Who is God?," December 1990

As the twentieth century nears completion America sits at the brink of potentially massive disruptive changes. A health care "system" that underserves almost half of its citizenry; an educational establishment universally assailed for its shortcomings in content and pupil achievement; almost unprecedented economic dislocations of its middle class; expansive violence to its natural environment and human inhabitants, and, through crime and deceit, the potential for widespread racial and ethnic physical confrontation—all characterize the America about to enter a new century.

Since the author of this book takes the position that all things are related, that whatever of significance happens in one sector or geographic region profoundly affects all others, and that, logically, blacks are impacted by all manner of occurrences, an effort was made to present a "wholistic" rendering of African American realities. The questions "how we are" and "how we came to be *where* we are" were central to the development of the work. It is impossible to discuss black realities in abstraction from American realities, and vice versa.

As noted in the book's introduction, a major motivation for undertaking the work was my sense that a large segment of America was attempting to ignore or turn its back on the continuing plight of its black citizens. Prominent individuals, black as well as white, who should have known better, were literally writing blacks out of their best-sellers. Or pretending in scholarly works that blacks were either responsible, almost entirely, for their plight or that society (governments, corporate and institutional leaders, other powerful individuals) had done about all that could be reasonably expected to relieve black pain and promote access to the nation's rewards and opportunities. Following "benign neglect," such misleading terms as "the declining significance of race" became prominent as codes heralding in the new silence. As late as December 1991 a prominent Alaskan news columnist averred that as "Allegations of Racism are Emotional and Useless" (title of article), and the term "'racist' is not a word I can use to communicate anything," it was his "hope I can go at least another 18 years before using it again." Once again, obscuring through intellectualism phenomena one doesn't care to openly and honestly deal with does not in fact make it go away. The reality is that racism and racists are the active ingredients of white supremacy—a complete system of thought and action historically (including presently) linked in this country to denial of humanhood to African Americans.

In concluding this work attention is refocused on certain topics all Americans need to begin thinking about. Violence as an expression of personal disaffection and desperate loneliness as well as race hatred; our vaunted and mythic individualism; and individual responsibility in a society driven by group thinking and inertia. The flip side of the coin shows promising actions by individuals reflective of some of our major strengths and promises. This section concludes with an abbreviated summary of problems and prospects for African Americans.

Beyond all the other "explanations" of the black experience in America stands the quality of national leadership. It has shaped, and been shaped by, so very much of the nation's direction. To the African American, the American experience has been one continuous perplexity, due, in large measure, to inconsistency between stated beliefs and moral precepts (Judeo-Christian) and behaviors actually prevailing in the "real" world. Without understanding the impact of the hidden informal strata of motivations, attitudes, and outlooks, running throughout American history an observer can never make sense of how we came to be as we are.

America has been and is, a continuing dilemma for black Americans: honest and dishonest; violent without conscience or remorse yet miserly in sharing meaningful resources and power. Malcolm X said that the greatest crime committed against blacks by white America was convincing us that we had no value and should be self contemptuous. What he could have added as equally tragic in its consequences is the gross uncertainty with which African Americans have had to approach whites in virtually all encounters, the behavioral imperatives of legal slavery notwithstanding. It is the "never knowing" what to expect from whites (whose power is inherent) in any given situation at any given moment in time. Being unable to anticipate a stimulus from those with real or perceived or imagined power often induces less than appropriate responses.

Despite its great success in welding diverse populations into a giant political amalgam, America remains a nation in the process of becoming, a collectivity riding the success of abundant resources, unparalleled entrepreneurial opportunities, geopolitical expansion, and abundant faith in the future, the paradox remains: on the one hand, having overcome an early struggle between those wishing for a nation led by what Harry Truman called an elite coterie similar to Europe's royal houses, and the democratically inclined such as Jefferson, the one great mass of people totally excluded from the dynamic—blacks—gave lie to all the impressive rhetoric penned in the Declaration of Independence. That virtually all our great leaders of the colonial era were slave holders who could nonetheless express democratic ideals set the stage for the dilemma the nation currently faces. Hypocrisy is not a term too strong to apply to the actions of the Founding Fathers, for, in retrospect, the chattel slavery they practiced and supported was not the worse curse.

The ultimate tragedy was establishing a mind-set which could simultaneously accept "equality and fraternity" and "life, liberty and the pursuit of happiness" yet deny democracy to a great number of human beings. Even the otherwise enlightened Harry Truman could include Jefferson and Andrew Jackson on his personal list of favorite presidents, in the process almost apologizing for their ownership of slaves and Jackson's murderous decimation of Creek Indians and treacherous use of Cherokees then forcing them onto the Trail of Tears. The discerning reader can argue with Pulitzer Prize winning historian Barbara Tuchman's assertion that such leaders should not be judged by "present-day values," leaving to their contemporaries, she demands, the job of evaluating "these episodes" of "injury to self-interest." Having laid down the basic structure of American society the fathers have made their sons responsible for their—the father's—sins.

Thus, even as various forces converged to give definition to the American character—success in war, religious diversity and tolerance—the converse to this political development occurred. American political, industrial, religious, and educational leaders could extol the virtues of a budding democracy yet turn a blind eye to the anti-democratic strains flowing, often unvoiced but recognized, on a parallel course. Above the populist/democracy oratory, for instance, historian Hubert Bancroft could write of another world:

...for innate wickedness and cold-blooded barbarities in the treatment of savages and the half-civilized nations no people on earth during the past century have excelled men of Anglo-Saxon origin.

Manifest Destiny, while ultimately responsible for the American acquisition of most of the North American continent, was inherently anti-democratic. It "opened up the west" and gave countless thousands an opportunity for land ownership and prosperity probably unparalleled in modern history. But in its wake white America developed the notion that they were somehow the world's "chosen" people, God-ordained to rule over all dominions including those of darker hue. Retired Army Col. Hackworth's grandmother captured this spirit: "Thanks to her," he wrote, "I grew up believing that my family made this country—with an axe in one hand, a rifle in the other—chopping down Indians, trees, or anything else that stood in the way of progress, of manifest destiny, and what was 'rightfully' ours."

The dual standard imbedded in the white American psyche is arguably the most profound historical dilemma confronting African Americans. And though there is evidence to suggest the nation is beginning to move in the direction of closing the gap between rhetoric and reality so much remains to be done that to hope for quick reconciliation is as risky as not believing or understanding the duality in the first place.

Along with greed and racial prejudice, the American social character has historically contained a large dose of violent propensities. This violence is displayed not only against persons of color, particularly blacks, but is turned outward against the very environment without which none of us could survive. It's a violence that can be seen when men will take loads of weapons and ammunition to isolated lakes in Alaska and decimate the waterfowl just for the fun of it; or murder a John Lennon, or kill sixteen people while on a "killing spree"; or become a Hillside Strangler, or "Son of Sam". Psychiatrist Rollo May says of this kind of apparent random violence that its perpetrators have poor self-images, and their acts are intended to say "that they too, are significant." In this context, "killing is killing", whether bird or person; its common irrational (without motive) quality is its outstanding feature.

Some commentators have explained this form of violence as alienation and estrangement which are logical consequences of living in social groups characterized by extreme individualism, and the "strong man taking on the world" image portrayed in the popular western writer Louis L'Amour's novels, have contributed to what Saul Bellow called a lack of "permanent connections" among individuals in Western society. Long before Bellow's insight, a Sioux chief and medicine man arrived at a similar conclusion. On his trip in Europe with the Buffalo Bill Show, Chief Black Elk noted that "Wasichus (whites)…would take everything from each other if they could, and so there were some who had more of everything than they could use, while crowds of people had nothing at all and maybe were starving." Will and Ariel Durant commented in The Lessons of History that not even the law protected men from one another in civilized Western society, for "men consume one another by due process of law."

We stand alone as individuals, and are afraid of other individuals. The more they differ from us, the greater our fear. Everyone becomes a potential adversary to be bested "by any means necessary." A L'Amour character tells what winning means:

> He fights his way, I mine. And mine's Injun. No man in his right mind risks losin' his hair to stand up to a man.

No one is to be truly trusted; friendships are not enduring. The individual, like the group, must adapt his weapon to the situation at hand. "To exist is to adapt, and if one could not adapt, one died and made room for those who could." These words by L'Amour were written in reference to the survivability of the American Indian, and, by extension, to other minority groups including blacks. To "adapt" was to ultimately become white.

The American quest continues to be a full realization of its ideals—the convergence of the great hopes of its Declaration of Independence and the Bill of Rights to the "deeds men do" in their everyday lives. At a time when people in even the ex-Communist world are demanding those freedoms and liberties we say are available as a matter of course in this country, so many wrongs need to be righted here before the world will believe we are not still hypocrites and liars.

If we can not rely on politicians and "experts" to act responsibly in guiding our efforts through enlightened, unselfish, leadership, then we as citizens must assume greater responsibility for what happens in our communities as well as the nation. As Doris Lessing has written in *Prisons We Choose to Live Inside:*

> It is individuals who change societies, give birth to ideas, who, standing out against the tides of opinion, change them. This is as true in open societies as it is in oppressive societies.

We must somehow defy the "lessons of history" and realize that each of us, individually, becomes our own leader relying far less on experts and charismatic leaders to chart our course. The *individual in community* as opposed to "rugged" individualism. We must prove Eric Fromm in error by demonstrating that people can defy the psychology of both wanting to be led and wanting to be autonomous and free of Big Brother. Americans have to understand that neither the likes of the late Jim Jones (of Jamestown infamy) or a Jim Bakker can save us; nor can charismatic political leaders, whether a Hitler, John Kennedy, or Malcolm X. Abe Lincoln warned us that the best of leaders have vices as well as virtues:

> My experience has taught me that a man who has no vices has damned few virtues.

And the sometimes sagacious L'Amour cautions that many "great men...are fine men, enough to be admired, but often they are sadly, weakly human, too".

We must change our attitude toward the poor and disadvantaged. In 1991 one in ten of us needed food stamps to survive and 33.6 million (13.5%) were poor. The Census Bureau's Division of Household Economic Statistics reported

African Americans had the highest rate at 32 percent. No longer can we afford a callous unconcern toward those who sleep in garbage dumps, or rot away in overcrowded prisons and filthy nursing homes. They are Americans, too, and many could be productive if given the opportunity.

That too many of our "better classes" have callous sentiments toward the millions of American poor can be seen in the experience of a popular Alaskan writer—who prior to visiting the nation's capitol had sympathetic views of the homeless—melting into the flow of cosmopolitan thinking. He wrote that upon arriving in Washington, he was horrified to observe street sleepers, and felt deep compassion. By the end of the fourth day he too had become "callous, dispassionate, and uncaring, and like other residents had become "cosmopolitan and enjoying it", and could "wave off" those begging for money "with one quick backhanded motion."

Americans have shown that they can be a compassionate people, but many of us are no longer impressed by hip-shoot gestures. To bring a seven year old Ecuadorian girl to Boston for orthopedic help is fine, but the contradiction of having so many needy unserved in the same city begs the question of just who do we think we are fooling!

Our contradictions are manifest; some are harmless, others dangerous. Mazuire, as we noted, has called Western whites the "greatest creators of ugliness in human history", but admits that they "are probably also the greatest appreciators of beauty in the contemporary world". Many people may not be able to recognize the expensive beauty ($39.9 million worth) in Van Gogh's "Sunflowers", but can appreciate a Norman Rockwell. That many whites would not see equal artistic value in a Charles White or other black artists represents hypocrisy in its more base form. Nationally syndicated columnist Tom Teepen wrote of how his Southern bred mother, a great fan of novelist Frank Yerby, "made a dramatic declaration to the family that she would read no more of his books...when she discovered he was black...her whole upbringing told her no black man could possibly write books to her liking." Americans imprisoned certain of their fellow citizens in concentration camps during World War II, called them Japs and Nips and have since argued over whether they should be compensated for property lost, ("compensation" was provided in 1990) even while we applaud West Germany's payment of $47 billion in reparations to Israel. Even more perplexing, we hail as hero the WWII Japanese fighter plane ace who shot down our own ace, Gregory "Pappy" Boyington, and a score of other American pilots. Yet even more confusing to one who might not understand our forgiveness and compassion, we have permitted the Japanese pilot to immigrate and live unmolested in this country! And, adds news columnist Anthony Lewis, Americans fought and died saving the world from Hitler and Nazism yet today "overlook a politician's (David Duke's) attachment to that evil, or would believe his thin claims to have found redemption, is to know something is deeply wrong in this country!"

Almost as if in compensation for some of the "rough edges" of our rugged individualism with its loneliness and estrangement, Americans take on voluntary charitable work in great numbers. According to Stephanie Buckhanon, more than 84 million of us over fourteen years of age participate in some kind of helping activity, more than any other nation, up to 43 percent in 1991 from the 38 percent in 1989, according to Jack Rosenberger. From the religious Reconstructionist Movement and Moral Majority to Neighborhood Watch and Big Brothers/Big Sisters, we give of ourselves and our resources. *USA Today* reported that Americans gave more than 2 percent of total income to charity in 1992, a level not matched since 1971. Individuals were the biggest contributors. By a large margin poorer Americans give more and volunteer more than the better off do. Unknown to (or ignored by) most Americans is the relatively high level of black charitable contributors. Rosenberg estimates that in 1991 African Americans gave almost 30 percent "of all household income …compared to 2.2 percent for whites." *Chicago Tribune* columnist Robert Greene need not be so concerned about the reader who wrote to encourage television viewers to help "save *Starman*", which the columnist saw as a trite undertaking when people could be volunteering "at a soup kitchen and helping feed" the hungry.

America will survive because of the character of its people. Because of the whistle blowers who have the courage to keep government honest from the inside (such as the Army's Colonel Hackworth who catalogued the causes of our human waste and military defeat in Vietnam and a Paul Biddle who, against Establishment brandishments, "blew the whistle" on the billion dollar scandal of universities overcharging the federal government for research contracts); because of corporate leaders like An Wang, a Chinese born American who can rise from Shanghai obscurity to wealth and power and give back to his community in moral leadership far more than he takes out, and who believes that "corporate behavior should be judged by the same standards as personal behavior".

America will survive because, greater than any other factor, the spirit of entrepreneurial risk-taking and adventure is instilled in its people—like the young Alaskan who dared to attempt a solo climb of Mt. McKinley in *winter,* "a feat nobody has – ever accomplished and lived to tell about". He did. Or like the young black adventurer who refused to let severe frostbite stop his trek as the only American in a team pioneering a different trail to the North Pole. The nation will survive because of people like the 64 year old man who radio commentator Paul Harvey praised for spending twenty years trying to swim the breakwater of Lake Erie and who died in his last, and successful, attempt. Because of individuals like Nobel chemist Donald Cram who, in his spare time, surfs the big breakers, exclaiming, "I like the fear of a big wave…To catch a big wave and to be scared to death while being able to handle it is just a lot of fun to me". Only an American could make such a pronouncement.

While nuclear holocaust is possible, Three Mile Island, the Russian nuclear disaster, and numerous near misses in other facilities, have aroused world opinion of the dangers of the "mighty atom". Greed and aggrandizement as acceptable modes of behavior—of achieving—while deadly if left uncurtailed or contained, often feeds on itself and is self-correcting, provided Americans are willing to look beyond their own individual interest to the greater good in combating it. Hackworth calls greed "the major growth industry in our land of opportunity." New York's Tammany Hall and countless lesser mini-dynasties established in the name of a handful of greedy men will continue to surface unless a concerned citizenry remains vigilant, which Americans have a tendency to forego until almost too late. Historian Bruce Catton's father told him that "'this problem of the overthrow of greed is absolutely the greatest problem that ever confronted any people'…and that the effort would require 'virtues superior to those demanded in contests that are settled by the sword.'" A sentiment vastly at odds with that of Chicago *Sun-Times* columnist Mike Royko who praises greed as the critical motivator that made America great!

Only racial prejudice and its behavioral manifestation, discrimination, have the very real potential to bring the nation down from within. No nation can remain strong and viable while divided against itself along the irrational lines of "race". W.E.B. Du Bois was prophetic in 1903 when he acknowledged the Color Line as being *the* Problem of the Twentieth Century. National public opinion polls show a continuing decline in white racial prejudice, a trend accelerated by the Civil Rights movement of the 1960s, when, according to journalist Leon Reese Cleghorn, many whites were struggling with the conflicts between their prejudicial stereotypes and their egalitarian inclination to accept everyone on the basis of individual merit. That so many whites have been confronting their own racial prejudices is evidence of both greater tolerance of racial differences and the extent of the problem remaining: Millions of other whites remain adamant and resist all efforts to be persuaded that blacks belong to the fraternity of humankind.

At any given period of American history there has been evidence of both a continuing "race problem" and the antithetical efforts to rectify it. And contrary to statements by neo-apologists, evidence of the magnitude of the "problem" mounts rather than diminishes. From the time when the "dominant employer in Rochester, N.Y. wouldn't hire Italians, blacks, or Jews",America has moved to the point where only blacks remain on the truly excluded list. Actions of the Reagan administration assured that overt racism and discrimination had come back strong again, and some of President Bush's actions tended to extend that tradition, which informed the hopeful that the "hump" was not yet overcome.

> After nearly two decades, five presidents, periods of both activism and apathy, largess and laissez-faire, the result has been at best stagnation…white America, left to its own devices, will never complete the unfinished task of creating racial equality.
> Walter Shapiro, "Unfinished Business," *Nation,* a review of National Research Council's *A Common Destiny: Blacks and American Society,* 1991

Desperate economic conditions prevailing during the last decade of the twentieth century do not point to a prosperous beginning of the twenty-first century. USA Today's Julia Lawlor projects that as the century closes, a college degree will not be worth what it was at the beginning, adding that one-third of "college graduates will hold a job that does not require a college degree," with some major employers such as General Motors doing no campus recruiting at all. Not only will all Americans without real wealth be affected but improved relations between black and white Americans, around which so much hope has been invested, are not likely to move forward. Suffering severe changes of lifestyle due to worsening economic conditions, millions of middle class white Americans cannot be expected to extend sympathy to the massive inequality still visited upon the majority of African Americans, even when it is from this white group—the middle class—that support for civil rights has traditionally come.

Indeed, the reverse is likely to be the case: many can be expected to join the ranks of the truly disaffected—the David Dukes—who attribute most or all of America's ills to civil rights and affirmative action (whatever the latter's intent, reality, or accomplishments.) At a social function of educated people this writer overheard a prominent white university professor exclaim to a white colleague that "affirmative action has torn this country apart." To highlight the twisted thinking and irrational emotionalism of such whites, this person had conveniently forgotten that his own university, the state's "flagship" institution of higher education, has had only two black *tenured* professors in its entire eighty-plus years history, one of whom had to take legal action to secure justice, the other achieving the exalted status of tenure through institutional reorganization—she was simply caught in the net at the right time and place. The truth of former Supreme Court Justice Thurgood Marshall's remark that "there is not a white man in this country who can say, 'I never benefited by being white'" is so obvious that many whites will consider it trash to be dumped on the pile of other garbage from the liberal do-gooders and hands-out fringe of the political left.

> ...no white American, including those who insist that opportunities exist for persons of every race, would change places with even the most successful black American...(Being white is) a security which is worth so much that not one who has it has ever given it away.
> Andrew Hacker

Yet we must never underestimate, as the Durants have cautioned, the economic fall from grace back into biology—the "law of the jungle"—characteristic of any person (or people), certainly in Western cultures, hemmed in by permanent unemployment, hunger and impacted despair. The Supreme Court Dred Scott decision not only said that blacks "had no rights which the white man was bound to respect," it added that the black man "might justly and lawfully be reduced to slavery for his benefit." Many whites, not alone in the South, have not forgotten this "remedy". No new laws are required to stymie black aspirations. Anti-black prejudice, being endemic in white American attitudinal makeup, has a life-force of its own. It is a *sentiment* that colors all aspects of white-black existence.

186

Economic fulfillment for most Americans will mean gainful employment. A drastically reduced supply of "decent" jobs will increase the already keen competition of the 1990s. Job discrimination against blacks that prevailed in the 1990s will appear tame compared to what will happen as the twenty-first century opens, for competition will come from quarters not considered significant only a generation ago. Discrimination in employment on the basis of *which* social group controls access will impact blacks in new ways. Jobs will be America's crucible in the twenty-first century.

John F. Kennedy appointed the nation's first black cabinet member, Dr. Robert Weaver, over strident Southern opposition. Bill Clinton appointed more African Americans (and women) than all other presidents combined. With anticipated economic demands from whites as the crisis deepens and grater visibility and political clout of Asians and Hispanics at century's end, it is doubtful that blacks will ever again be so prominent in the non-elective political mainstream.

Though intended to remedy race discrimination in employment *against blacks,* equal employment opportunity laws and affirmative action programs never achieved what many whites (out of ignorance or malice) and some blacks, believed or *willed.* As tools to address not past but *present* discrimination, these remedies in fact had very limited success particularly after the Reagan court achieved dominance. In the major battleground that is American higher education, for instance, despite a pervasive belief by whites that blacks are "over-represented" on faculties, nationally less than two percent of faculty are black. When faculty at historically black institutions are factored out less than one percent black faculty are present in predominately white institutions. And when black faculty working in community and junior colleges are subtracted—the less prestigious rung of the higher education ladder—what's left is an infinitesimally small group of black teachers in America's more than 3,000 colleges and universities. To the extent that equal opportunity and affirmative action have, with help of feared federal sanctions (more "paper" than real after Reagan), forced large employers to be more cautious (and subversive!) in personnel actions, these programs have enjoyed a degree of success, after the numerical successes of the early 1970s. Without them, Cornel West asserts, active and open discrimination against women and minorities "would return with a vengeance."

Whites are going to absurd lengths to discredit programs designed to benefit people of color through anti-discrimination programs. (Interestingly, the rhetoric of the right always targets *blacks* rarely including other "covered" groups.) In her *New York Times* column of January 19, 1992, "Young White Men Irked by Losing the Edge," Anna Quindlen noted how irrational and hate-filled much of the inflammatory anti-affirmative action rhetoric is. It's irrational because in almost all instances where blacks are said to be "taking over" or getting positions through "reverse discrimination" or preferential treatment, all one has to do is look around the workplace, whether "construction sites, the precinct houses, the investment banks," schools or almost any other place of work to discern the absurdity of these charges. In her encounters with college students, Quindlen remembered one white male who told her white men "don't have a chance," yet on his own campus "a scant five percent of his classmates were black."

Another illustration of the public having been misled as to the impact of affirmative action lies in the federal government itself. As reported previously, fewer than 20 blacks hold senior policy making positions in the federal Civil Service. In its December 16, 1991 issue, *Jet* magazine disclosed that of approximately 11,000 Senate and House staff jobs blacks occupy fewer than 400, with most of these working for the 26 black representatives in the House. Only one black law clerk has worked in the Supreme Court, he for Thurgood Marshall; all four of Clarence Thomas' clerks are white. In 1993 Blacks made up 22 percent of the workforce of the National Institutes of Health (NIH), yet only 3 percent of senior management. When a congressional committee held a hearing in response to black complaints, NIH director Healy said she sensed something amiss when assuming the position. The federal government cannot pretend to enforce anti-discriminatory laws when it is also guilty.

Most white Americans who parade their immigrant fore relatives out as successes who "arrived penniless and pulled themselves up by their bootstraps" apparently have no idea of the degree of economic oppression suffered by blacks throughout our history. Not only have individuals been barred from competition in much of the workplace but untold numbers have been denied access to financial and other resources necessary to building viable business enterprises. How many whites have been lynched because they dared open a grocery store in *their* neighborhood in competition with whites whose stores were elsewhere? It happened to blacks in Memphis. How many thriving white business districts have been bombed from the air and their residents carted off to internment camps? It happened to blacks in Tulsa. How many whites, simply because they were white, have been denied life insurance by the "ninth largest nonprofit health and welfare insurance company" in the nation, as alleged in a lawsuit brought by the Southern Poverty Law Center on behalf of a former top salesman "because he violated a company policy of not selling life insurance to blacks"? And how many white business persons with cash in hand, have had to hire a person of another "race" to make their major purchases when not in their neighborhood? It happened several times to multimillionaire black entrepreneur John Johnson. Until all forms of economic discrimination are eradicated, or at least sufficiently suppressed, equality of economic opportunity is a fraud.

Beginning with the Irish in the mid-19th century, virtually every wave of immigrants has been detrimental to black American welfare. As Du Bois and others concluded from systematic study, many stable, even though powerless and harassed, black communities have been torn asunder by immigrant ascendancy and preference.

Contemporary massive immigration especially from "South of the Border" (including South America) and Asia, coupled with pronounced increases in European, White South African, and Jewish newcomers (Russian and Israeli, with many perhaps most of the Russian Jews initially emigrating to Israeli eventually settling in the United States), can be expected to, again, strip more of the economic pie away from African Americans. The turmoil in what was the Soviet Union gave impetus to mass emigration of whoever could get out! One immigrant Soviet scientist predicted that if economic well-being continued to decline in the latter part of the 1990s as it had in the early years of the new republics, "you're going to see scientists coming over here by the tens of thousands and driving taxicabs." Whether America will permit their entry seems to have already been decided. Already by 1992 Russian teachers and researchers in American higher education had reached significant levels.

This new wave of immigration does not bode well for black America. The Cuban exodus to Miami has been detrimental to black Floridians as has the one-half million Salvadorians and millions from various Asian groups in Southern California and elsewhere. The Asian impact alone has begun to have great influence on some major American institutions. How will whites keep the Harvards "white" when they can't keep Asians out by claiming low test scores or inability to pay? UC at Berkeley Professor Troy Duster points out that Asian students—from places like Hong Kong, Korea, and China ("students with higher GPA's and SAT's") as well as Asian American students are putting the crunch on white student prospects for admission. Duster cites applicant flow records to illustrate the dilemma: In 1980 all applications to UC—Berkeley totaled 8,000. "In 1988, about 7,500 Asians alone applied," for about the same number of freshman seats. {This writer will devote a future volume to relations between African Americans and other influential—for blacks—social groups.}

Without a concerted organizational effort on the part of black leadership, blacks in the next century could very well be the forgotten Americans without even a pretense of public concern for our welfare. Others will have garnered all the attention and visibility. An illustrative case: At the urging of the affirmative action officer, a new white female chancellor at a major public university convenes a meeting of minority—non-white—faculty to provide a forum for raising issues needing institutional attention. In obviously muted voices all, except for the sole black professor, said things were okay. The black professor spoke of differential treatment she had experienced and of the lackadaisical treatment of black students. When asked by the affirmative action officer what she planned to do about the professor's concerns, the chancellor indicated that things seemed to be going smoothly and despite the black professor's complaints, there didn't appear to be any cause for alarm. Thus a non-black majority, albeit minority individuals, not generally known for their willingness to speak publicly of ill treatment, an institution turns a deaf ear to legitimate complaints.

On the positive side of the economic front, blacks can be expected to continue to show respectable gains in certain economic endeavors. Aside from the successful entrepreneurs and entertainers, the military and professional athletics will absorb a significant proportion of young blacks, even though there will be fewer in absolute numbers in each because of military cutbacks brought on by the end of the Cold War and new college athletic eligibility rules that will drastically reduce opportunity for young blacks to advance to the professional ranks in some fields.

In education, as in employment, there will be setbacks as well as advances. Ex-University of Wisconsin law professor Patricia Williams adds her voice to that of many others who express perplexity over the curious phenomenon of rising black high school graduation rates and *decreasing* black college attendance. Aside from fewer financial aid dollars, heightened campus racial conflict, and supposed disaffection with American institutions in general, young blacks are not battering at the doors of American higher education. Ex-Education Secretary Lamor Alexander's 1991 prohibition against using public money to fund race designated scholarship programs cannot but help to exacerbate the problem. Black leaders must develop a strategy to combat *any* policy or action that will act to limit black access to educational opportunity. At the same time much more attention must be given to the question of "education for what?" Part of that answer has to be a concern for matching *predicted* career opportunities and black youth aspirations. William F. Buckley, Jr.'s idea of a voluntary national service program for American youth to whet "the appetite to contribute to the health and morale of the republic" thereby fulfilling "a running debt to one's homeland" is sound. Given the condition of contemporary black youth, however, such a program should be mandatory for certain categories, as described in a previous section and it should train for *real* jobs, as ex-chiefs or staff chair Colin Powell told an audience in February 1994. With almost twice as many young black men in jail as in college in 1990, the need is clear.

The burgeoning black male and ethnic academies form another piece of the revised educational puzzle. Beset by concern over low and lack of academic achievements, apparent low self-esteem and obvious listlessness in direction of many inner city black youth, particularly young males, concerned adults are pursuing their own educational avenues outside public school curriculums. In Detroit, Boston, Milwaukee and other larger cities. The principal of a black high school in a Southern city explained his program:

> My purpose is to save the African American child. I call my action plan Operation Access—a Cultural Offensive—the Dream of Freedom Transformed to Action...the key element of my plan...is to infuse and flood the community with ethnicity...ethnicity is the basis ingredient in being an American. I understand how other ethnic groups use their ethnicity as a basis for achievement in scholastics and economics.

What an earlier generation of black leaders—including Booker T. Washington, W.E.B. Du Bois and Marcus Garvey—called "group effort" is back in vogue and may well be an important element in black striving in the next century. To move beyond mere survival to "liberation," in Kesho Scott's terms, African Americans must devote attention to *group* strategies. After experiencing the devastating effect of America's vastly superior artillery and air power, the Vietnamese communists adopted a battlefield strategy of "hugging the belt." In lay terms this meant: "I will stay so close to your forces that if you bomb me, *you* will also be hurt." African Americans, certainly many of our leaders, seemed to have adhered implicitly to such a strategy through our great emphasis on *integration*. It is now time for a reassessment and re-evaluation of options.

Related to greater black input into and decision making in education will have to be group generated programs to deal with the self esteem issue. Much of black on black pathology is, many experts contend, driven by the forces of external racism. Factors seemingly internal to the group are also at play. Intra-group caste segregation is still evident, for instance. In a major research effort spanning the decades beginning with the 1960s through the 1980s, two black sociologists confirmed that piece of folklore relegating the darkest of blacks to the bottom of the social and economic hierarchy. Skin tone, the researchers found, continues to be a major factor in the distribution of good jobs, praise, and rewards in black America. Light skinned blacks earn more money and have higher "occupational standing" even "when such factors as amount of educa-tion, marital status, sex, age, and parents' economic and social status were held constant."

> If you're light you're alright
> If you're brown stick around,
> If you're black get back!

Louis L'Amour's blue-eyed blond and Alice Walker's *black* black woman represent extremes in the American appearance game. Without across the board economic opportunity for all Americans, there is great doubt that this most irrational of phenomenons can be overcome. Even as black parents and educators must constantly make an effort to do so. The unfortunate situation for blacks in the America of the 1990s is that, unlike Paul Robeson, so few blacks *want* to be black.

In some African American communities black on black crime is of epidemic proportions. Even while the general American public mistakenly believes that most crime in the nation is committed by blacks in contradiction of the facts. (Law professor Patricia Williams, when confronted with this myth, points to U.S. Bureau of Justice Statistics which show, for instance in 1986, that "whites were arrested for 71.7 percent of all crimes; blacks and others...accounted for the remaining 28 percent.") It is of note that blacks have been spared the more heinous crimes such as mass murderers like Ted Bundy (killer of dozens of women) and Chicago's Charles Gacy (sex molester and murderer of scores of young boys) and the "organized gang of (teen) devil-worshipers (that) killed their parents" and "puzzled authorities." Some black youth join gangs and commit murder to "protect" turf and for other unacceptable reasons. But there has **never** been a reported case of black teenagers engaging in ritualistic "Satanic" crimes involving mutilation of sex organs and murder of younger males, as was alleged against three white 18 year old males in Arkansas in January 1994. Blacks do not kidnap, commit political terrorism, or "pull off big bank jobs." Nor do we engage in large scale fraud. It is worthy of note that the material or monetary value of *all* the crimes committed by blacks since our arrival in America does not equal the monetary value of theft committed by an Ivan Boesky *or* a Michael Milken. And outside of the 1973-73 so-called Zebra "political" murders in Los Angeles by the Black Angles wing of the Black Muslims, in which 14 whites were randomly killed, there had not been any black mass killing of whites since Nat Turner's legitimate rebellion to rid the South of slavery in the 1830s. (A Jamaican immigrant killed six whites and wounded a score of others, including Asians, on a New York subway train in December 1993.) In March 1994 a black man was arrested and charged with murdering at least seven young women. He had not been convicted as of the publication of this book.) Nor do blacks engage in incest or sexual child molestation at the same rate as whites. No Jim Jones or David Koresch has surfaced in the black community.

Whatever the national data, in order to have the stable communities and neighborhoods prerequisite for harmony and progress, crimes committed by blacks, homicides in particular, must be curtailed. This effort has to assume the combined forces of community leadership and broad participation and the active, fair commitment of municipal police agencies. It also takes into consideration the undeniable role played by external economic and political factors in fostering, sometimes promoting, criminal activity.

The criticism leveled against law enforcement and the entire criminal justice system merits serious attention and suggests that, at least those segments touching the lives of blacks (which is the majority), sincere overhauling needs to be undertaken. The Rodney King incident in Los Angeles and the killing of a 16 year old male African American by white new Orleans police officers (a local American Civil Liberties Union official said it sounds like the teen "was executed in cold blood"), the "suicide" hangings of black inmates in Mississippi jails, are actually frequent occurrences in black communities. Professor Williams (among others New York Judge Bruce Wright) has observed, "black and Hispanics are less likely to be given probation, more likely to receive prison sentences, more likely to receive longer sentences, and more likely to serve longer time" than similarly situated whites.

Many blacks and white observers of American law enforcement suggest the very racial make-up of police agencies patrolling minority neighborhoods is a factor in the discriminatory treatment they receive. Citing a study conducted by the Council on Interracial Books for Children, Professor Williams points out, for example, that as late as 1982, in New York City, with a 50 percent black and Latino population, "86.8 percent of police officers are white; 8.6 percent black; 4.5 percent Latino; 0.1 percent Asian or American Indian." Even having a black police commissioner (Benjamin Ward, followed by another black commissioner), himself under closer scrutiny than any past commissioner, could not undo damage caused by a police force constituted so apparently arbitrarily.

Ralph Ellison has spoken eloquently about the pain and paranoid suffering induced by fear that can visit at any time under threat of violence. In an interview he told novelist John Hersey:

"Human beings cannot live in a situation where violence can be visited upon them without any concern for justice—and in many instances without possibility of redress—without developing a very intense sense of the precariousness of all human life, not to mention the frailty and arbitrariness of human institutions."

Without reform there will be an inevitable reckoning.

As a reader I like western fiction, particularly those novels dealing with Plains Indians and their struggles with whites. I have yet to find a satisfactory way of telling, let alone convincing, my white friends who are also fond of westerns and to a person unhappy about their inevitable unhappy endings, that the same treatment is being meted out to blacks today on the streets of our cities and on the dusty back roads of the rural South.

Hard experience has taught black people this: Only those you know and trust can truly hurt you to the quick in this life. You expect to be hurt by everybody else.
Ralph Wiley, *Why Black People Shout,* 1991

A major concern of African Americans throughout our history has been the manner in which we have been perceived, studied and portrayed by whites. The present book's first chapter attempted to show that even as certain events occurred early in the nation's history to bring unity to a motley collectivity of similar, and dissimilar, human communities, that anti-black sentiment was a cementing cornerstone of the social, political, economic, and intellectual (including scientific) leadership. Indeed, the racism leveled upon black Americans has been so great that, according to eminent historian John Hope Franklin, in an early essay entitled "The Dilemma of the American Scholar," blacks, not viewed as capable of joining the select company of scholars in America" by virtually *all* white Americans, had not only to establish their credentials in chosen professions and disciplines but who, at some early point, felt compelled, as Franklin comments, "they *had* to combat the contentions of Negro inferiority," no matter what discipline they had been trained in—W.H. Crogan in Greek literature, physician C.V. Roman, Benjamin Brawley in English literature, Julean Lewis in biological science, among others. Black scholars in the waning years of the twentieth century feel the same compulsion: Thomas Sowell and Walter Williams in economics, Shelby Steele in English literature, Stephen Carter and Patricia Williams in law, (*not* civil rights law, by deliberate choice, but tax and commercial law respectively), among many, many others.

Unlike earlier generations of black scholars, serious divisions of perspective, portrayal, prescriptions and prognosis exist among the latest arrivals. Without repeating an earlier discussion about differences among them, suffice to say they all should be heard and judged on the extent to which they present accurate descriptions and useful and realizable remedies for the black American condition. Blacks and whites need to hear our diverse voices no matter how distasteful some of their views. A Leonard Jeffries of City College of New York, whom some consider anti-Semitic and excessively romantic about Africa, must be heard. So must a Thomas Sowell.

A warning: most black American political and media leaders, joined by

193

influential Jews and a segment of the larger white community, wish to discredit Louis Farrakhan, many wishing that he would simply "go away," in the words of a black newspaper publisher. They all vastly underestimate Farrakhan's appeal not only to the "underclass" but his growing support among black professionals and elements of the white working class. The "fifty" converts among the throngs of young blacks who flock to Farrakhan lectures, Cornel West contends, represent his true influence. Prominent black columnist Clarence Page calls him a fringe leader. Both are in gross error. Public silence or disapproval of Farrakhan based on fear of retaliation obscures a very large reservoir of covert agreement with the Nation of Islam leader. Until the rage on which his appeal is derived is addressed, a Farrakhan will have a large black audience. Understanding his appeals, more than attacking his biases, has yet to be achieved. In a March 1994 public address in Alaska, Page noted he had covered numerous Farrakhan speeches, several exceeding two hours. When the media reported on them at all, they gave attention only to the "15 seconds he engaged in anti-Semitic 'rhetoric.'" Indeed, Page contended, only Farrakhan and rapper ICE-T are considered true leaders by a large segment of black youth "because they are not compromisers."

A growing worry among black intellectuals and community leaders is that white conservatives have *appointed* certain of our scholars as *the* spokespersons for all the rest of us. (Thomas Sowell makes the claim that white liberals have "adopted black as mascots, in order to 'make a statement' against American society," a charge other blacks make of him and other black conservatives like Walter Williams.) And they are rewarded with prizes, lecture tours, and important posts in government and academe. Essayist Wiley says of Alice Walker that she was awarded a Pulitzer (for the derogatory *The Color Purple*) while James Baldwin never won one "even though he could write rings around Alice." And of Thomas Sowell, arguably the most quoted black scholar by whites of the left and right, Wiley says:

> Dr. Sowell is always turning up at some university or in some newspaper, talking in impressive academese about how black people can't do this and won't do that. Invariably, he is telling this to white people. It seems you cannot be a scholar without going by white people first...Dr. Sowell probably thinks it's his own brilliance that causes him to be so popular. I've got news for him. It's his – act.

One noted black scholar has gone so far as to posit "two kinds of blackness," roughly representing the two poles of black scholarship and culture celebration. Those who garner the prizes are "racial blacks," race being "essentially a group identity which is imposed on individuals by others," while the "cultural blacks" are those who collectively forged their own identities out of "the traditions, rituals, values and belief systems of African American people."

Not who by, but *how* our story is told is of obvious importance. Of equal importance is the willingness of white America to lend it's ears to the wide array of voices that would speak of and for us.

While the tug of war rages within the walls of academe between opposing forces (more often, most don't know, between black and white than among blacks) in the interpretation and projections about African American life, a more visible struggle is waged in our most popular medium—television. Again, not to go over ground already covered, it is important to add that this is one of the more promising educational vehicles for social change. Television portrayal of blacks has evolved from denigrating stereotypes to a much more realistic (though still circumspect in matters of interracial sex and political striving out of the mainstream) picture. When one considers all the competing ethnic and other interests desiring air time, it is nothing short of phenomenal that in the 1992 season nine additional black oriented programs were added with the loss of none from 1991. (Bill Cosby did announce that he was on his own pulling *The Cosby Show* after the 1992 season.) Speaking roles for blacks have increased dramatically, one survey found. Of 569 such roles "on 56 network shows…17 percent of characters are black," more than any other nonwhite group. So, while the pressure must continue to make television more responsive to the array of our demands, and, critically, employ more blacks in all aspects of the industry, it is entirely in error to claim no progress has been made. Combined with a new generation of blacks inspired, produced and *controlled* feature films, visual media has advanced far beyond print as a positive communication vehicle, even with setbacks represented by the films like Tina Turner's autobiographical *What's Love Got To Do With It?* and Oprah Winfrey's television movie *There Are No Children Here,* both of which glorify black male bashing. Winfrey's film, if taken to its logical conclusion, accuses black men of in fact creating black public housing projects since it is by their absence that black women are forced into these unlivable habitations.

Corporate television is making belated but important adjustments to black America. Having learned through viewer surveys that African Americans, per capita, constitutes the medium's largest viewing public, a BBDO Worldwide advertising survey, confirming that blacks and whites don't like the same kind of programs -" the top 10 favorite prime-time shows among blacks are completely different from the overall top 10," is forcing network executives to offer more realistic programming. *Cheers* doesn't make a lot of sense to most blacks.

Since its founding America has been inexorably evolving, at a greater or lesser pace, toward inclusion and utilization of all its human resources. Though blacks continue to "bring up the rear" in acceptance and opportunity, the closing years of the twentieth century witnessed prospects for despair rarely known on the North American continent. Never before have so many been forced to feel a basic insecurity and fear of the future.

Yet even with the widespread sense of foreboding some Americans are pressing forward with a progressive agenda regarding race and racism. That some whites have taken it upon themselves to both recognize and act on the divisive racial issue is shown in this excerpted segment of a resolution passed at the 1991 Kiwanis International convention:

"encourages racial harmony and calls on all Kiwanians and Kiwanis clubs to help bring about an end to racism globally by: examining their attitudes toward races and the treatment of others as a result of these attitudes; raising the awareness level of other adults and children about racism and its negative affects; promoting the position that racism is not permanent, unalterable human condition and is no longer a viable option in human interaction; and making efforts to end racism a top priority of educational systems, organizations, and communities worldwide."

Having about 400,000 members worldwide Kiwanis is a service organization of upwardly mobile professionals and business people. It once barred blacks and women from membership.

It is my heart...not my ancestry, leading me to believe that if Almighty God ever set a single test by which to judge the republic's ability to fulfill its promise of liberty for all men, that test is race.
John Jakes, *Heaven and Hell*

"People will do great things if you will only set them free."
President George Bush, State of the Union Address, January 28, 1992

INTO THE 21ST CENTURY

On Moral Values

On the subject of moral values, a Vermont neurologist misses something when he claims, in an article condemning white racism, that "the black ghetto is nothing more than white upper middle class America overlaid on poverty: and that "the values are ours, the actions simply mimed in a setting of sewage and rodents." He misses the fact that even though present in black communities, homosexuality, and the AIDS derived from that form of sexual activity; abortion (as a moral decision); incest; murder without motive, conscience or remorse; treason; suicide (until-recently); child abandonment by teen mothers; and "disrespect" for the human body as evidenced in the wearing of bikinis, are all held in implicit disdain.

Black ex-Harvard conservative social scientist Glenn Loury was closer to the truth than the neurologist when he told television commentator Bill Moyers that "blacks no longer need our white values of convenient divorce, child estrangement, neglect of elderly members, unbridled violence and absent sexual restraint in our newspapers, television programs and movies". Social historian Lerone Bennett echoes this view adding that blacks cannot afford to "uncritically and completely" accept the values "of his oppressors" if we would survive.

In reality, in the way of things, as Dr. Loury points out, blacks need little of what whites have: not their culture, life style, sex life, religion. What we do need, the *only* real need is money, and the prerogatives it provides. Baseball great Jackie Robinson summed it well in his autobiography *I Never Had It Made:*

Money is America's God, and business people can dig black power if it coincides with green power.

In the end what whites will have to understand is that no matter what our differences of culture, color or class, African Americans, in the words of ex-National Urban League Director Vernon Jordan, struggle for the "same thing white people take for granted…a safe neighborhood, a good job with fair wages, food in the refrigerator, beer in the cooler, tuition for their children, a two-week vacation, a pension, insurance, a quiet funeral and a debt-free estate."

> …a people who for four hundred years waged a battle for the right to be ordinary, to be as individuals, like everybody else; some good, some bad, some wise, some foolish, here and there a genius, now and then a fool.
> the late publicist Louis Lomax

A quest for bringing back traditional values, sometimes in new clothing, is underway in large segments of black America. The African American post-Christmas holiday celebration of unity and love called Kwanzaa (devised by university professor Ron Karenga in the late 1960s) has spread nationwide in popularity, as has the traditional family reunion.

On Integration

One of the ostensible social goals of school integration was to give children a better opportunity to understand one another across racial lines, thereby reducing racial prejudice and misunderstanding based on stereotype. Given the amount of racial animus, hostility, and ignorance still prevailing after more than a generation of school (if not *social*) desegregation, that goal, clearly on a large scale, has not been achieved. (In December 1993 the Harvard Project on School Desegregation released a report that documented a return to pre-1968 segregation levels, finding that two-thirds of black children are attending predominately black schools. The report warned that "The civil rights impulse from the 1960s is dead in the water and the ship is floating backward toward the shoals of racial segregation.") Judge Wright notes that blacks are "as unknown to white thought as are the strange complications of Sanskrit to English-speaking hearers." Much evidence supports this contention. A high school counselor told writer Tony Parker that he was worried about a situation where whites pretend blacks don't exist, illustrating his point with a story of an encounter with a parent, "to all extent otherwise a reasonably intelligent well-educated person:"

> "Do you know, in all my life I've never met a black person and I wouldn't want to. Not because I'm color prejudiced or anything, because I'm not; it's just I don't like black people, that's all."

In Louis L'Amour's The Strong Shall Live the invisibility of people whose existence whites would rather not admit reaches high clarity. A man new to the western frontier looks for open range land to claim. He inquires of townspeople:

"What's off there?" gesturing toward the west.

A townsman replies, "Nothing but wilderness, some of the wildest, roughest country on earth and some bloodthirsty Indians."

"No people?"

"None."

Until whites admit of our visibility and our humanity, until they, in the words of judge Wright, no longer "perceive a darker skin color and find in that difference some comfort of superiority," there is no resolution of racial bigotry.

Representative of the degree of white resistance to integration is a discovery I made on a visit to Jackson, Mississippi in 1991. A native of the city explained that the proportion of white middle class children attending "Christian" academies is probably higher than those attending public desegregated schools. When asked if any blacks were enrolled in the private schools she remembered that one had enrolled but was dismissed when no other school would play football against his team. Over the years numerous black teachers in desegregated schools have related how white parents had their children transferred to classes with white teachers. A long-time black teacher friend related that a white first grader told her he didn't like black teachers.

Also indicative of white power of the old variety is that in what otherwise is a serious effort to develop an African American heritage museum in Jackson, there is not one artifact or other display of the white terrorism, such as lynching, that has been so much a feature of that state's history. I didn't need to inquire of the omission; the entire building and its contents would have been put to the torch. Even so, black Mississippians have reason to be proud of their achievement.

On Residential Segregation

A fundamental fact of race relations in 20th century America (as it will be in the 21st century) is that white Americans want distance between themselves and black Americans. Residential segregation is a fact of life that African Americans have to acknowledge and, rather than putting so much energy into complaining and litigating (though this is absolutely necessary since all Americans should be able to reside where they wish to and can afford to), black organizations should devote more of their resources to bread and butter issues like jobs and employment discrimination.

Blacks must look again at Booker T. Washington's "drop your bucket where you are" dictum and W.E.B. Du Bois's "Nation Within a Nation" idea. Building strong, viable communities rather than running away from those needing leadership (and running away, in fact from blackness). Beautiful black communities exist all over this country—well maintained by prideful owners. Historian John H. Clark and multimillionaire entrepreneur Percy Sutton have between them almost 100 years continuous residence in Harlem. They wouldn't live anywhere else although they can afford to. Sutton says, "there's a warmth about Harlem" that he wouldn't trade for a "penthouse downtown."

My friend Iola expresses a similar attachment: "I too felt warm in Chicago's 'black belt.' Today, I'm afraid on the streets which once gave me comfort, yet I too wouldn't trade my community for a penthouse anywhere."

On Campus Racial Tensions

Campus violence stemming from racial and religious bigotry flared at many colleges and universities in the last two decades of the 20th century, but its objective of fomenting widespread rejection of minorities was not achieved. Institutional programs have surfaced and been supported on the national level by such relatively new groups as the National Institute Against Prejudice and Violence, the National Organization of Black Law Enforcement Executives, the National Center for the Study and Prevention of Campus Violence, and the Center for Democratic Renewal. Nathan Rutstein's more than 100 Healing Racism Institutes in the U.S., Canada and Great Britian are available to colleges and universities. For younger children, the Southern Poverty Law Center has developed a "Teaching Tolerance" kit which as of January 1992 had been "sent free to educators in public and private schools across the country." Future mailings are planned.

One of the most disappointing and shortsighted pieces of news from the education front comes from an unexpected source: the liberals. During a one month period in 1990 the *Chronicle of Higher Education,* the most widely read periodical by college and university professionals, three major essays appeared decrying the clustering together of black students on campus. Add these to popular black professor Shelby Steele's piece about black students ruining their life chances by self-ghettoization, a casual observer of campus race relations could conclude that institutions are not harming black students, they are the cause of their own downfall. The problem with all of these essays is that they ignore substantial research all of which point to the utility of students banding together. It is when they do not or when they associate *exclusively* with only other blacks that they tend to miss opportunities. There is absolutely no reason why a black student cannot associate socially with other blacks and not at the same time have various kinds of ties across racial lines with other groups. To suggest otherwise is to engage in the most insidious form of racism. A black Harvard coed explains:

> "Here we have a small minority community that sticks together. We depend on each other for support. Harvard can be very cold emotionally and physically. I'm used to warm people and warm weather."

bell hooks (she does not capitalize her name) teaches at a white institution and has commented on criticism of black students unity: "…all social manifestations of black separatism are often seen by whites as a sign of anti-white racism, when they usually represent an attempt by black people to construct places of political sanctuary where we can endure, if only for a time, white domination." A graduate of such an institution told the author that black students need "a sanctuary where we can *escape*."

When Native American, Hispanic, and Jewish students associate freely within their own groups, no complaint is heard. Indeed, colleges in many areas of the country applaud the positive role played by ethnic based student organizations. At the University of Alaska there is general acknowledgment that without such programs retention of Alaska Native students would be almost impossible. Why is that only when African Americans come together for bonding (and increasingly for protection) is there an outcry?

Research providing reasons for Asian student success concluded that "studying together" was a major factor.

In the Tony Brown film *White Girl*, a new (transfer) student at a predominately white college asks another black female, if she would be joining the black student organizations and says "If it weren't for the Black Student Union I don't think I could stand this place." To which the new student replies, "Why come to a white college to set up a Black group." Because says her companion, "we're trying to survive—that's why."

A law school student, one of 11 blacks in a class of 200, giver further testimony of the dual burden with which black students have to cope. "If I had gone to a black law college,: he wrote, "I wouldn't have had to deal with racism but could have spent my time concentrating on being the best I could be."

Much of American higher education is indeed hostile territory for African Americans. The extent to which blacks "feel" the rejection is reflected in, for example, the theme of the Association of Black Women in Higher Education 15th annual conference (June 1993): African—American Women in the Academy: Developing an Agenda or Empowerment In An Unfriendly Climate.

I and other black higher education careerists have noted over the years how when even two blacks walk openly together, or eat together—whatever—there are always stares of curiosity, stares of hostility, and stares of "blank expressions" from whites. Even Shelby Steele has commented that he always makes sure he is dressed properly professorially so as to not draw the wrong kind of attention to his blackness.

Racial unrest is not confined to the college campus. In tiny Oregon, Wisconsin, just minutes away from "progressive" Madison, overt racist hostility is an everyday obstacle course for the handful of black students in the high school. I know this personally because my 15 year old son is a freshman there. Name calling is the least of his worries. Fear of using the restroom, being pushed into lockers and otherwise physically intimidated, having to endure "white power" blockades in school corridors, are daily items on the racial menu. Enduring and prevailing (he proudly sent me a commendation earned for scoring high—96%—on a math test), he and the three other black and biracial students are monuments to enduring American values — courage, pride, faith, stick-to-it-ness. About white parents and other adults who promote, support, and condone (even in silence) racist student behaviors, my friend Iola has written, "Oregon High School has a problem. (Its black students) are not its problem. If their parents pay taxes these moneys help to finance (the School). It appears that the OHS community (and many, many others) wants no part of African Americans ... (However) when and if the objects of contempt (black students) are gone Ed, these people will turn to the differences among themselves (as sources of friction).

However heroic my son's actions in dealing with that environment, he will not return next year, even as I know his detractors will be effusive in self congratulation. In my mind he will have met and bested the enemy.

On Positives for Public Education

On the public education front the most heartening news is the growing number of corporations and individual industrialists who in recognition of the reality of a changing racial demography are insisting that education address real world needs. Philanthropists like New York's Eugene Lang and Kansas City billionaire Ewing Kauffman have joined with other moneyed individuals from around the country combatting in concrete terms the practice of trying to compete in a global economy while denying opportunity to a large segment of the nation's citizenry. By 1993, at least one state higher education agency had joined this struggle with a creative program. Rhode Island's commission of Higher Education promises its third graders "from needy families" a deal they can't afford to bypass. Students sign a 10-year agreement to "remain in school, stay off illegal drugs, and avoid pregnancy." For all who keep the pledge the state will guarantee a "tuition-free post secondary education."

On Black Resistance to Racist Violence

White racists who would commit physical violence against blacks are encountering a new form of black resistance. Klanwatch's *Intelligence Report* chronicles increasing confrontations between racist demonstrators and black counter-protestors. Maya Angelou's mother's expression of outrage characterizes this group. She told her daughter:

> "Animals can sense fear. They feel it. Well, you know that human beings are animals, too. Never, never let a person know you are frightened. And a group of them...absolutely never. Fear brings out the worse things in anybody. (Those) whites in the (hotel) lobby knew you were scared as a rabbit...But something about me told them, if they mess with either of us, they'd better start looking for some new asses, 'cause I'd blow away what their mommas gave them'."
> Maya Angelou, *The Heart of a Woman*

While the black struggle is unlikely to employ violence as a major weapon, white racists can no longer with impunity and without thought of consequence to themselves practice physical intimidation against blacks.

A report released by the Southern Poverty Law Center in late 1993 documents increased frequency of hate crimes of blacks *against* whites, noting that "not long ago it was extremely rare to find cases that even hinted of blacks attacking whites in hate-crime type situations."

On the Plight of Young Black Men

During the sixties I, like most Black middle income Americans, participated in civil rights demonstrations, joined the march on Washington and did all the other things that a good Black citizen was expected to do at the time. Although extremely critical of the status quo and often bitter in its denunciation, in the back of my mind, there was always a belief that, given time and intelligent struggle, this nation would come to its senses and accept the Black man as a human being. I no longer believe that.
quoted in *Betrayal By Any Other Name*, by Khalid Al-Mansour

Problems faced by young black men are similar to those confronting their age peers. Young men the world over, cultural anthropologist David Gilmore discovered, somewhat to his surprise, have to vindicate their manhood through "tests and challenges." When there are few culturally acceptable challenges available the young create their own, thus explaining why young black men join gangs and father children they cannot support. Until the larger society values them as much as it does young white men and until black adult men assume a larger share of responsibility for guiding their younger brothers, there is not much hope that the rate and nature of involvement with the criminal justice system, low educational achievement, and high fathering rates will change.

When you have no home, you forget everything, even who you are.
James Thom, *Panther In the Sky*

Given the undesirability and unsuitability of many black communities in terms of their lack of stability and general inability to nurture the young, particularly males, a massive program of remediation must be undertaken. While responsible black adults work to bring security and stability to neighborhoods, the federal government in concert with industrial leaders must institute a massive Job Corps-like effort. Jointly funded by the government and the private sector such a program would remove, through voluntary recruitment supplemented by certain classes of those already incarcerated, large numbers of black youth, including females, from their social environments, relocate them to residential training camps, where programs designed by companies who will hire them will be provided. Adult blacks would provide the critical training in social skills needed to survive and achieve in the larger society. The jobs provision must be "real" and remunerative to the extent of making "believers" in the promise of the "system." Training not connected to real jobs—a "place"—will only serve to reinforce low self esteem and deepened cynicism about being left out. These young men and women have to come away from the experience believing, if not knowing, that they are valued, respected, wanted, needed, and appreciated.

Gang activity, especially among young black men, is of increasing concern. In a survey by the University of California Center for Research on Crime and Social Control, in 94 percent of American cities, gangs were identified, a 50 percent increase since 1984. The survey researchers were surprised not only at the number of gangs—more than 1000 in Los Angeles alone ("gang capital of the world")—but that, while black gang membership was greater, Asian, Hispanics and white youth had their own gangs.

Why do youth join gangs rather than traditional groups such as Scouts, Boys Clubs, YMCA, etc.? Aside from the fact that many middle class-oriented youth organizations have no branches in many inner cities, young blacks join for some of the same reasons alienated white youth join skinhead groups. Rapper ICE-T said the first time he found love was in a gang. Floyd Cochran said young whites join white supremacist groups in search of "a family and a place to belong"…and they are "given a structure and told what to do."

A "war against gangs" will be even less successful than the so-called war on drugs. The drug traffic in inner city communities is not controlled by the gangs who traffic them; that's the preserve of well endowed and protected (out of the line of fire) whites. Inner city residents, nevertheless, have to use every means at their disposal to combat this pestilence. Under present economic and social conditions, attempting to eliminate gangs would be folly. *It's not the gang but what it does that should be attacked.*

Gangs can be constructive forces in a community. Black youths have to become *warriors* acting on behalf of the total community against all internal and external adversaries. Black churches have to somehow connect to gangs, for as Tucker Carlson wrote,

"church attendance is the most accurate indicator of whether black men will become criminals."

On Black-On-Black Crime

Most observers of urban crime agree that much of the increase over the past two decades is drug related. The earlier introduction of heroin by whites into black communities has been far surpassed by cocaine. The *60 Minutes* (Nov. 21, 1993), expose of the CIA's role in massive drug trafficking points to an enormous task which black leaders will have to tackle before true "safe neighborhoods" will become a reality. It is clear that white America is not inclined to take on this monstrous betrayal of trust.

Blacks must (and are beginning to in many communities) take steps to design innovative strategies for policing their own neighborhoods. Because of the sheer magnitude of the problem, many police departments cannot, or will not, do the job. Since most of our communities do not exist in "less violent times" that were "largely absent of the prevailing pathology of poverty, despair, drug abuse, and violent death, and where social reinforcements sustained a supportive cultural environment," in James Edward's words, we have to adopt methods to what presently *is*. Anytime a black community can sustain 16 homicides in *one* week, as did the District of Columbia in 1993, drastic action is called for. The black community has to decide what form that action will take.

As many black neighborhoods are literally combat zones, only a civilian-military response employing whatever weapons are required for particular situations can effectively curb the criminally inclined. Vigilantism, with all its inherent dangers, is the weapon of last resort but there appears to be no alternate to its use in many communities. Well meaning rhetoric about crime being a function of poverty, thus implying the former cannot not be curbed without first attacking the latter, must give way to a new set of imperatives calling for Safe Neighborhoods at any cost!

Whatever else may be said of black-on-black crime, it is a certainty that young homicide victims are providing much needed organs for transplanting into individuals who would otherwise die, such as the governor of Pennsylvania.

On Police Abuse of Authority

The most effective short-term means of curtailing police brutality is to make *individual* officers liable and accountable for their conduct on duty. The City of Los Angeles has paid out millions of dollars in settlements and court judgments because of police abuse of citizens. Until individual abusers are also fined—out of their own pockets, they will continue to misuse authority and snicker about their actions. Just as the Southern Poverty Law Center had enjoyed great success putting Klan and other white supremacist organizations and their leaders out of business by seeking judgments and organizational assets, so too can individual officers have to pay for their own violation of law.

The long-term solutions requires restructuring police leadership and better screening of recruits.

On Black Self-Help Organizations

Blacks have no national organizations or leaders, save perhaps Jesse Jackson, who can speak and act with real authority and power on their behalf. Were this not the case, the falsely accused black engineer in Texas and the marine unjustly convicted of rape would not have had to be saved through the exposés of *60 Minutes*. If the National Association for the Advancement of Colored People were more than a membership organization with shrill voice, it could effectively intervene across a broad spectrum of critical cases and issues affecting black individuals and the collectivity. Any organization in existence almost one century that never even owned its headquarters building for most of that period (even threatened with eviction) can hardly be expected to exert willful, consistent effort on behalf of its constituents. Any national organization claiming power status that cannot persuade an American president (Reagan in this case) to meet even once in eight years with its leaders cannot lay claim to having any real power or influence. Until a black national organization emerges that rivals, say, the Anti-Defamation League or the American Jewish Congress in influence and power, it is foolish even embarrassing for blacks to parade their organizations around as though they can work miracles. It is to be hoped that Ben Chavis, Jr., NAACP's new executive director will understand, among other things, that no organization with a constituency as affluent as Black America, has a right to exist if that constituency refuses to fund it. (The same pertains to other facets of black life. "The largest Afro-American museum in the country," in Los Angeles, is threatened with closure due to lack of funding. If blacks will not keep it open, it should be closed.)

Once acknowledged as one of the most organized social groups in America blacks in late 20th century America have witnessed a gross and dramatic decline in neighborhood based support organizations. Prior to the late 1960s virtually all black communities, no matter their economic status, were characterized by the presence of not only numerous denominational churches but mutual aid societies, women's and men's benevolent and fraternal organizations. Networks of support spawned formal as well as ad hoc avenues to which an individual could turn. Behavioral norms were set and reinforced through a system of rewards and lenient "punishments." The "triangle of love" was much in evidence with churches, their ministers, deacons and ushers always available to respond to community need. There was mutual respect if not mutual admiration between churchgoers and the few wayward and non-believers.

While churches in abundance are still to be found in African American communities their role as peacemakers, emergency relief agencies, a place for socializing (and youth socialization), and, most important, as carriers of the cultural tradition, has dissipated. In contemporary black America virtually all of these traditional functions (except in remnant form) are now assumed by others and, it is said, no longer provide quality leadership or serve as mentors, counselors, and role models. A black male acquaintance informed the author that his minister makes a point of periodically reminding his audience to "do as I say, not as I do" to excuse some of his excesses. Perhaps a measure of black youth estrangement and alienation from an institution desperately needed is found in low attendance or affiliation and a high degree of church vandalism and theft.

As the new century emerges, African Americans of all social groups need communal support structures. Informed, interested and committed adults will have to come forward to replace those who made the exodus from the inner cities and rural towns when racial integration seemed the ticket to salvation.

On Black Political Leadership and Economics

Black political leadership is in disarray. Yes, there has been progress. Mississippi, of all places, for instance, can boast of a black chair of the State Democratic party, the "only black state chairman in either party," as Tom Baxter observes. The national Democratic Party "made history" by picking Ronald Brown as its first African American chairman. A progressive, highly educated black man from Baltimore has joined the ranks of other big city black mayors; and black elected officials are showing up in places least expected such as the Oregon statehouse and an Ohio Assembly district that is 65 percent white. In 1986 there were more than 6,500 black elected officials compared to fewer than 200 before passage of Lyndon Johnson's 1965 Voting Rights Act. By 1993 that number had surpassed 7,000.

The disarray is evidenced by lack of both consensus on just what the black agenda should be, or even if there is a *black* agenda. Maverick leader Roy Innis of the Congress of Racial Equality told the U.S. Civil Rights Commission that the goals of the civil rights movement of the '50s and '60s have been achieved and urged the Commission to direct more of its attention to "black prejudice against Asians…and whites."

Much of the leadership of the "Movement" era is unavailable to the current generation of blacks. Of those who had a degree of influence such as Martin Luther King and Malcolm X, many have gone the way of the Black Panthers 'Lil' Bobby Hutton and Hewy Newton—the assassin's bullet. Bobby Seale sells cook books; Eldridge Cleaver converted to the Mormon Church (which a popular black magazine penned as the church considered most racist by blacks); Julius Lester, formerly one of our better "propagandists" is now an embattled black Jew, considered an anti-black black by his African American colleagues at a major Eastern university.

Confusion reigns also because political gains have not been followed by economic opportunities and advances. Ghana's Kwame Nkrumah dogma that "Seek you first the political kingdom and all other things will be added unto you" has not worked in Africa or in America's blighted cities. What has in fact happened in cities controlled by black mayors, reports Georgia Persons, is that a few individuals are getting rich while little is done "to ameliorate the perilous conditions of the black poor," the bedrock of the politicians' careers. TransAfrica's Randall Robinson and the Hoover Institute's Thomas Sowell are in agreement on at least one issue: political power without economic power is illusory power—no power at all.

With some justification, blacks like to point with pride to Atlanta as the black mecca, a city controlled politically by blacks and supposedly brimming over with blacks who have "MADE IT." Yet Ron Taylor reports that Atlanta is bested by only Newark, New Jersey, another black led city, in proportion of poor people. And a *Frontline* report concluded that Chicago has a million people (when Washington was mayor) who "suffer from severe hunger often going to bed unsure whether they have food for the next day."

In defense of black mayors it is true that not even the best connected *white* leader could work the miracles necessary to overcome the inherited blight of our metropolitan areas. But pointing that out does not excuse the actions of some of our mayors, most notably the former mayor of the nation's capitol. While exercising the rights of citizenship to attain political influence, blacks must come to understand the relationship between politics and economics realizing the limitations imposed on mayors by a shrinking tax base, deteriorating infrastructures, and, at best, rhetorical expressions of concern from Washington and most of their state capitols. Black citizens, recognizing the massive nature of the problems facing their communities, must demand an economic agenda on the scale of A. Philip Randolph's "Freedom Budget," a comprehensive plan to address the dire problems of "the least of us," the vast and growing underclass. We do not have to be as optimistic as the late Ralph Abernathy, a former King aide, who told a Fairbanks, Alaska, gathering that in another generation blacks will have almost reached the economic millennium, "owning banks, sitting on (corporate) boards, and have a stronger stake in the social and economic life of America." We do have to recognize the leverage which could be gained from utilizing the several billion dollars in real money at our disposal each year to build solid black economic enclaves that would potentially influence and redirect the course of American economic and political life.

On Black Child-rearing

The confusion in the leadership extends down into child-rearing. Black parents no longer know "how to explain discrimination to their children," wrote Thomas Morgan (although unlike whites, according to a black female physician, "black people as a whole don't teach their children to hate white people, or look down on white people.") Black parents of earlier generations knew who the "enemy" was; and leaders could explain from whence they came and where they were trying to get to. Marcus Garvey sought a "New Negro...proud racially conscious and ready to fight back, but also hard-working, well-behaved and frugal." He wanted to make being black a "virtue" rather than the "crime" it appeared to many whites and some blacks. The late educator Benjamin Mays thought of the "heroic deeds" of his father and "of those captives who fought and died on board ship...rather than become slave" and acclaimed them responsible for having "driven me on." Before he was ten years old Jesse Jackson knew he would be an achiever "the day the white grocer stuck a .45 revolver in his face" because blacks were not permitted the privilege of whistling in his store. A true to life black mother in Michener's *Chesapeake* admonishes her only son:

"Your job is to stay alive, Keep away from notice. Doan' do nothin'to attract attention...Doan' never challenge a white man..."

On relations with white women: "They don't exist. They ain't there."

Black adults must train the young to be warriors. Warriors are disciplined; know who the enemy is; can anticipate problems—with police, educators, employers, and others meaning them harm. They know how to set goals, and how to achieve them. They respect legitimate authority and know how to deal with the illegitimate. They have been trained to *out-think* not *out-react* their adversaries. One of their texts will be Sun Tzu's much translated *The Art of War.*

In the 21st century the black males who survive will be those who have warrior skills and attitudes, the totally submerged waifs, and the few who are lucky.

I have personally taught young black men who became warriors:

Phil Donahue
The Phil Donahue Show

Dear Phil:

Yesterday an elderly white male friend reported to me that your March 3 show featured an African American female who, in his words, "was really tough on you (black) guys. She called you shiftless, dishonest, womanizers, and a lot of other unnice names." I said to my friend that that person (could it have been Alice Walker? He couldn't recall the name) was one of a parade of black women currently engaging in black male bashing who evidently cannot see the forest for the trees, meaning they tell only part of the story.

I was prompted to write this letter by a telephone call from a former student of mine who gives lie to her testimony. Without going into a long biographical statement about many of my former black male high school students, I challenge you to randomly select any from the class of 1974-75, bring them on your show and let them tell the rest of the story in their own words. These guys for the most part came from the *inner* inner cities of Milwaukee, Detroit, Chicago, and St. Louis, yet with few exceptions (notable among them the sons of prominent black families, obviously not from inner cities), they have "made it", presently working as bankers, attorneys, physicians, fire fighter executives, self-employed businessmen, and so on. Their success also gives lie to much of the rubbish about preferential admissions, affirmative action, and other efforts designed to address severe race based inequities.

I dare you to bring them on your show!

Sincerely,

Needless to say, there was no reply from Phil.

Despite racial harassment from some fellow students, professors and later co-workers (as recently as the summer of 1993 a former student, now a physician, phoned to ask my opinion of his consideration of a relocation due to continued harassment by some white colleagues), these young men are success stories. They stayed the course and achieved what even in 1993 many

208

naysayers claimed couldn't be done by blacks of their background; and their "happy endings" continue, I know, because they have remained in touch with one another and they sometimes throw surprise reunion parties when I happen to be passing through.

Many similar "experiments" with inner city youngsters of the late 1960s and 1970s proved as successful as the one I participated in at the Jesuit boarding school; and they demonstrated (again) that with a little positive nudging African American children will excel. While most such programs faltered when the "window of opportunity" squeezed almost shut in the late 1970s and 1980s, a few, such as the A Better Chance program in the Northeast, still thrive.

It is tempting to believe that the success of such programs surprised and frightened many who are now anti-affirmative action spokespersons. For if it worked for my students think of how many more of our trapped and tragedy— bound kids could be saved. One suspects that the ultimate threat to the neoconservatives was fear of loss of control of the educational establishment and access to jobs.

> "Fight them with all you have. Scratch the ground so that even if you are defeated, people passing will say, 'Two people fought here.'"
> Chinua Achebe

In 1993 two important books by black experts were published on the subject of black child-rearing. They are *Raising Black Children* (reissued) by the psychiatrists James Comer and Alvin Poussaint, and *Different and Wonderful: Raising Black Children in a Race-Conscious Society* by the clinical psychologist husband-wife team Darlene and Derek Hopson. My own *Black Students in Interracial Schools* (2nd edition 1994) promotes achievement in high school and college.

On Equal Employment Opportunity and Affirmative Action

Americans need to understand several things about affirmative action. It was not intended nor has it generally operated to force employers to hire unqualified persons. No massive gains have been made by blacks in employment, a fact supported by data on black un- and under-employment and the two-thirds of us still living below, at, or just above the poverty line. We also need to understand that millions of whites believe, erroneously unfortunately, that passage of the 1964 Civil Rights Act eliminated race discrimination though millions of others know, through their own experiences, observations and reading that that is not the case.

Blacks should also realize that when whites speak of how hard they, their parents and grandparents might have had to work to tame the land, make careers, or hold onto jobs, they speak (many, that is) the truth. The poverty dramatized in Loretta Lynn's *Coal Miner's Daughter* was, and is, real.

Even with the advantage of "white" skin coloration in a race conscious society life "ain't (necessarily) been no crystal stair" for millions of whites, either. True, the land was brutally wrestled from the Indians, but beyond this "gift" what has been achieved came at heavy cost.

In the early implementation of Lyndon Johnson's executive order mandating affirmative action in hiring and promoting women and minorities, major gains were made by blacks in major corporations and some public institutions, a period a Harvard acquaintance agreed was a "brief window of opportunity." Since the mid 1970s those gains have steadily eroded due to lack of enforcement by the U.S. Labor Department and growing resistance from whites fueled by unscrupulous politicians and neoconservative educators and media pundits. Without an enforceable affirmative action effort there is little evidence to support a view that employers will offer job opportunities in an across-the-board fair and equitable manner. The most definitive research on the government's affirmative action requirement clearly demonstrates that for those organizations operating under the legal mandate (which *excludes* about 80 percent of employers) the level of black employment was significantly higher than in those firms and institutions not required to take affirmative action.

Despite the worthwhileness of the government's efforts on behalf of black employment, an effort seriously curtailed under the Reagan administration and the current Supreme Court, blacks can expect minimal government sanctioned efforts in the future.

For conservative whites like Rush Limbaugh (*The Way Things Ought to Be*) and David Brock (*The Red Anita Hill: The Untold Story*), affirmative action programs are "reverse discrimination" because, in Limbaugh's words, they "transfer discrimination from one race to another." In the "real" world, however, there is good affirmative action and bad affirmative action. Anita Hill represents the "bad" because, in their view, she didn't take to Yale Law School the necessary academic tools to be successful without some unspecified special boost. Clarence Thomas, on the other hand, was a special black who made it on his own—all the way to the Supreme Court (about which Hispanic educator David Ochoa had this to say: "I doubt that a person who graduated from law school in the middle of his class, has only 16 months of judicial experience and is not a recognized legal scholar even comes close to being the 'best' person to be nominated.")

As previously mentioned, affirmative action has not been a god-send for blacks; and, Hacker points out, if there has been any harm to white males, it has been "relatively small." More important, in Hacker's view, is how so many whites have been convinced that it is a giveaway for blacks: "there is something about the race of the recipients that bothers conservatives in ways they cannot always articulate in a coherent manner."

Whites don't seem to be aware of, or wish to be reminded of, how much "affirmative action" has always worked to their benefit in this country. Simply *being* white, without *doing* anything, is rewarded. More specifically, notes Marilyn Geewax, programs such as the new Deal's Works Progress Administration, the GI Bill after World War II which provided not only grants for college but "loans for homes, farms, and businesses," Medicare, Social Security, rural electrification, free homesteads, and so on. In short, Geewax contends, white men's "success in life grew out of a combination of his own efforts and help from the government at each critical stage of his life." Farm subsidies, tariff protection, tax breaks to businesses, and on and on.

"Affirmative action" has also been employed in political wars in ways never anticipated by the executive order. Lee Atwater, George Bush's 1988 campaign chairman used the Willie Horton case to scare whites and boost Bush's chances. As he lay dying of brain cancer, Atwater sought forgiveness for using such a bad rap against blacks. Rush Limbaugh thought it a proper tactic that demonstrated how misguided liberal reformers were.

Throughout the life of the executive order, white females have been the major beneficiaries. So much so that many black observers attribute black male losses in employment to this tremendous influx of white females into the workforce. In recognition of this new status of the white female as a key employment authority, blacks will have to devise means of influencing her.

> Blacks are (the) first of the postindustrial discards...Even though the African Americans have taken the highest proportion of casualties, they are merely the frontline troops. All low income and working-class Americans, of every ethnic group, are involved in this battle; few are likely to escape unscathed, whatever their family traditions or values.
>
> Stephanie Coontz, *The Way We Never Were: American Families and the Nostalgia Trap*

Inasmuch as anti-black employment discrimination is massive and pervasive with no indication of decreasing in the foreseeable future, some means external to the employer will have to be used to at least moderate its impact—call it affirmative action or any other name.

On Higher Education

American higher education is embroiled in an *ideological* war. The forces arrayed against each other are those on the Right led by the National Association of Scholars, whose membership comes mainly from senior white male faculty, and those of the Center and Left. The war is ideological because it doesn't permit of deviation from the "party line," is not open to debate and dialogue (supposedly the hallmark of higher education), and is unforgiving of any who question the methods, means, and aims of strategies employed. From the Right (where the money is, coming as it does from the same sources as funding for conservative think tanks and destabilization programs, some observers claim) come the heavy hitters—men like George Will, Pat Buchanan and a score of none academics who support and supply their academic friends. Also allied with this group are the Allan Blooms whose agenda is to "save" Western Civilization from the barbarians who would dismantle curriculum, lower standards, and bring in undeserving students. Ishmael Reed has made the interesting observation that in his visits to the major universities in Europe, he has never heard the term "Western Civilization."

Also joining this group are disaffected white males who feel left out. As Ellis Case wrote of the movie *Falling Down,* "When Michael Douglas's deranged character…prays for 'everything to be just like it was before', he is speaking not only for himself but for every frustrated white man who has found his once comfortable world collapsing." For such white men seeing even one black man in a non-traditional position causes them to "feel aggrieved." Ann Quindlen has written that much of the white male backlash to affirmative action and changes—what few their are or are proposed—is merely a reaction to attempts to dismantle a system—good-old-boys—falsely publicized as merit based when in fact it is "simply a system that once favored him, and others like him."

Victory in this war will probably go to the strongest—those with political clout, money muscle, and media access. Center—left academics enjoy few of those. But this victory will also bring cosmetic changes such as a few more black faculty (but a lot more Hispanic, Asian, even African, and immigrants); a few additional "multicultural" courses and programs; and more minority students (but not significantly more blacks), because of sheer numbers not out of the goodness of someone's intentions.

On the Demise of Black Colleges

Black colleges were established at a time in the nation's history when, put simply, there was no place else for blacks who wanted higher education to go. Over the decades, most of these schools have done admirably—even remarkably—in preparing young African Americans to lead productive lives as doctors, lawyers, teachers, and ministers. For example, at one point there were 17 African American law schools; today there are four. Even with integration, when so much "brain drain" took a large percentage of the more able students and faculty (not administrators) away to predominately white schools, black schools have held their own and were enjoying by 1993 a resurgence of interest by black youngsters.

But with all of that I do not expect that, optimistically, more than a few of the 100 plus operating in 1993 to survive as *black* institutions beyond the first decades of the 21st century. Aside from deferred maintenance and other fiscal problems, danger lurks in two quarters: Title VII of the 1964 Civil Rights Act prohibits discrimination based on race (and other classifications). This law was based on a recognized need to address massive employment bias against blacks. So long as black colleges were seen as unattractive career choices by most whites and faculty positions were available in predominately white colleges in white communities, black colleges were not the recipients of large numbers of applications from whites coming out of graduate school. With a rapidly shrinking job market in higher education nationally and more graduates available, black schools are being deluged with white applications. The ensuring race discrimination lawsuits, in which whites are winning substantial judgments, can only portend a dire future for these schools.

The other quarter from which danger can be anticipated is desegregation. Black public colleges in several Southern states are caught in the bind of declining public support for higher education and legal mandates from federal courts to desegregate "dual" higher education. The success of desegregation schemes in states like Alabama, Mississippi, Louisiana, and Georgia can only work to the detriment of black colleges.

Desegregation will mean the virtual end of a distinct education enterprise and tradition. One black female student said of the formerly black Lincoln University in Missouri that the only thing "black" about the place anymore was the black studies department (which she appreciated). A black Texas Southern University faculty member complained that "Americans think that the way you desegregate is to wipe away everything black."

Racism in American society is real. The apparently unorchestrated effort to deny that it is a factor can only delude, mislead, and anger the American citizen. The exasperation induced by misinformed conclusions of such respected groups as the World Future Society and the publishers of the *Futurist* magazine that essentially ignore the presence (let alone the problems) of African Americans is becoming widespread. When 20 million people go hungry as they do in the United States, and when a large proportion are black, it's ludicrous to say race is not a factor. When of the estimated 40,000 infants who die in the country each year and the largest segment is black, race must be a factor. When the prison population increased to almost three-quarters of a million inmates in the late 1980s, most of whom were black, there must be a "racial" explanation. When a large number of white investors refuse to site plants in predominately black areas even when all other conditions are favorable. When *60 Minutes* applauds the efforts of a black farmer to build an impressive personal library only to have it arsoned when publicized (and burned again when irate viewers donated books for restoration). When wealthy blacks like Chicago's John Johnson cannot purchase downtown property even with cash and has to have a white front man do it for him. Or when African Americans, especially males, are being decimated by bigoted law enforcement practices, particularly in the war on drugs, which a *USA Today* study concluded was really a war on blacks. ("Racial inequality in the drug war can be found in some of America's most liveable cities.") And when the major banks in a so-called progressive city conspire to deny mortgage and home improvement loans to blacks. The widespread employment discrimination and customer maltreatment of blacks alleged against the Denny's restaurant chain is symptomatic of deep racial fissures remaining.

For African Americans the 21st century challenges will be mindboggling. Our very survival will depend on meeting the world as skilled, resourceful, aggressive people, understanding that for us—as it was for Du Bois in 1903 the problem of the 21st century will be the problem of the color line. As a short time resident of a YMCA on Chicago's South side during the late 1950s, I saw first hand what racial discrimination could do to men professionally trained and educated—in law, the sciences, and at least one in medicine—who had to settle for work in the U.S. Post Office alongside people with fewer or no academic credentials. By 1994 I had met dozens of well educated blacks, some graduates of prestigious professional schools, who had not been able to obtain state certification or a license in their fields. (Thus my reservations about education as *the* answer.) As a returning Peace Corps Volunteer, from Ghana in 1964, my first thought in exiting the place and seeing the contrasting hues of black Americans compared to the Africans I had worked and lived among, was whether we black Americans would achieve all the rights of American citizenship *before* we were literally obliterated as a group.

That is still a valid question.

"Black People Have No Permanent Friends, No Permanent Enemies...Just Permanent Interests."
Motto of the Congressional Black Caucus

...as a longtime critic of American institutions, I know, based on my experiences in other countries, that the United States, despite its problems, is still one of the most creative, experimental, and dynamic societies in the world. Even James Baldwin's stinging criticism of the United States was always tinged with sadness, because Baldwin, like many of us, knew that this society could do better and measure up to its great promise. Even the hostile jabs at American Society one hears in rap music are based more on disappointment and frustration than a desire to see the United States, in the words of Pat Robertson, "crash and burn."

Rodney King, who showed more class in defeat than those who beat him did in victory, said it all: "Can we get along?" I believe that we can.
Ishmael Reed, *Airing Dirty Laundry,* 1993

At the risk of appearing an alarmist my candid opinion about the condition of my people in the United States can be summarized as follows:

I know of no racial group on the face of the earth who is more ravaged, depleted, broken spirited and hopeless than the African American.

On the other hand,

I know of no group more promising, tender hearted, responsive and anxious to please than the African American.
Khalid Abdullah Taig Al-Mansour, *Betrayal By Any Other Name,* 1993

APPENDIX

A TALK WITH MY PEOPLE

Fellow race men, your attention,
For I want to talk with you.
Now, you listen very closely,
For what I will say is true.

We as a race are in serious trouble,
From the old down to the young.
We've been asleep on our job,
We've been asleep almost too long.

To the Christians first of all,
We've slept on our job,
While the president and his cabinet
Set out to really rob.

The notion of prayer in the school
Which was our basic hope,
Of saving our little boys and girls,
Which was a sure way to cope.

Many parents never prayed
With their children in the home.
So the teacher prayed with them in school
Before she sent them home.

Our young people are in utter chaos
Not knowing just what to do,
"Give your child a sense of direction -
Before he leaves home," still is true.

God gave each one a brain,
To really think for himself.
With help from God and parents
He can really be "something else".

Saying no to drugs and sex,
And really meaning no.
A strong will and determination,
Will make him do just so.

Black boys can do more in this life,
Than just play games of sport.

Trying to excel in academics,
Will give him a good report.

As a race, we are doomed my friends,
Unless God intervenes.
He is able to make all things right,
Just don't give up on him.

This world really belongs to God,
And all there is within -
And God is still in charge of his world,
Why not depend on him.

Black people, come back to God,
And stop your life of sin.
One day God will bring you into the judgment,
Do you think that your life will win -
A home in Heaven, that is?

Composed by Mrs. Artie Brown (Used by permission)

Race Progress Destroyed by Four Types of Blacks

by James E. Alsbrook
Prof. Emeritus. Ohio U.

If you think Black slavery in America is gone, you'd better think again. The legal ownership and physical control of blacks are gone. They involved whips, guns, chains and gestures symbolizing absolute subjugation.

But a new slavery has emerged. It involves voluntary self-humilation, the prostitution of personal dignity, the deliberate degradation of other Blacks and the implicit or explicit adoration of White skin.

This new slavery seems astonishingly out of place 130 years after the Emancipation Proclamation. It is not enforced by the law, the whip, chain or gun. It is enforced by the internal mentality and mindset many Black people exert over their own bodies. It is voluntary. Advocates and victims of this mindset and new slavery are of four types:

Type 1.: This Black high school teacher claims Booker T. Washington urged Black people to "lighten" the race by producing babies having "white blood." She claims White people have genes conferring mental superiority over all other races and are naturally more intelligent. She has taught high school for many years and she gives extra attention to light-skinned Black students because she believes darker-skinned Black students are "almost hopeless."

Type 2.: This Black college professor with a doctorate degree frequently uses his favorite term, "A n—r ain't worth a s—t." He says it jokingly, but his behavior indicates he deeply believes it. He avoids using Blacks to get services or products and he glows when talking to Whites.

Type 3.: This president of a failing college attacked Thurgood Marshall and the 1954 desegregation decision by declaring "A Black student does not have to sit beside a White student in order to learn anything in school." This statement is true, but it is only one part of the big picture. He was properly appealing to race pride but neglecting to mention shortfalls such as inadequate buildings, equipment, supplies, institutional ranking, teacher qualifications, crucial psychological effects and other problems.

Type 4.: These are Black actors, actresses and performers who gladly portray Black people as depraved, immoral, ignorant buffoons on the screen, stage, radio and television. They willingly obey White and sometimes Black directors and producers interested in quick money instead of intelligence and truth. They cater to the biases, vanity and low expectations of those Whites who need an ego boost, a scapegoat or reinforcement of their feelings of superiority. These Blacks are not concerned that wrong messages with misleading implications are sent to millions of people.

Enormous damages are being inflicted on young Black students by Blacks like the public school teacher, the professor and the college president. Instead of being good role models, providing helpful guidance and inspiring students with hope and optimism, these so-called educators are misleading and damaging young Black minds. Their students are getting the message that "White is right," Black is bad and racial discrimination is desirable.

Black performers who portray disgraceful stereotypes are found mainly on the Fox network. NBC, CBS and ABC are not stereotype-free, but Fox is worst because it appeals to Uncle Tom Blacks, midget-brained Blacks, White bigots and Blacks who deceive themselves into the ridiculous belief that they are so obviously superior that White people would never associate them with Black stereotypes. What vanity and stupidity!

Bill Cosby and Tim Reid are campaigning to improve the quality and respectability of Black roles on television. But the Uncle Tom, slavish mentality spread by the four types of Blacks listed above brings a few tainted "pieces of silver" to Black performers. These race traitors pollute the thinking and sabotage any worthwhile opportunities of many thousands of young, respectable Blacks.

Do you know an educator or performer like one of the types above? Do something about it!

(Reprinted by permission of South Carolina Black Media Group)

SELECTED BIBLIOGRAPHY

BOOKS

Adams, Richard. *Traveller*, 1988.

Al-Mansour, Khalid Abdullah Tariq, *Betrayal By Any Other Name*, 1993

Amaker, Norman, *Civil Rights and the Reagan Administration*, 1988.

American Council on Education, *Minorities on Campus: A Handbook for Enhancing Diversity*, 1989.

Angelou, Maya, *The Heart of a Woman*, 1982.

Ashe, Arthur, *Days of Grace: A Memoir*, 1993.

Baker, Mark, *Nam*, 1981.

————, *Cops*, 1985.

Baldwin, James, *The Evidence of Things Not Seen*, 1985.

Bancroft, Hubert. *The Native Races*, 1967 reprint.

Battle-fields of the South, from Bull Run to Fredericksburgh; with Sketches of Confederate Commanders, and Gossip of the Camps, by an English combatant, 1984 reprint from the 1864 edition.

Beesley, Stanley, *Vietnam: The Heartland Remembers*, 1987.

Bell, Derek, *And We Are Not Saved: The Elusive Quest for Racial Justice*, 1987.

Bellant, Russ, *The Coors Connection: How Coors Family Philanthropy Undermines Democratic Pluralism*, 1991.

Benjamin, Anne. ed., *Winne Mandela: Part of My Soul Went with Him*, 1984.

Benjamin, Lois, *The Black Elite: Facing the Color Line in the Twilight of the Twentieth Century*, 1991.

Bennett, Lerone, Jr., *The Negro Mood*, 1969.

Berry, Mary F. and Blassingame, John W., *Long Memory: the Black Experience in America*, 1982

Berry, Don, *A Majority of Scoundrels: An Informal History of the Rocky Mountain Fur Company*, 1961.

Berry, F. Clifton, Jr., *Sky Soldiers*, 1987.

Bilbo Theodore, *Take Your Choice. Separation or Mongrelization*, 1947.

Bilotta, James D., *Race and the Rise of the Republican Party, 1848-1865*, 1993.

Bingham, Howard, *Muhammad Ali: A Thirty-Year Journey*, 1993.

Bly, Robert. *Iron Men: a Book About Men*, 1990.

Bodett, Tom, *Small Comforts*, 1987.

The Book of Mormon, 1986 edition.

Bowers, John, *Stonewall Jackson: Portrait of a Soldier*, 1989.

Boyte, H. C., Booth, S., and Max, Steve, *Citizen Action and the New American Populism*, 1986.

Brace, Ernest C., *A Code to Keep: The True Story of America's Longest-Held Civilian Prisoner of War in Vietnam*, 1988.

Breitman, George, ed., *By Any Means Necessary: Speeches, Interviews, and a Letter by Malcolm X*, 1970.

Brown, Jim, with Steve Delsohn, *Out of Bounds*, 1989.

Browning. Rufus, Marshall, Dale, and Tabb, David, *Protest Is Not Enough: The Struggle of Blacks and Hispanics for Equality in Urban Politics*, 1984.

Bunch, Chris, and Cole, Allan, *A Reckoning for Kings*, 1987.

Burch, Ernest, Jr., *The Eskimos*, 1988.

Burchard, Peter, *One Gallant Rush: Robert Gould Shaw and His Brave Black Regiment*, 1965.

Burnham, James, *Suicide of the West: An Essay on the Meaning and Destiny of Liberalism*, 1985.

Business-Higher Education Forum, *Three Realities: Minority Life in the United States*, 1990.

Caldicott, Helen, M.D., *Nuclear Madness*, 1978.

Carrington, G. A., *Arrow and Saber: Battle at Thunderhorse Mesa*, 1989.

Carter, Forrest, *Gone to Texas*, 1973.

Carter, J., and Carter, R., *Everything to Gain: Making the Most of the Rest of Your Life*, 1988.

Carter, Stephen, *Culture and Disbelief*, 1993.

————, *Reflections of an Affirmative Action Baby*, 1991.

Catton, Bruce, *Reflections On the Civil War*, 1982.

Chai, Ch'u, and Chai, Winberg, eds. and trans., *The Sacred Books of Confucius and Other Confucian Classics*, 1965.

Clark, Johnnie M., *Guns Up!*, 1988.

Clarke, John Henrik. *Notes For an African Revolution: Africans at the Crossroads*, 1991.

Clay, William. *Just Permanent Interests: Black Americans in Congress 1870-1991*, 1992.

Collins, Marva, and Tamarkin, Civia, *Marvin Collins' Way*, 1982.

Comer, James, M.D., *Maggie's American Dream: The Life and Times of a Black Family*, 1988.

Coontz, Stephanie, *The Way We Never Were: American Families and the Nostalgia Trap*, 1992.

Council for the Advancement and Support of Education, *Attitudes About American Colleges*, prepared by the Gallup Organization October 6, 1989.

Counter, Alan, *North Pole Legacy: Black, White & Eskimo*, 1991.

Crewdron, John, *By Silence Betrayed: Sexual Abuse of Children in America*, 1988.

Cross, Theodore, *The Black Power Imperative: Racial Inequality and the Politics of Nonviolence*, 1984.

Cruse, Harold, *Plural But Equal: Blacks and Minorities in America's Plural Society*, 1987.

Cullop, Floyd G., *The Constitution of the United States: An Introduction*, 1969.

Davis, Burke, *They Called Him Stonewall: A Life of Lt. General T. J. Jackson, C.S.A.*, 1954.

Davis, F. James, *Who Is Black?: One Nation's Definition*, 1991.

Deloria, Vine, *God Is Red*, 1979.

Dixon, Thomas, *The Leopard's Spots*, 1902.

Donahue, Phil, *The Human Animal*, 1987.

Dooley, John, *Trump: The Building of an Empire*, 1988.

Dorn, Edwin, *Who Defends America? Race, Sex, and Class in the Armed Forces*, 1989.

Douglas, Kirk, *The Ragman's Son: An Autobiography*, 1988.

Douglas, Paul, *In the Fullness of Time: The Memoirs of Paul H. Douglas*, 1972.

Douglas, William O. *The Anatomy of Liberty: The Right of Man without Force*, 1963.

————, *Go East Young Man-The Early Years: The Autobiography of William O. Douglas*, 1974.

Dover, John W., *War without Mercy: Race and Power in the Pacific War*, 1986.

Du Bois, W. E. B., *Against Racism: Unpublished Essays, Papers, Addresses*, 1887-1961, Aptheker, H., ed., 1985.

————, *Prayers for Dark People*, Aptheker, H., ed., 1980.

Durant, Will and Ariel, *The Lessons of History*, 1968.

Dye, Dole A., *Platoon*, 1986.

Early, Tom, *Sons of Texas*, 1989.

Edleman, Bernard, *Dear America: Letters Home from Vietnam*, 1985.

Einstein, Albert, *Ideas and Opinions*, 1982.

Ezrorsky, Gertrude, *Racism & Justice: The Case for Affirmative Action*, 1991.

Fabre, Michael, *From Harlem to Paris: Black American Writes in France, 1840-1980*, 1991.

Fallaci, Oriana, *An Interview with History*, 1976.

———, *A Man*, 1979.

Forbes, Jack D., *Black Africans and Native Americans*, 1988.

Franklin, John Hope, and Moss, Alfred A., *From Slavery to Freedom: A History of Negro Americans*, Sixth Edition, 1988.

Frost, David, *The Americans*, 1970.

Gandhi, M. K., *An Autobiography: On the Story of My Experiments with Truth*, 1945.

Garrison, Webb, *A Treasury of Civil War Tales*, 1981.

———, *Civil War Trivia & Fact Book*, 1992.

Garrow, David J., *The FBI and Martin Luther King, Jr.: From Solo to Memphis*, 1981.

Gerburg, Mort, *The U.S. Constitution for Everyone*, 1987.

Ghost, Gray: The Memoirs of Colonel John S. Mosby, 1992 edition.

Gibbs, Jewel Taylor, ed., *Young, Black, and Male in America: An Endangered Species*, 1988.

Glasser, Ronald J., M.D.. *365 Days*, 1971.

Goell, Milton, *The Wall That Is My Skin: Poems Inspired by the Negro's Fight for Democratic Rights*, 1945.

Goldwater, Barry, *With No Apologies*, 1979.

Gould, Stephen Jay, *The Mismeasure of Man*, 1983.

Greely, Andrew, *Confessions of a Parish Priest: An Autobiography*, 1987.

Green, A. Wigfall, *The Man Bilko*, 1963.

Grizzard, Lewis, *Elvis Is Dead and I Don't Feel So Good Myself*, 1984.

Groom, Winston, *Better Times Than These*, 1978.

Hacker, Andrew, *Two Nations: Black and White, Separate, Hostile, Unequal*, 1992.

Hackworth, David (Col.), and Sherman, Julie, *About Face: The Odyssey of an American Warrior*, 1989.

Hare, Nathan, and Hare, Julia, *Bringing the Black Boy to Manhood: The Passage*, 1985.

Hemenway, Robert E., *Zorn Neale Hurston: A Literary Biography*, 1977.

Henry, Charles P. *Culture and African American Politics*, 1990.

Henry, Will, *Chiricahua*, 1973.

Hill, Robert, ed., *Marcus Garvey: Life and Lessons*, 1987.

Hobstadter, Richard. *Anti-Intellectualism in American Life*, 1966.

Hooker, Robert, *Displacement of Black Teachers in the Eleven Southern States*, Race Relations Information Center, 1970.

Hooks, Bell and West, Cornel. *Breaking Bread: Insurgent Black Intellectual Life*, 1991.

Horsman, Reginald, *Race and Manifest Destiny: The Origins of American Racial Anglo-Saxonism*, 1981.

Hostetler, Joseph A., *Amish Society*, 1980.

———, ed., *Amish Roots: A Treasury of History, Wisdom and Lore*, 1989.

Hughes, Langston, "The Big Sea," in David Jay, ed., *Black Joy*, 1971.

Hurston, Zora N., *Moses, Man of the Mountain*, 1939.

———, *Dust Tracks on a Road*, 1942.

———, *The Sanctified Church*, 1983 edition.

Iacocca, Lee, *Iacocca: An Autobiography*, 1984.

————, with Kleinfield, *Sonny, Talking Straight*, 1988.

Jackson, Reggie, *Reggie: The Autobiography of Reggie Jackson*, 1988.

Jakes, John. *North & South*, 1982.

Jameson, Perry, and McWhiney, Grady, *Attack and Die: Civil War Military Tactics and the Southern Heritage*, 1982.

Jefferson, Thomas, *Notes on Virginia*, excerpted in Ward, Baldwin H., ed., *Pictorial History of the Black American*, 1973.

Jelinek, Pauline, "Blacks Most Likely to Find Housing Discrimination, Says Researcher," *Black Issues in Higher Education*.

Jensen, Oliver, ed., *Bruce Catton's America: Selections from His Greatest Works*, 1979.

Johnson, James Weldon, *God's Trombones: Seven Negro Sermons in Verse*, 1927.

Johnson, John H., with Bennett, Lerone, III, *Succeeding against the Odds*, 1989.

Johnston, Terry C., *Dying Thunder*, 1992.

Johnston, William and Packer, Arnold . *Workforce 2000: Work and Workers for the 21st Century*, 1987.

Jones, K. C., with Warner, Jack, *Rebound*, 1986.

Jordan, Barbara, and Hearon, Shelby, *Barbara Jordan: A Self-Portrait*, 1979.

Katz, William Loren, *Black Indians; A Hidden Heritage*, 1986.

Kearns, Doris, *Lyndon Johnson and the American Dream*, 1976.

Kidd, J. H., *Personal Recollections of a Cavalryman: With Custer's Michigan Cavalry Brigade*, 1908.

Killian, Lewis, *White Southeners*, 1985.

King, Martin L., *Where Do We Go from Here— Chaos or Community?*, 1968.

Kochman, Thomas, *Black and White Styles in Conflict*, 1981.

Koestler, Arthur, *Dialogue with Death*, 1942.

Lamm, Richard, *Megatraumas*, 1985.

Lanker, Brian. *I Dream A World: Portraits of Black Women Who Changed America*, 1989.

Lanning, Michael Lee, *Vietnam 1969-1970: A Company Commander's Journal*, 1988.

Leckie, William, *The Buffalo Soldiers: A Narrative of the Negro Cavalry in the West*, 1967.

Lewis, David L., *W.E.B. DuBois: Biography of a Race*, 1993

Levin, Robert, *Bill Clinton: The Inside Story*, 1992.

Life at Cornell, 1986.

Lightfoot, Sara, *Balm in Gilead, Journey of a Healer*, 1988.

Loving, T. S., *And Brave Men, Too*, 1985.

Madhubuti, Haki R., *Black Men: Obsolete, Single, Dangerous? The Afrikan American Family in Transition. Essays in Discovery, Solution, and Hope.* 1990.

Mangold, Tom, and Penycate, John, *The Tunnels of Cu Chi: The Untold Story of Vietnam*, 1985.

Mays, Benjamin F., *Lord, the People Have Driven Me On*, 1981.

Mazuri, Ali A.. *The Africans: A Triple Heritage*, 1986.

McClenney, Earl H., Jr., *How to Survive When You're the Only Black in the Office*, 1989.

Mead. Chris, *Champion: Joe Louis, Black Hero in White America*, 1985.

Moon, William Least Heat, *Blue Highways: A Journey into America*, 1982.

Naisbitt, John, and Aburdene, Patricia, *Megatrends 2000: Ten New Directions for the 1990s*, 1990.

Nash, Jay R., *Citizen Hoover*, 1972.

National Commission on Crimes and Prevention of Violence, *Report*, 1970.

National Urban League, *State of Black America*, annual reports.

Neihardt, John, *Black Elk Speaks*, 1979.

Nizer, Louis B., *Thinking on Your Feet,* 1940.

Nolan, Keith W., *Death Valley: The Summer Offensive I Corps August 1969,* 1988.

Orfield, Gary, *The Growth of Segregation in American Schools: Changing Patterns of Separation and Poverty Since 1968,* A Report of the Harvard Project on School Desegregation to the National School Boards Association, 1993.

O'Reilly, Kenneth, *Racial Matters,* 1989.

Overstreet, Everett Louis, *Black on a Background of White: A Chronicle of Afro-Americans' Involvement in America's Last Frontier, Alaska,* 1988.

Page, Clarence, *A Foot in Each World: Essays and Articles by Leanita McClain,* 1986.

Parks, Gordon, *To Smile in Autumn: A Memoir,* 1979.

Pelfrey, William, *Hamburger Hill,* 1987.

Perot, Ross, *United We Stand,* 1991

Phillips, Robert, *Louis L'Amour: His Life and Trails,* 1989.

Pickens, T. Boone, Jr., *Boone,* 1987.

Pinkney, Alphonso, *The Myth of Black Progress,* 1984.

Porter, Horace, *Campaigning With Grant,* 1991 edition.

Reed, Ishmael, *Writin' is Fightin': Thirty-Seven Years of Boxing on Paper,* 1988.

———, *Airing Dirty Laundry,* 1993.

Reeves, Richard, *American Journey: Traveling with Tocqueville in Search of Democracy in America,* 1982.

Remington, Frederic, "A Scout with the Buffalo Soldiers," in *Frederic Remington's Own West,* 1960.

Ritter, Bruce, *Sometimes God Has a Kid's Face: The Story of America's Street Kids,* 1988.

Robinson, Jackie, *I Never Had It Made — Jackie Robinson: An Autobiography,* 1972.

Rosengarten, Theodore, *All God's Dangers: The Life of Nate Shaw,* 1975.

Rothmiller, Mike and Goldman, Ivan, *L.A. Secret Police: Inside the LAPD Elite Spy Network,* 1992.

Russell, Bertrand, *Education and the Good Life,* 1922.

Said, Edward, *Culture and Imperialism,* 1991.

Segal, Ronald, *The Race War,* 1966.

Simmons, Edwin, *Marines: The Illustrated History of the Vietnam War,* 1987.

Sinkler. George, *The Racial Attitudes of American Presidents: From Abraham Lincoln to Theodore Roosevelt,* 1971.

Skimin, Robert, *Gray Victory,* 1988.

Smith, Ed, *Where to, Black Man? - An American Negro's African Diary,* 1967

———, *Black Students in Interracial Schools: A Guide for Students, Teachers and Parents,* 2nd edition 1994.

Smith, Errol, *37 Things Every Black Man Needs to Know,* 1991.

Sowell, Thomas, *Race and Economics,* 1975.

Stacy, Palmer, and Lutton, Wayne, *The Immigration Time Bomb,* 1988.

State Higher Education Executive Officers, *A Difference of Degrees: State Initiatives to Improve Minority Student Achievement,* 1987.

Stein, Max, ed., *Abe Lincoln Jokes: Wit and Humor,* 1943.

Takaki, Ronald, *Strangers from a Different Shore: A History of Asian Americans,* 1989.

Taylor, Jared, *Paved With Good Intentions; The Failure of Race Relations in Contemporary America,* 1992.

Taylor, Lawrence, in Beiderson, John and Jackson, Heidi, Compl., *Voices of Struggle - Voices of Pride,* 1992.

Teacher, Lawrence, and Nicholls, Richard, *The Unabridged Jack London,* 1981.

Terry, Wallace, *Bloods: An Oral History of the Vietnam War by Black Veterans*, 1984.

Thom, James A., *From Sea to Shining Sea*, 1984.

Trembley, Ray, *Trails of an Alaskan Game Warden*, 1985.

Troupe, Quincy, ed., *James Baldwin: The Legacy*, 1989.

Walker, Margaret, *For My People*, 1942.

———, *This Is My Century: New and Collected Poems*, 1989.

Wang, An, *Lessons: An Autobiography*, 1986.

Weatherby, W. J., *James Baldwin: Artist On Fire*, 1989.

Webb, G.L. *Conviction & Sentencing: Deception & Racial Discrimination*, 1979.

Welsing, Frances C. *The Isis Papers: The Keys to the Colors*, 1991.

West, Cornel. *Race Matters*, 1993.

Wilder, L. Douglas, Governor of Virginia, Forward to Congressman William Clay, *Just Permanent Interests: Black Americans in Congress 1870-1991*, 1992.

Williams, Patricia . *The Alchemy of Race and Rights: Diary of a Law Professor*, 1991.

Williams, Walter, *The State against Blacks*, 1982.

———, *All It Takes is Guts: A Minority View*, 1987.

Williamson, Joel, *The Crucible of Race: Black-White Relations in the South since Emancipation*, 1984.

Wilson, George, *Mud Soldiers: Life Inside the New American Army*, 1989.

Work, John W., *Race, Economics, and Corporate America*, 1984.

Zionism, University Service Department, American Zionist Youth Foundation.

ARTICLES, SPEECHES, ETC.

KEY

Afro-American	Baltimore Afro-American
Amsterdam News	New York Amsterdam News
Black Issues	Black Issues in Higher Education
Chronicle	Chronicle of Higher Education
Daily News	Anchorage (Alaska) Daily News
Free Press	Burlington (Vermont) Free Press
Hispanic Link	Hispanic Link Weekly Report
Monitor	Christian Science Monitor
Multicultural Banner	National Multicultural Banner
News-Miner	Fairbanks (AK) Daily News-Miner
U.S. News	U.S. News and World Report

Aig, Marlene, "Yonkers Threatened with Bankruptcy," *Anchorage Daily News*, August 3, 1988.

Alleyne, Reginald, "They-all-look-alike Syndrome Imperils Justice," *Capital Times*, April 17, 1984.

Anderson, Charles, "The Thing Most Missed" and "Black and White," in Greenberg, M., and Norton, A., *Touring Nam: The Vietnam War Reader*, 1989.

Anderson, Ed, "Plans to Foster Black Judgeships Fail in Senate," *The Times-Picayne*, New Orleans, June 6, 1989.

Ankofer, Frank, "Unequal Justice: Report Outlines Minority Mistreatment," *Milwaukee Journal*, May 9, 1982.

Bailey, Peter, "Need for Black Nationalism," *New York Amsterdam News,* January 11, 1986.

Baker, Derick, "Sex Means Never Having to Stick Around, *N'Digo,* June 1993.

Baker, Donald, and Melton, R. H., "Virginia Gets Ready for a Historic Election–A Black Runs for Governor in the Southern Heartland," *Washington Post,* National Weekly Edition, June 19-25, 1989.

Baldwin, James, "On Being 'White'... and Other Lies," *Essence,* April 1984.

Barber, Lionel, "The Paradox of the Black American: Political Success without Economic Progress," *World Press Review,* January 1988.

Barber, Red. "One Who Was There Recalls Branch Rickey's Fight for Civil Rights." *Monitor,* February 26, 1986.

Barnes, Fred, "Can We Trust the News?," *Reader's Digest,* January 1988.

Barnes, Peter, "Jackson to Attend CBS Annual Meeting in Campaign for More Minority Hiring," *Newsweek,* April 16. 1986.

Barreiro, Dan, "Hiring of Black Not News in NBA," *Houston Chronicle,* June 11, 1989.

"Barriers," Interviews with Prominent Blacks (The Dream Then and Now), *Life,* Special Issue, Spring 1988.

Barry, E. Jeannie, "Share the Wealth: Who Will Teach the Black Children?," *Black Collegian,* March/April 1986.

Bauer, Fran, "Flyers Accuse Palestinian Grocers of Exploiting Black Neighborhoods," *Milwaukee Journal,* January 4, 1983.

Baxter, Tom, "Black Bridges Racial Gap to be Mississippi Chief," *Atlanta Journal and Constitution,* December 13, 1987.

Bean, Joe P., "Confronting the Prejudice that Lingers," *Monitor,* February 25, 1987.

Bedard, Paul, "NAACP Hints Racist Plot Against Barry," Washington Times, January 23, 1990.

"Bellow, Saul, Foreword to Bloom, Allan, *The Closing of the American Mind,* 1987.

Bennett, William J., "American Education: Making It Work," A Report to the President, reprinted in *Chronicle,* May 4, 1988.

Berger, Joseph, "Children Embrace Faith of Fathers," *New York Times,* April 3. 1985.

Berkow, Ira, "Sayers Will Always Remember the Value of Brian Piccolo," *Fairbanks Daily News-Miner,* November 9, 1988.

Billingsley, Andrew, "Black Families in a Changing Society," in *State of Black America,* 1987.

Blow, Steve, "System Leaves Black Doctor Heartsick," *Dallas Morning News,* June 5, 1989.

Bonedetto, Richard, "Black Mayors Integrate City Jobs," *USA Today,* April 19, 1985.

Booker, Simeon, "Ticker Tape USA," *Jet,* June 20, 1988.

———, "Colin L. Powell: Black General at the Summit of U.S. Power," *Ebony,* July 1988.

Bowman, LaBarbara, "Poll: No Immunity from Racism," *USA Today,* Special Report, September 5, 1989.

Brock, Pope, "Chief Anderson," (Pioneer Black Aviator), *People,* November 28, 1988.

Brown, Tony, "The Irony of Black Rhetoric about Racism," *Tri-State Defender,* June 3, 1989.

Brown, Wesley, "About People: Nobel Laureate Wole Soyinka," *Essence,* August 1987.

Browne, J. Zangba, "Fear of Blacks Earns Man $$?," *Amsterdam News,* July 6, 1985.

Buchanan, Patrick, "Paddle, the Prime Cause of Racial Woes," *Lowell* (Mass.) *Sun,* February 5, 1981.

Buchwald, Art, "LA Police Chief Gets Backing from Kluxclan," *Capital Times,* May 25, 1982.

Buckhanon, Stephanie, "Making a Difference: What Will We Become," *Black Collegian,* January 1988.

Bushkoff, Leonard, "Garvey Quest Remembered in N.Y. Exhibit," *Atlanta Journal and Constitution,* December 13, 1987.

Bussey, John, "Fighting the Tide: Detroit Ghetto Area Tries Self-Reliance, and Learns Its Limits," *Wall Street Journal,* April 7, 1989.

Butler, Richard, "This Is a Court for White Aryans Only," *USA Today,* September 26, 1985.

Byrd, Robert, "Hypertension Heredity Link Is Established," *Burlington Free Press,* September 6, 1986.

Caldicott, Helen, "Environmentalism, Global Harmony, and Citizen Action," Address delivered at the University of Alaska Fairbanks, April 9, 1990.

Campbell, Angus, and Schuman, Howard, "Racial Attitudes in Fifteen American Cities," in *Supplemental Studies for the National Advisory Commission on Civil Disorders,* 1968.

Capps, Kris, "Kleinfeld Takes Oath as New Federal Judge," *News-Miner,* July 15, 1986.

Carlson, Tucker, "That Old-Time Religion: Why Black Men Are Returning to Church," *Policy Review,* Summer 1992

Celis, William, III, "Japanese Set Sights on American Farmland," *Wall Street Journal,* May 1, 1989.

Cerstvik, John, "William A. Blakey: Key Figure on Capitol Hill," *Black Issues in Higher Education,* October 1986.

Cetron, Marvin; Rocha, Wanda; and Luckins, Rebecca, "Into the 21st Century: Long-Term Trends Affecting the United States," *The Futurists,* July-August 1988.

Clancy, Paul, "Our Dream Is Their Dream," *USA Today,* October 10, 1985.

———, "Park Forest: Integration's Proud Legacy," USA Today, October 15, 1985.

———, "USA's Richest," *USA Today,* October 15, 1985.

Clark, Anita, "'Wrong Man' Assault Charge Dropped," *Wisconsin State Journal,* May 14, 1982.

———, "Killer in Court," *Wisconsin State Journal,* November 8, 1985.

Clark, Hattie, "Mother against Gangs: New Chicago Group Says 'Enough!' to Teen Violence," *Monitor,* April 28, 1986.

———, "The Verdict: Back to School," Monitor, January 13, 1987.

Clark, Kenneth R., "Fate Hands Gossett a Son and a Cause," *Chicago Tribune,* TV Week, December 13, 1987.

Cleghorn. Reese, "Blacks and Whites Over 30 Years," review of Bob Blauner's *Black Lives, White Lives: Three Decades of Race Relations in America,* 1989, in *Washington Post,* National Weekly Edition, May 22-28, 1989.

Cobb, Charles, "NCAA Action–It's Racially Motivated," *Crisis,* March 1983.

Cobb, Paul, "Moon Victim of Gov't. Conspiracy," *Washington Post,* July 15, 1985.

Cogdill, Ingrid, "Abernathy Holds on to the Dream," *News-Miner,* January 26, 1988.

Cohen, Richard, "This Nation Has Gone Slack on Racial Bigotry," *Capital Times,* July 7, 1982.

Coleman, Daniel, "Black Child's Self-View Is Still Low, Study Finds," *New York Times,* August 31, 1987.

Coleman, Milton, "Dexterous Miami Mayor Faces Stiff Fight for His $6,000 Job," *Washington Post,* October 3, 1985.

———, "Blacks Help Elect Republicans in New Jersey, Cleveland," *Washington Post,* December 21, 1985.

Collie, Tim, "Blending Tampa's Ethnic Hues," *Tampa Tribune,* May 28, 1989.

Conciatore, Jacqueline, "Prison Devouring Multitude of Young Black Males," *Black Issues,* August 31, 1989.

———, and Rodriguez, Roberta, "Blacks and Hispanics: A Fragile Alliance," *Black Issues,* October 11, 1990.

Connell, Christopher, "Panel Says U.S. Losing Racial Fight," *Capital Times,* May 23, 1988.

Cordes, Colleen, "Chicago Sociologist Challenges 'Culture of Poverty' as Explanation for Plight of Inner City Poor," *Chronicle*, March 11, 1987.

Coughlin, Ellen, "Segregation Changed Little over 1970's, Study Shows, *Chronicle*, January 27, 1988.

Crongoli, A. Kenneth, M.D., "Urban Blacks Need No Morality Lessons from Upper Crust," *Burlington Free Press*, February 7, 1986.

Crowe, John, "NCAA Votes Stiffer Academic Requirements for Participants in Intercollegiate Sports," *Chronicle*, January 19, 1983.

Cummings, Judith, "White Nationalist Leader Says He Had Contacts with Farrakhan," *New York Times*.

"Current Facts," Big Brothers/Big Sisters of America, 1984.

Daly, Matthew, "Howard U. Graduate Is 18 and Heading for Medical School," *Washington Post*.

Daniels, Lee A., "Bill Cosby Donates $20 Million to College," *Daily News*, November 8, 1988.

Davidson, Joe, "Black Candidates Debate Pursuing White Vote When House Races Hinge on Broader Turnout," *Wall Street Journal*, April 8, 1986.

Davis, Angela, "Radical Perspectives on the Empowerment of Afro- American Women: Lessons for the 1980's," *Harvard Educational Review*, August 1988.

Dean, Cory, "Plan for a University Panel Eases Racial Tension at Brown," *New York Times*, April 30, 1985.

Dedman, Bill, "Atlanta NAACP Calls for Boycott, Federal Probe of Banks," *Atlanta Constitution*, May 10, 1988.

Degler, Carl N., "In Pursuit of American History," presidential address to the American Historical Association, reprinted in *American Historical Review*, February 1987.

Delpit, Lisa D., "Skills and Other Dilemmas of a Progressive Black Educator," *Harvard Education Review*, November 1986.

Dennis, Raoul, "Racism on the Rise," *Black Enterprise*, April 1987.

Denton, Nancy, and Massey, Douglass, "Residential Segregation of Blacks, Hispanics, and Asians by Socioeconomic Status and Generation," *Social Science Quarterly*, December 1988.

Douglas, William O., "My Credo."

Downey, Charles, "Overseas Adoption: A Family Portrait," Cover Story, *Kiwanis Magazine*, April 1990.

Duke, David, "Race: A Time for Truth," videotape, 1986.

Duncan, Amy, "Great Blacks in Wax Museum Aims to Institutionalize Black History," *Monitor*, February 20, 1986.

Dunn, William, "Stress Increasingly Pushes Seniors to Suicide," *USA Today*, September 11, 1986.

Duster, Troy, "They're Taking Over! - and Other Myths About Race On Campus," *Mother Jones*, Sept./Oct. 1991

———, "Study: Hispanics to Shape Nation More," *USA Today*, November 26, 1986.

Eastland, Terry, "What the Next President Should Do about Civil Rights," *Chronicle*, September 21, 1988.

Eberlhart, Richard. "How I Became a Royal White Elephant, Third Class," *American Heritage*, February-March 1987.

Edmond, Alfred, Jr., "Journalists Win Bias Suit," *Black Enterprise*, July 8, 1987.

El Nasser, Haya, "As US Ages, Mags Want in on Action," *USA Today*, February 9, 1988.

Elias, Marilyn, "Whites More Liberal on Race, Not on Laws," *USA Today*.

Evans, Gaynelle, "NAACP Legal Defense and Education Fund's Phyllis McClure Fights the Good Fight," *Black Issues*, November 10, 1988.

————, "Harold Cruse on 'Plural But Equal'," *Black Issues*, May 11, 1989.

————, "Opening Another Door: The Saga of Harvard's Barack H. Obana," *Black Issues*, March 15, 1990.

Farley, Reynolds, "North More Segregated than South," *Anchorage Times*, October 29, 1986.

Farrell, John A., "Mormon Power Still Prevails in Utah, but Change is Afoot," *Milwaukee Journal*, November 31, 1982.

Faulkner, William. Addressed Southern Historical Association, Memphis, TN. 1955.

Feinsilber, Mike, "Americans Most Conservative, Survey Shows," *Capital Times*, January 9, 1982.

————, "Sociologist Says Sports Still Full of Racism," *News-Miner*, September 17, 1989.

Fields, Cheryl, "High Court Opens Civil-Right Suits to All Ethnic Groups," *Chronicle*, May 27, 1987.

Fields, Rubye, "Lack of EEO Enforcement: A Barrier to Equal Opportunity," *Management Review*, December 1987.

Fisher, Susan, "Japanese Pilot Recalls Downing of Boynton," *News-Miner*, January 16, 1988.

Fiske, Edward, "Ranks of Minority Teachers Are Dwindling, Experts Fear," *New York Times*, February 9, 1986.

Fogelson, R., and Hill, R., "Who Riots? A Study of Participation in the 1967 Riots," in *Supplemental Studies for the National Advisory Committee on Civil Disorders*, 1968.

Forrer, Eric, "A Perspective on Alaska Native Education," Address delivered to the University of Alaska Board of Regents, August 17, 1990.

Franklin, John Hope, "Founders Didn't Fight for Rights of Blacks," Barbara Reynolds interview, *USA Today*, February 4, 1987.

Franklin, Stephen, "Detroit Wages All-Out War against Crack," *Chicago Tribune*, December 13, 1987.

Gamarekian, Barbara, "Blacks Rate Capital an Equal Opportunity City?," *New York Times*, July 21, 1982.

Gandhi, Natwar, "Still the Promised Land," *Washington Post*, National Weekly Edition, June 19-25, 1989.

Garza, Crystal H., "Mary Church Terrell 'Kept on Insisting'," *Press Connection*, November 16, 1979.

Gates, Mireille, "Minority Lifestyle Blamed for Death Rate," *USA Today*, October 17, 1985.

Gauss, John, "Give the Blacks Texas," *Civil War Times Illustrated*, May/June 1990.

Gilliam, Dorothy, "The Threat of Church Power," *Washington Post*, February 17, 1986.

Gilmore, David, "Manhood: Why Is Being a 'Real Man' So Often a Prize to be Won?." *Natural History*, June 1990.

Gittlesohn, John, "FBI Files Tell It Like It Was," *Free Press*, April 24, 1985.

Glasgow, Douglas, "The Black Underclass in Perspective," in *State Of Black America*, 1987.

Gonzalez, Juan, "3,000 Victims Marched on Washington," *National Multicultural Banner*, November 1986.

Graves, Earl, "How to Deal with Corporate Downswing," *Black Enterprise*, March 1987.

————, "What the Constitution Means to Black America," *Black Enterprise*, July 1987.

Greenhouse, Linda, "Court, Ruling 5 to 4, Eases Burden on Employers in Some Bias Suits," *New York Times*, June 6, 1989.

Grimsley, Mark, "Ulysses S. Grant: His Life and Hard Times," Special Issue, *Civil War Times Illustrated*, February 1990.

Gupta, Udayan, "From Other Shores," *Black Enterprise*, March 1983.

Hamill, Pete, "Black and White at Brown," *Esquire*, April 1990.

Hanburg, David, "Prejudice, Ethnocentrism, and Violence in an Age of High Technology," President of Carnegie Corporation of New York, annual address, 1984.

Harper, Peter A., "His Dream Opens Doors to the Future for Inner City Kids," *Free Press,* February 13, 1986.

Harris, Louis, "Alienation Returns to Record Level in U.S.," *Milwaukee Journal,* March 17, 1983.

Harvey, L. P., "'Bad Paper' Vets–America's Discarded Warriers," *Monitor,* November 10, 1986.

Hearde, Basil, "Blacks in 'Nam," Cover Story, *Chronicle of War: Vietnam,* Spring 1990.

Helmore, Kristian, "Racism: Main Cause of Inner-City Poverty," *Monitor,* December 20, 1986.

Henry, William A., III, "Beyond the Melting Pot," *Time* Cover Story, "America's Changing Colors," April 9, 1990.

Hentoff, Nat, "Strategic Silences on Farrakhan." *Washington Post,* October 5, 1985.

Higgs, Shelia, "2 Decades of Discrimination at NIH" (National Institutes of Health) *Washington Afro-American,* July 17, 1993

Hillinger, Charles, "After 2 Million Miles, He Stops to Smell Roses," *Milwaukee Sentinel,* May 4, 1982.

Hilts, Philip, "25% of Americans Slip In and Out of Poverty," *Capital Times,* March 8, 1984.

Hirsh, Michael, "Ties That Don't Bind, U.S.–Japan Relations," *News-Miner,* April 8, 1990.

Hodgkinson, Harold, "Demography of the 21st Century," Keynote address to the 3rd Annual National Conference on Racial and Ethnic Relations In American Higher Education. June 4, 1990.

Holden, Matthew, Jr., "Reflections on Two Isolated Peoples," in Washington, Joseph, Jr., ed., *Jews in Black Perspective: A Dialogue,* 1984.

Hornflower, Margot, "Farrakhan Draws Huge Crowd," *Washington Post,* October 8, 1985.

Hughes, Langston, "The Big Sea," in Jay, David, ed., *Black Joy,* 1971.

Hunt, Albert, "Special-Interest Money Increasingly Influences What Congress Enacts," *New York Times,* June 26, 1982.

Huston, Zora Neal. "How It Feels to Be Colored Me," in Alice Walker, ed., *I Love Myself When I Am Laughing... and Then Again When I Am Looking Mean and Impressive: Writings of Zora Neat Huston,* 1979.

Jackson, Jesse, "From Battleground to Common Ground to Higher Ground," speech to joint session of the Alabama legislature, in Hatch, R. D., and Watkins, F. E., eds., *Reverend Jesse L Jackson: Straight from the Heart,* 1987.

———, "Excellence in the Press: Freedom, Fairness, and the Future," in Hatch, R. D., and Watkins, F. E., eds., *Reverend Jesse L. Jackson: Straight from the Heart,* 1987.

———, "Farewell to a Superstar and a Declaration of War: Eulogy for Don Rogers," in Hatch, R. D. and Watkins, F. E., eds., *Reverend Jesse L. Jackson: Straight from the Heart,* 1987.

———, "Forty Years Later–Hibernation, but Not Yet Joy," speech in West Berlin on 40th anniversary of end of WW II, May 8, 1985, in Hatch, R. D., and Watkins, F. E., eds., *Reverend Jesse L. Jackson: Straight from the Heart,* 1987.

———, "It's Not the Bus–It's Us," in Hatch, R. D., and Watkins, F. E., eds., *Reverend Jesse L. Jackson: Straight from the Heart,* 1987.

———, "Liberation and Justice: A Call for Redefinition, Refocus, and Rededication," in Hatch,

R. D., and Watkins, F. E., eds., *Reverend Jesse L. Jackson: Straight from the Heart,* 1987.

———, "Our spiritual and Prayer Roots," in Hatch, R. D., and Watkins, F. E., eds., *Reverend Jesse L. Jackson: Straight from the Heart,* 1987.

———, "Protecting the Legacy: The Challenge of Dr. Martin Luther King," in Hatch, R. D., and Watkins, F. E., eds., *Reverend Jesse L. Jackson: Straight from the Heart,* 1987.

————, "Religious Liberty, Civil Disobedience, Conscience, and Survival," in Hatch, R. D., and Watkins, F. E., eds., *Reverend Jesse L. Jackson: Straight from the Heart,* 1987.

Jackson, Reggie, "We Have a Serious Problem that Isn't Going Away, *Sports Illustrated,* May 11, 1987.

James, Willie Mae, "Why Block Black Progress?," letter to the editor, *Amsterdam News,* January 2, 1986.

Johnson, Alicia, "Black Managers Still Have a Dream," *Management Review,* December 1987.

Johnson, J., and James, Curtis, eds., "My Greatest Challenge: Thirteen Men Discuss the Obstacles They Seek to Surmount," *Essence,* November 1987.

Johnson, Kathy, "Debts, Broken Dreams Drive Many Adult Children Back Home," *Daily News,* December 29, 1987.

Jordan, June, "Nobody Mean More to Me than You and the Future of Willie Jordan," *Harvard Educational Review,* August 1988.

Kailen, Clarence, "The Ultra-Right," *Madison* (Wis.) *Forum,* June 12, 1980.

Kazi-Ferrouillet, Kirumba, "Guns, Butter and Affirmative Action: An Interview with General Bernard Randolph," *Black Collegian,* January 1982.

Kelly, James M., and Studley, Edward, "Has Busing Been a Help?," *Boston Globe,* April 16, 1988.

Kilpatrick, James, "Social Security Found Bad for Blacks," *News-Miner,* August 14, 1987.

Klaidman, David, "Farrakhan: A Message Based on Hate," *Washington Post,* November 9, 1985.

Kozol, Jonathan, "The New Untouchables," (Poor Children), *Newsweek,* Special Issue, Winter/Spring 1990.

Lacayo, Richard, "Between Two Worlds, the Black Middle Class *Time* cover story, March 13, 1989.

La Franchi, Howard, "Texans' Racial Attitudes Changing–for the Better," *Monitor,* January 19, 1987.

Lambro, Donald, "Reagan Years Meant Prosperity for Blacks," *News-Miner,* July 7, 1988.

Lamm, Richard D., "The Melting Pot: Half Empty," *Monitor,* September 19, 1985.

Langer, Gary, "Concerns about Racism Persist," *Juneau* (Alaska) *Empire,* August 8, 1986.

Larsen, Genelle, "Orem Citizens Go Out on Patrol: Academy Teaches Residents about Police–and Vice Versa," *Desert News,* 1989.

Learig, Walter. "Innocent Man's Eight Year Prison Ordeal," *Ebony,* March 1987.

Leavy, Walter, "Eddie Murphy's Princely Role," *Ebony,* July 1988.

Lester, Sheena, "100 Men Plus, CYGS, Block Clubs Unite to Rid Area of Criminals," *Los Angeles Sentinel,* December 14, 1989.

Locus, Carl, Capt., "Tuskegee Airmen Remember Black Pioneers," *Goldpanner* (Eielson AFB, Alaska). February 5, 1988.

Lynch, Lorrie, "Marva Collins: Education's Wonder Woman Keeps Books and Doors Open for Chicago Kids," *USA Today,* January 4, 1987.

Maguire, Daniel, "The Erosion of Affirmative Action," *Crisis Magazine,* March 1981.

Malcolm X, "Black Man's History," In Goodman, Benjamin, ed., *The End of White World Supremacy: Four Speeches by Malcolm X,* 1971.

Marable, Manning, "Black Education and the Myth of Equality," *Multicultural Banner,* March 1, 1986.

————, "The Paradox of Desegregation," *Multicultural Banner,* November 1986.

————, "The Beast Is Back: An Analysis of Campus Racism," *Black Collegian,* September/ October 1988.

Marcus, Ruth, "DAR to Reprimand Two Members Who Leveled Racism Charges," *Washington Post,* October 11, 1985.

Marquand, Robert, "Wanted: Black Schoolteachers," *Monitor,* April 4, 1986.

Martin, Hosea, "Choosing Heroes: A Lesson in American Black History," *Monitor,* February 25, 1987.

Matthews, Joan, "Profile of an Expatriate: Dr. David James on Life as a Physician in Switzerland," *Black Issues,* December 15, 1987.

Mauro, Tony, "Lack of Minority Lawyers Probed," *USA Today,* February 15, 1985.

———, "High Court Overturns '62 Murder Conviction," *Free Press,* January 15, 1986.

May, Lee, "Blacks Behind the Badge," *Milwaukee Sentinel,* June 6, 1982.

Maynard, Robert, "A Strong-Willed Black Woman Can Move Even DAR " *Free Press,* March 21, 1986.

McBride, Nickolas, "Going to Bat for Minorities in the Media," *Monitor,* October 31, 1986.

McCall, Alexander, M.S., "The Warring Image," *Soldier of Fortune,* January 1981.

McClain, Leonita, "How Chicago Taught Me to Hate Whites," in Page, Clarence, *A Foot in Each World: Essays and Articles by Leonita McClain,* 1986.

———, "Jews and Blacks Still shipmates," in Page, Clarence, *A Foot in Each World: Essays and Articles by Leonita McClain,* 1986.

———, "There Are No White People," in Page, Clarence, *A Foot in Each World: Essays and Articles by Leonita McClain,* 1986.

McDonald, Kim, "The 'Real' Donald Cram: Surfer, Folk Singer, Chemist, Nobelist," *Chronicle,* July 27, 1987.

McFadden, Robert, "Group Recommends More Judges and Police to Fight Crime in City," *New York Times,* March 7, 1986.

McManus, Doyle, "The Boston Syndrome: Racial Tension Keeps City on Edge," *Milwaukee Journal,* March 16, 1982.

McRae, F. Finley, "Officials Condemn Racial Overtones in Beach Attack," *Los Angeles Sentinel,* June 30, 1988.

Mehrenz, Elizabeth, "American Family Continues to Erode," *Daily News,* July 21, 1988.

Merkel, Amy, "Black Enlistment is Not Choice, but Means of Survival," *Free Press,* April 28, 1986.

Messe, Deborah, "Study Cites Success of Blacks in Military," *Free Press,* April 24, 1986.

Mooney, Carolyn. "Affirmative-Action Goals, Coupled with Tiny Number of Minority Ph.D.'s Set Off Faculty Recruiting Frenzy," *Chronicle,* August 2, 1989.

Morgan, Joan, "Supporting Black Education is Moral Duty, Says Black Businessman," *Black Issues,* March 29, 1990.

Morgan, Thomas, "The World Ahead: Black Parents Prepare their Children for Pride and Prejudice," *New York Times* magazine October 27, 1985.

Moskos, Charles. "Success Story: Blacks in the Army," *Atlantic Monthly,* May 1986.

Mouat, Lucia, "City Jobs, Are Blacks Shut Out?." *Monitor,* February 4, 1986.

Murray, Alan, "Losing Faith: Many Americans Fear U.S. Living Standards Have Stopped Rising," *Wall Street Journal,* May 1, 1989.

Niebuhr, Gustav, "Sunday Morning at 11 Remains Most Segregated Hour of Week," *Atlanta Journal and Constitution,* August 9, 1987.

Nix, Crystal, "Housing Family in Shelter Costs City $70,000 a Year," *New York Times,* March 3, 1986.

Norment, Lynn, "The Truth about AIDS," *Ebony,* 1987.

Okazawa-Rey, Margo, "Women Challenging Racism: The Third Wave of the Women's Liberation Movement," address delivered at Women Challenging Racism Conference, printed in *Forum,* National Institute Against Prejudice and Violence, March 1989.

Olivas, Michael, "An Elite Priesthood of White Males Dominates the Central Areas of Civil-Rights Scholarship," *Chronicle,* May 24, 1989.

Overbea, Luix, "Reagan Aide: Black, Republican, and Proud of It," *Monitor.*

————, "Growing Numbers of Black Women See Military Service as Ticket to a Stable Career," *Monitor,* September 26, 1985.

————, "Boston Blacks Face Opposition to Their Plan to Form Separate City," *Monitor,* October 27, 1986.

————, "Secession Scare Has Boston Mayor Mending Fences with Blacks," *Monitor,* November 20, 1986.

————, "Blacks Need to 'Renew the Spirit' of Black Power's Glory Days," *Monitor,* January 28, 1987.

Overstreet, Louie, "More Money for More Prisons Won't Solve Crime Problem," *All-Alaska Weekly,* May 18, 1989.

Page, Clarence, "Race Relations: Do We Really Have Any?," public address delivered at the University of Alaska Fairbanks, March 28, 1994

Page, Dave, "U. S. Grant's Spirit Still Pervades Historic Galena, Ill., the Town He Left for Civil War Glory," *American Civil War,* January 1989.

Parks, Ronald, "Mayor Arrington and the Grass Roots Movement Find Common Ground," *Birmingham Times,* March 10-16, 1994.

Passley, Maurice, "All-White Juries Draw Focus," *Chicago Tribune,* January 3, 1986.

Patterson, Demetrius, "U. of C. Professor Cites Keys to Enduring Poverty," *Chicago Defender,* January 26, 1988.

Patterson, Dorsey, "We Should Flood Our Community with Ethnicity," *Commercial Appeal,* Memphis, June 7, 1989.

Pavala, Gary, "The Students Accused of Racism on Campuses Can Become a Force for Social Justice," *Chronicle,* August 1, 1990.

Perot, H. Ross, "Educating Our Children for the Next Century," *Educom Review,* Spring 1989.

Pritchard, Chris, "South Africans Bring New Dimensions to Australian Racial Issues," *Monitor,* April 15, 1986.

Purnick, Joyce, "Ward Disputes Claim by Goetz of Self-Defense," *New York Times,* February 22, 1985.

Radin, Charles, "Philosopher Hits Streets," *Boston Globe*

Randolph, Laura, "Black Health," Interview with U.S. Surgeon General C. Everett Koop, M.D., *Ebony,* September 1988.

Rangel, Charles, Cong., "Denunciation on Demand Ruins Black-Jewish Links," *Amsterdam News,* October 12, 1985.

Ravitch, Diane, "Multiculturalism Yes, Particularism No," *Chronicle,* October 24, 1990.

Raymond, Chris, "Global Immigration Will Have Widespread Impact on Society, Scholars Say," *Chronicle,* September 12, 1990.

Reed, Ishmael, "... and the Maligning Male," *Life,* Special Issue, Spring 1988.

Reeves, Richard, "Blacks and Whites Work Together in Atlanta," *Daily News,* July 20, 1988.

Reider, Jonathan, "Inside Howard Beach," *New Republic,* February 9, 1987.

Renseberger, Boyce, "Race, Class Discounted as Factors in Youth Crime," *Daily News,* August 26, 1988.

Rich, Spencer, "Asian Americans Outperform Others in School and Work," *Washington Post.*

————, "Census Shows Big Drop in Two-Parent Households," *Capital Times,* May 4, 1982.

————, "Study: Non-White Adoptees Do Well," *Free Press,* December 26, 1985.

————, "Panel Sees Bleak Future for Half of U.S, Youth," *Daily News,* November 18, 1988.

————, "And the Poor Keep Getting... the Wealth-Poverty Gap Is Growing In America," *Washington Post,* April 3-9, 1989.

Rickey, Warren, "Supreme Court Asked to Look at Racial Bias in Death Penalty," *Monitor,* September 11. 1985.

————, "Racial Bias Found in Death Penalty Cases," *Monitor,* September 12, 1985.

————, "US a Haven for Paramilitary Groups that Provide Legal Mercenary Training," *Monitor,* October 8, 1985.

————, "Militant Racism Growing In US," *Monitor,* January 15, 1986.

Robeson, Paul, "I Want to Be African," (1934), in *Paul Robeson Speaks.*

————, "Negroes–Don't Ape the Whites," 1935, in *Paul Robeson Speaks: Writings, Speeches, Interviews, 1918-1979.*

Rogers, Phil, "Rangers Owners Revealed–Cottrell Is First Black Part- Owner," *Dallas Times Herald,* June 3, 1989.

Rorne, Jonathan, "Indianapolis's 'Masters of Disaster'," *Monitor,* April 7. 1986, review of Indiana University film, "The Masters of Disaster," about an inner-city school's national champion chess team.

Rosenberg, Jack, "Brighter Than 1000 Points of Light," *Emerge,* March 1993

Rossi, P., Berk, R., Boesel, D., Edison, B., and Groves, W., "Between White and Black–The Faces of American Institutions in the Ghetto," in *Supplemental Studies for the National Advisory Commission on Civil Disorders,* 1968.

Rossides. Daniel, "What Is the Purpose of Education?," *Change,* April 1984.

Rowan, Carl, "Study on Black Higher Education Adds Up to 'Social Science' Bunk," *The Atlanta Constitution,* February 25, 1985.

————, "Just More Slander of the Black Family," *Washington Post,* February 1, 1986.

Rowe, Jonathan, "Will the 'Lang Solution' to Affordable College Catch On?," *Monitor,* February 10, 1986.

Royko, Mike, "Fear Not, Ivan Boesky Will Manage to Tough It Out," *Daily News,* December 28, 1987.

————, "'Mississippi Burning' Not History but It Does Justice to the Times," *News-Miner,* January 21, 1989.

Rudin, A. James, "On Bigotry and the Need to Keep Marching," *Monitor,* February 12, 1987.

Ruffin, David, "Picking Federal Judges: Color Blind or Blind to Blacks," *Black Enterprise,* April 1987.

Rule, Sheila, "Divorce Rate Soaring for Black Couples: Experts on Family Cite Special Strains," *New York Times,* May 24, 1982.

Ryan, Bob, "Some NBA Troubles Are Black and White," *Milwaukee Journal,* June 5, 1982.

Ryan, Michael, "'You Just Have to Try,' Two Everyday People, in Different Communities, Saw a Problem and Believed They Could Do Something about It," *Tampa Tribune,* Parade Magazine, May 28, 1989.

Sanford, G. D., and Rohde, M., "Officers Sketch a Racist Force," *Milwaukee Journal,* March 3, 1980.

Santoli, Al, "How They Saved a Neighborhood," *Parade,* August 14, 1988.

Saunders, Marguerite, "Alcohol Is Number One Black Health Problem," *Minority Business and Employment Times,* January-February, 1989.

Schilling, Thomas, "Coors Cans Blacks Intellectual (Ability)," *Rocky Mountain News.*

Schreiner, Tim, "Our Roots: English, German, Irish, Afro-American...and 13 Million Say Plain 'American'," *USA Today,* June 1, 1983.

Seaberry, James, "College Educated Blacks Said to Confront Discrimination," *Washington Post,* April 22, 1985.

Selcer, Richard, "Youthful Innocence Shattered," *America's Civil War,* March 1989.

Semerod, Roger, "Work Force 2000," *Nuestra,* January/February 1987.

Shapiro, Walter, "Unfinished Business: A Sweeping Survey of Race Relations......," *Time,* August 7, 1989.

Siegel, Barry, "Will New Wave of Immigrants Transform US?," *Milwaukee Journal,* December 29, 1982.

Simmons, Carole, "Just Call Me Colored," *Atlanta Tribune,* July 1, 1993

Sinclair, Abiola, "S. African Prof. Denied Tenure in Zionist Tiff." *Amsterdam News,* September 31, 1985.

Sinclair, Ward, "Black Farmers a Dying Minority," *Washington Post,* February 18, 1986.

Sizemore, Barbara, "Separatism: A Reality Approach to Inclusion?," in Robert L. Green, ed., *Racial Crisis in American Education,* 1969.

Smith, Carlton, and Guillen, Thomas, "An Epidemic of Murders," *Seattle Times/Seattle Post Intelligencer,* December 13, 1987.

Smith, Wes, "FBI Agent Remembers Harassment, Pain," *Chicago Tribune,* December 6, 1987.

Smothers, David, "Marva Collins: 'I Have No Apologies to Make'." *World News Examiner,* April 23, 1982.

Smyth, David, "Pecking Order in Everything In Japan," review of Hall, Edward, and Hall, Mildred, *Hidden Differences: Doing Business with the Japanese* (1987), *News-Miner,* December 20, 1987.

Sneider, Daniel, "Prejudice In Japan," *Monitor,* November 21, 1985.

Sowell, Thomas, "Civil Rights History Lesson," *Washington Times,* June 12, 1993

Spolar, Chris, "Schools Look for Minority Instructors," *Washington Post,* September 14, 1985.

Steele, Shelby, "I'm Black, You're White. Who's Innocent? Race and Power in an Era of Blame," *Harpers Magazine,* June 1988.

———, "Ghettoized by Black Unity," excerpt in *Harper's,* May 1990.

Stelly, Matthew, "'Q & A': Movie Addressing Police Corruption and Race Relations the Best in Years," *Milwaukee Courier,* June 2, 1990.

Sterritt, David, "Film Quest for Black Dignity and Identity," *Monitor,* January 24, 1986.

Stuart, Reginald, "In Changing Birmingham, Rotary Votes to Stay White," *New York Times,* May 31, 1982.

Sullivan, Cheryl, "New Extremists Exceed 'Jim Crowism' of KKK," *Monitor,* January 12, 1987.

———, "Racists Take Violent Path," *Monitor,* January 12, 1987.

———, "White Supremacists Test Limits of US Rights to Free Speech, Assembly," *Monitor,* January 14, 1987.

Swetzok, Paul, "'State (AK) Should Punish Discrimination," *Tundra Times,* August 1, 1988.

Taylor, Robert, "Big-City Police Forces Shoot Less, Talk More, Easing Racial Tension," *Wall Street Journal,* December 28, 1982.

Tenoria, Vyvyan, "Rising Racism in Sri Lanka's Ethnic Strife Weakens Fabric of Nation," *Monitor,* November 22, 1985.

Tidwell. Billy, "A Profile of the Black Unemployed: A Disaggregation of Analysis," in *State of Black America,* 1987.

Tolchin, Martin and Susan, "Foreign Money, U.S. Fears," *New York Times* magazine, December 13, 1987.

Tuck, Ron, "Harlem's Fighting Spirit," *Washington Post,* December 12, 1985.

Turner, Renée, "Postal Union President Robert L. White: The Civil Rights Crusader of the Labor Movement, *Ebony,* February 1988.

Unger, Arthur, "Hard-Hitting Special about Black Families," *Monitor,* January 23, 1986.

Van Horne, Winston A., "Integration or Separation: Beyond the Philosophical Wilderness Thereof," in W. A. Van Horne and T. Tonnesen, eds., *Race: Twentieth Century Dilemmas–Twenty-First Century Prognoses,* 1989.

Vivian, C. T., "The Social Cost of Racism," Keynote address to the 3rd Annual National Conference on Racial and Ethnic Relations in American Higher Education, June 2, 1990.

Vobejda, Barbara, "Black P.G. Group Opposes Busing," *Washington Post,* April 15, 1985.

Wallace, I., Wallace, A., and Wallechinsky, D., "First U.S. City to be Bombed from the Air," *Parade* magazine, March 13, 1983.

Ward., Geoffrey C., "Up by the Bootstraps from Slavery," *American Heritage,* December 1986.

Washington, J. Leon, "Black Students, White Campuses: The Plight, the Promise," *Black Collegian,* September/October 1988.

Wharton, Clifton R., Jr., "Public Higher Education and Black Americans: Today's Crisis, Tomorrow's Disaster?," speech to the National Urban League, printed in *Minorities in Public Higher Education,* 1988.

Wheeler, Louanne, "Promoting the Health of Black Americans," *Black Issues,* December 15, 1987.

Whitaker. Charles, "The New Mississippi: Is It Really Better 'Up North'?," *Ebony,* August 1989.

White, Evelyn, "How Paul Stewart Mines Lost 'Gold' with a Tape Recorder," Founder of Black American West Museum, *Smithsonian,* August 1989.

Whitmore, Wando, "Breaking Stride in the Corporate Marathon," *Black Enterprise,* March 1987.

Wickham, DeWayne, "Thanksgiving Is Bittersweet for Most Black Americans," *Free Press.*

Wilkerson, Margaret, and Gresham, Jewell, "Sexual Politics of Welfare: The Racialization of Poverty," *The Nation,* Special Issue, Scapegoating the Black Family: Black Women Speak, July 24/31, 1989.

Wilkins, Roger, "Keeping the Faith–The Black Church," *Frontline* television report, June 16, 1987.

Williams, Juan, "Black, Separatist Farrakhan Widening Support," *Washington Post,* March 4, 1985.

Williams, Linda, "New Black Politicians, Skillful and Pragmatic, Transcend Civil Rights," *New York Times,* January 9, 1986.

Williams, Walter, "Blacks Don't Need Quotas to Keep Pace," *Ethnic Enterprise News,* November/December 1989.

Winerip, Michael, "Catholic Learns Klan 'Wizardry'," *Daily News,* September 29, 1986.

Wolfman, Brunetta, "College Leaders Must Act Firmly to End Racial Resegregation on Their Campuses," *Chronicle,* September 12, 1990.

Yarborough, Marilyn, "Teaching the Lessons of the Past in a Contemporary Environment," *Black Issues,* May 11, 1989.

Young, Lawrence, "Isn't She Pretty?...," *Black Issues,* January 29, 1989.

Yurco, Frank, "Were the Ancient Egyptians Black or White?," *Biblical Archaeology Review,* September/October 1989.

EDITORIALS, UNATTRIBUTED ARTICLES, LETTERS, ETC.

"4.8% of Blacks Missed in Census," *Milwaukee Journal,* April 5, 1982.

"8 Held In L.A. Charges in Plot to Start Race War," *News-Miner,* August 16, 1993.

"25 Years Later: Is White Racism Still Dividing America Into Black and White Races - Separate and Unequal?," *Jet,* May 31, 1993.

"650 Athletes Who Failed to Meet New Standards Are in College, Most Are Black," *Chronicle of Higher Education,* May 13, 1987.

"3000 White Patriots March in Forsyth," *Thunderbolt,* February 1987.

"A Biracial Police-and Love-Story," *Milwaukee Sentinel,* January 10, 1984.

"A World Without Fathers: The Struggle to Save the Black Family," *Newsweek* cover story, August 30, 1993.

"African-American or Black: What's in a Name? Prominent Blacks and/or African-Americans Express Their Views," *Ebony*, July 1989.

"Agent Accuses FBI of Racism," *Anchorage Daily News*, November 6, 1987.

"Alabama Keeps Confederate Flag," *News-Miner*, February 13, 1988.

"All-Black Crew to Fly Mission," *Free Press*, January 2, 1985.

"Amerasians Claim Colleges Trying to Stay White, Keep Them Out," *National Multicultural Banner*, March/April 1987.

"Asian Americans Outnumber Blacks at Independent Schools," *Black Issues in Higher Education*, June 15, 1987.

"Belief in God, Religion Widespread among Blacks," *Milwaukee Journal*, July 10, 1982.

"Bias in Residency Laws," *Chicago Tribune*, January 3, 1986.

"Big Reunion Reminds Family of Achievements Grown from Slave Roots," *Atlanta Journal and Constitution*, July 5, 1987.

"Bigotry Carries Big Price Tag," *Milwaukee Journal*, March 21, 1984.

"Black and White in America," *Newsweek* Special Report, March 7, 1988.

"Black Army Surgeon Faces Loss of Job in Alabama After Race Is Exposed," *Jet*, July 12, 1993.

"Black Caucus Members Discuss Future Goals During Parley in Calif.," *Jet*, July 19, 1993.

"Black Hockey Player Faces 'Rednecks,' Racial Stereotypes," *Chronicle*, November 27, 1985.

"Black Job Applicants Win $53,960 From LSU," *Chronicle*, June 30, 1993.

"Black Lawyers Still Are Minorities in Profession," *Jet*, September 26, 1988.

"Black Men More Likely to Be Jailed," *Wisconsin State Journal*, July 29, 1985.

"Black Women in the Military: Facts and Figures," *Black Enterprise*, April 1986.

"Black-on-Black Crime Versus Self-Hatred," letter to the editor, *Chicago Defender*, June 12, 1993.

"Black-White Wealth Gap Narrows a Bit," *News-Miner*, July 27, 1989.

"Blacks Get $6 Million in Honda Job Bias Settlement," *Jet*, April 11, 1988.

"Blacks in Management: New Difficulties in Moving Ahead," *BNAC Communicator*, Fall 1988.

"Blatant Bias Findings," *Fair Employment Practices*, October 2, 1986.

"Bombing, Killings, Racist Spector of Anti-Semitism," *Daily News*, November 16, 1987.

"Brazilian Police Out to Curb Baby Trafficking," *News-Miner*, September 27, 1986.

"Bulls Add Kukoc to Championship Herd," *News-Miner*, July 20, 1993.

"Business Leader" (Joshua Smith, CEO Maxima Corp.), in "What Is The State of Black America?," *USA Today*, February 25, 1993.

"Camille Cosby Warns Spelman Grads about Use of Sex and Money," *Jet*, June 12, 1989.

"Center Files Suit Against Major Life Insurance Company," *Law Report*, January 1992.

"Children of the Underclass," *Newsweek* Cover Story, September 11, 1989.

"College Doesn't Close Blacks' Pay Gap," *USA Today*, September 16, 1993.

"Colleges Won't Name Building for Donor Linked to Hate Mail." *News-Miner*, March 2, 1988.

"Council on Interracial Books For Children," *Fact Sheets On Institutional Racism*, 1982.

"David Duke's Louisiana Victory Is Reflection of a National Strategy," *The Monitor*, Publication of the Center for Democratic Renewal, May 1989.

"David Duke: Taking Racism to the Louisiana State House," *Klanwatch*, April 1989.

"Despite Extremists, Polls Indicate Tolerance on Rise," *Anchorage Times*, April 23, 1989.

"Discrimination Charges Mount Against State Troopers on East Coast," *Jet*, June 28, 1993.

"Discrimination Exists among Blacks," *Daily News*, May 14, 1989.

"Dodgers' Campanaris: Blacks May Lack 'Necessities' to be Managers," *Chicago Tribune*, April 8, 1987.

"Donations to Charity Soar to $124 Billion in '92," *USA Today*, May 26, 1993

"Education Has Little Impact on Minority Unemployment, Study Finds," *Higher Education Daily*, November 29, 1982.

"Employers Said to Need Strategies to Recruit, Retain Minority Employees," *Affirmative Action Compliance Manual for Federal Contractors*, September 30, 1988.

"Ethnoviolence at Work," *Forum*, National Institute Against Prejudice and Violence, March 1989.

"ETS's Michael Nettles on the SAT, Secondary Preparation, College Selection and Retention," *Black Issues*, February 15, 1988.

"Ex-Skinhead Ties Metzger to Killing," *Law Report*, Publication of the Southern Poverty Law Center and its Klanwatch Project. March 1990.

"Fed Study" Bank Leaders Deny Minorities," *Anchorage Daily News*, October 14, 1991.

"Few Blacks in Top City Jobs, Study Says," *Fair Employment Practices*, September 4, 1986.

"GM Gives Black Schools $1 Million in Bias Case," *Monitor*, October 29, 1986.

"Health Care Update: The Good News and the Bad," *Black Issues*, May 15. 1987.

"HHH (Hubert H. Humphrey) Institute of Public Affairs Report Reveals Growing Incarceration of Minority Youth, *Black Issues*, September 18, 1986.

"High Court Rules Prosecutors Can't Disqualify Jurors on Basis of Race," *Monitor*, May 1, 1986.

"History of Minorities Is a Growth Industry," *USA Today*, February 23, 1988.

"'Hope and Fears' List," *Newsline*, a newsletter of the World Future Society, Spring 1989.

"Housing: Behind Segregation," *World Press Review*, March 1986, from *The Economist* of London.

"How Blacks' TV Viewing Habits Differ From Whites'," *Jet*, April 22, 1993

"How San Francisco Church Fights Crack Cocaine–and Wins," *Jet*, May 16, 1988.

"HUD Uncovers Discrimination," *Emerge*, February 1992.

"Hunger among Blacks Said Becoming Epidemic," *Amsterdam News*, March 29, 1986.

"Inadequate Preparation and Lack of Role Models Blamed for Minority Engineering Attrition," *Black Issues*, December 15, 1986.

"Is America Falling Behind?," Interview with Paul Kennedy by Robert Heilbroner, *American Heritage*, September/October 1988.

"Japan's Clout in the U.S.," *Business Week* Cover Story, July 11, 1988.

"Japanese Carmakers Hire Fewer Blacks than American Carmakers, Study Reveals," *Jet*, September 19, 1988.

"Jew Abandons His Heritage for Life in Klan," *USA Today*, December 27, 1985.

"John F. Kennedy, Jr.: The Sexist Man Alive (1988)," *People* Cover Story, September 12, 1988.

"Joint Statement: Constitutional Scholars' Statement on Affirmative Action After *City of Richmond v. J. A. Croson Co..*" *Yale Law Review*, 1989.

"Judge Says FBI Guilty of Discrimination against Hispanics," *News- Miner*, October 1, 1988.

"Juneteenth: Free to be ...., " *Houston Defender*, June 11-17, 1989.

"Jury Award for Lynching Likely to Hurt KKK Group," *Monitor*, February 17, 1987.

"Jury Awards $1 Million to Professor in Bias Suit," *Chronicle*, April 4, 1990.

"Khadafy Urges U.S. Blacks to Create Separate Army," *Free Press*, February 25, 1985.

"Kids and Cocaine," *Newsweek*, March 17, 1986.

"Klan Surfaces in AK," *Los Angeles Sentinel*, November 26, 1987.

"Last Black To Leave Town Killed By Gang," *News-Miner*, August 16, 1993.

"Lawmakers Cry Racism, Seek Ouster: (Gov.) Clements Defends Legal Advisor," *El Paso Times*, May 28, 1989.

"Life Expectancy in U.S. a Record 73.7 Years." *Milwaukee Journal*, October 13, 1982.

"Man Killed in Jail, Texas Jury Decides." *USA Today*, February 10, 1988.

Maning Marable interview with Ed Wiley III, "Intellectual Pursuits: Examining the Role of Black Thinkers In a Contemporary World," *Black Issues*, May 6, 1993.

"Marine Cleared in Rape Case to Quit," *USA Today*, February 22, 1988.

"Matters Have Gotten Out of Hand' in a Violent Society," *U.S. News and World Report*, June 28, 1982, Interview with Saul Bellow.

McClatchy News Service, "Report Blasts U.S. on Racial Disparities," *News Miner*, May 18, 1993.

"Memo Reveals Southern Whites Turning Republican," *Jet*, July 24, 1989.

"Most Illiterate Adults in U.S. Are White, Study Concludes," *New York Times*, December 13, 1987.

"Nakasone Apologizes for Racial Comments," *News-Miner*, September 27, 1986.

"National Campaign Seeks to Locate, Teach 27 Million Adult Illiterates," *Washington Post*, May 13, 1985.

"National Study Reports White Cops' Beating of Blacks 'Dirty Secret of Racism'," *Jet*, May 3, 1993.

"Navy Ponders Reasons for Lack of Black Advancement," *Anchorage Times*, July 26, 1988.

"Neglected Issue of Aging among Blacks Needs More Study, Researchers Warn," *Chronicle*, October 29, 1986.

"Newspaper: Racial Bias Pervades Jury Selection," *Free Press*, March 10, 1986.

"Nigeria Cancels Speech by Farrakhan," *Free Press*, February 10, 1986.

"Not Long Ago There Was Only One Way for a Black Woman to Have Office in Society," *Essence*, June 1988.

"OU (Oklahoma University) Holds Conference in an Effort to Provide Leadership in College Racial and Ethnic Relations," *The Black Chronicle*, Oklahoma City, June 1, 1989.

"Our Big Cities Go Ethnic," *US News*, March 21, 1983.

"Pickens Blasts 'Good Ol' Boys'," *USA Today*, February 3, 1987.

"Playboy Interview: Eddie Murphy," *Playboy*, February 1990.

"Police Action in Suburb of St. Louis Sparks Anger Over Questions of Racism," *Jet*.

"Police Officers: Are We Hiring the Wrong People?," Speech by Ron Dowell, former police officer; Director of Personnel and Labor Relations, Troy, Michigan. Reported in *N/ PELRA Newsletter*, February 28, 1987.

"Proposal for Separate Black District Sparks Controversy in Milwaukee," *School Law News*, September 17, 1987.

"Proposition 48 Casualties," *Black Issues*, September 15. 1986.

"(Pullman) Porters Made Most of Limited Options," *Chicago Sun Times*, August 1, 1993.

"Race and the South: How Blacks and Whites Are Remaking the Old Confederacy." *U.S. News*, Cover Story, July 23, 1990.

"Racial Incidents on Campus Rise," *News-Miner*, March 7, 1988.

"Racial Inequality Found in Chicago JTPA Program, Urban League Says," *Affirmative Action Compliance Manual for Federal Contractors*, December 23, 1988.

"Railroad Race Bias Case Is Settled For $10 mil," *Jet*, July 5, 1993.

"Remarks of Thurgood Marshall," Associate Justice, Supreme Court of the United States, at the Second Circuit Judicial Conference, September 8, 1989.

"Remembering 'Pops'" (Michael Jordon's father), *People*, August 30, 1993.

"Rep. Backs Bill to Give Blacks Medal of Honor," *Jet*, June 20, 1988.

"Reverend Martin Luther King on Open Housing," *Fair Housing Keys*, Metropolitan Milwaukee Fair Housing Council, Winter 1984.

"Robber Says He Funded Supremacists," *Daily News*, January 29, 1992.

"Skinheads: The New Wave of Racism," *The Ku Klux Klan: A History of Racism and Violence*, Third Edition, 1988.

"Spike to Spike: The Filmmaker Interviews Himself," *Essence*, July 1989.

"Study Exposes NYPD Hiring," *Emerge*, February 1993.

"Study Shows Juries Favor Whites," *Afro-American*, August 10, 1985.

"Support for Desegregation Declines, Study Says," *Black Issues*, March 1985.

"Survey Reveals Few Blacks Currently Hold Top Posts in Federal Bureaucracy," *Jet*, December 16, 1991.

"Tenure Denied at Stony Brook Upheld by SUNY Chancellor." *Chronicle*, February 11, 1987.

"Texas Police Investigating Gang of Teen-Age Vigilantes," *Free Press*, April 6, 1985.

"The Blacks and the Blues: A Special Report on Police Brutality, *Essence*, September 1985.

"The Last Mafia Marriage," televised May 1993.

"The Young and the Racist–White Supremacy Exploits 'Hot' Television," *The Monitor*, Center for Democratic Renewal, May 1989.

"They Aren't Crazy or Lazy, Just Poor," *USA Today*, February 5; 1988, Interview with Jonathan Kozol.

"Thinking About Tomorrow," Caroline Bird interview of John Naisbitt and Patricia Aburdene, *Modern Maturity*, June-July 1993.

"Transracial Adoption Seen as Positive Experience," *Chronicle*, February 18, 1987.

"Two Women Highlighted in $105 million Bias Settlement" (with Shoney's Restaurants), *Jet*, April 8, 1993.

"U.S. Prison System Called Racist," *Washington Post*, October 25, 1987.

"University of Michigan Professor Documents Black-White Disparity," *Black Issues*, January 15, 1988.

"University of Michigan Researchers Chronicle Childbirth Fatalities for Black Women," *Black Issues*, September 1, 1986.

"UW Researcher Finds No 'True' Integration," *Milwaukee Journal*, May 13, 1983.

"Washington Lobbyist Tells V.C. Students to Remember History" *Black News*, February 20-26, 1992.

"Western Frontier Remains America's Most Dangerous Region," *Atlanta Journal and Constitution*, December 13, 1987.

"White Supremacists Seeks U.S. House Seat from Wyoming," *Klanwatch*, April 1989.

"White Teachers Who Used *Ebony* in Class, Keeps Her Job," *Jet*, June 14, 1993.

"Women With Fear of Blacks Fights to Keep Disability Award," *Daily News*, October 4, 1991.